The Gates of Hell

Confessing Christ in a Hostile World

Edited by Scott R. Murray

CONCORDIA PUBLISHING HOUSE • SAINT LOUIS

3558 S. Jefferson Ave., St. Louis, MO 63118–3968
1-800-325-3040 • www.cph.org

Manufactured in the United States of America

Library of Congress Cataloging-in-Publication Data

Names: Murray, Scott R., editor.

Title: The gates of hell / edited by Scott R. Murray.

Description: Saint Louis : Concordia Publishing House, 2018.

Identifiers: LCCN 2017048929 (print) | LCCN 2017050561 (ebook) | ISBN 9780758659149 | ISBN 9780758659132

Subjects: LCSH: Lutheran Church--Doctrines. | Lutheran Church--Missouri Synod--Doctrines. | Christianity and culture. | Apologetics.

Classification: LCC BX8065.3 (ebook) | LCC BX8065.3 .G38 2018 (print) | DDC 230/.41322--dc23

LC record available at https://lccn.loc.gov/2017048929

---

1 2 3 4 5 6 7 8 9 10 26 25 24 23 22 21 20 19 18 17

TABLE OF CONTENTS

Abbreviations iv

Introduction v
by Rev. Dr. Scott R. Murray

Convention Sermons

1. "Upon This Rock" (Matthew 16:13–20) 1
by Rev. Dr. Matthew C. Harrison
2. "Saying What God Says" (1 John 1:8–2:2) 7
by Rev. Dr. Herbert C. Mueller Jr.
3. "Held Fast to Hold Fast" (Hebrews 10:23) 11
by Rev. Dr. John C. Wohlrabe Jr.
4. "Joy in Jesus" (1 John 1:1–4) 15
by Rev. Dr. Scott R. Murray
5. "It's All about Love" (Leviticus 19:15–18) 19
by Rev. Nabil S. Nour
6. "Saints and Faithful Brothers" (Colossians 1:1–14) 23
by Rev. Christopher S. Esget

Convention Essay

7. "Built on the Rock—Confess" 27
by Rev. Dr. Daniel O. S. Preus

Articles

8. The Gates of Hell and the Religion of Sex 41
by Rev. Dr. Scott R. Murray
9. The Gates of Hell: Luther and the Two Kingdoms 73
by Rev. Dr. Matthew C. Harrison
10. The Gates of Hell and the Status of the Church in Western Society...... 105
by Rev. Dr. John C. Wohlrabe Jr.
11. The Gates of Hell: Defying the Devil in International Mission Work 141
by Rev. Dr. Daniel O. S. Preus
12. The Gates of Hell and the Table of the Lord 167
by Rev. Christopher S. Esget
13. The Gates of Hell and the Urgency of Preaching 197
by Rev. Nabil S. Nour
14. The Gates of Hell and Defending the Faith against Them 219
by Rev. Dr. Herbert C. Mueller Jr.

Abbreviations

AC Augsburg Confession
Ap Apology of the Augsburg Confession
Ep Epitome of the Formula of Concord
FC Formula of Concord
LC Large Catechism
LW Luther's Works, American Edition
SA Smalcald Articles
SC Small Catechism
SD Solid Declaration of the Formula of Concord
Tr Treatise of the Power and Primacy of the Pope
WA Weimar Edition of Luther's Works

Introduction

Christ Promises

The status of the Church is changing. She is not the darling of the culture. The Church is no longer perceived to be a supporter of the cultural goods such as stability, honor, honesty, hard work, and marriage. Many of those goods have been precipitously abandoned on account of the elites'[1] assault on what, until less than a generation ago, were considered truths vital to the ongoing success of our nation and its people. Now those who have the courage to confess the Bible's truths about sex, marriage, the value of human life, and so on are labeled as haters, enemies of culture, and hurtful to the state.

The changed status of the Church from being a cultural darling to being a cultural enemy is causing increasing anxiety for those who still confess the truth of the Christian faith. For example, the court cases mounted against pious believers who make a stand against moral depravity causes us all to shiver, because we are committed to the same faith that incites such rage against these courageous believers. What can we do and how should we live in the face of these fraying verities? How will we respond to these attacks on our faith and fellow believers?

It is helpful to learn that the Bible was written in a cultural situation far worse (at least for now) than the one we face in our day. Institutional depravity led to vicious persecution of believers during the first three centuries of our era. The Letter to the Hebrews was written to people who were afraid of approaching persecution. We are no different, both in the sense that the adversarial relationship with culture is not unlike the one faced by the Fathers in the earliest days

1 Victor Davis Hanson of the Hoover Institution provides a helpful definition of the word *elite* as it is used here: "An elite is also defined by education (preferably Ivy League and its coastal counterparts), residence (primarily between Boston and Washington on the East Coast, and from San Diego to Berkeley on the Pacific), profession (executive positions in government, media, law, foundations, the arts, and academia), celebrity (name recognition from television, Hollywood, network news, finance, etc.), and ideology, such as those prominent in the progressive movement" ("Who Are Those Darned 'Elites'?" *Defining Ideas: A Hoover Institution Journal*, September 8, 2016, http://www.hoover.org/research/who-are-those-darned-elites). In keeping with the progressive agenda, an elite is usually overtly or covertly anti-Christian, anti-life, and, of course, has a pro-homosexual agenda.

of the Church and also in the sense that the sexual/moral devolution of culture looks much like the situation in the first three centuries of our era. We are afraid for many of the same reasons those past heroes of the faith were afraid. Jesus' response to them is the same as it is to us. Just when we begin to fear that Satan is having his way with us, we must hear our Lord tell us that He will build His Church, and the gates of hell shall not prevail against it (Matthew 16:18). So even though it seems like Satan is winning, Christ promises that he will not prevail.

The essays and sermons in this book will testify to the power of Christ's promise to defend His Church. This is not a time to despair of God's help. In the midst of suffering, Christ promises to be with us. How could it be any different? Hasn't Christ offered Himself into suffering and death for our sake? Why wouldn't He be with those who suffer for His sake? Of course He will!

The authors who have collaborated on this book are writing to confess their confident hope for the future of the Church under God. These seven men are the elected leaders of The Lutheran Church—Missouri Synod (LCMS), serving together as the president and vice presidents of the church body: Rev. Dr. Matthew C. Harrison, president of the LCMS; and Rev. Dr. Herbert C. Mueller Jr.; Rev. Nabil S. Nour; Rev. Dr. John C. Wohlrabe Jr.; Rev. Dr. Daniel O. S. Preus; Rev. Christopher S. Esget; and the undersigned; who are the vice presidents of the LCMS. They have an abundance of experience serving the church, having served, or now serving, as parish pastors, teachers, and leaders of church auxiliary institutions. The volume also includes sermons full of hope and encouragement in Christ that were preached by the president and vice presidents at the 2016 convention of the LCMS in Milwaukee, Wisconsin. Luther tells us that Satan hates nothing more than to have the Word of God preached, and that he therefore flees from it.[2] The essays and sermons definitely belong together as a way of beating back the kingdom of our enemy. The Word of God does what it says and the gates of hell will never prevail against the kingdom of Christ, the Church. Christ promises.

Rev. Scott R. Murray, PhD

Houston, Texas

NINTH SUNDAY AFTER PENTECOST 2017

2 AE 18:401

1

"Upon This Rock"

Matthew 16:13–20, Sermon

Rev. Dr. Matthew C. Harrison, LCMS President

66th Regular Convention of The Lutheran Church—Missouri Synod

JULY 9, 2016

> He said to them, "But who do you say that I am?" Simon Peter replied, "You are the Christ, the Son of the living God." And Jesus answered him, "Blessed are you, Simon Bar-Jonah! For flesh and blood has not revealed this to you, but My Father who is in heaven. And I tell you, you are Peter, and on this rock I will build My church, and the gates of hell shall not prevail against it. I will give you the keys of the kingdom of heaven, and whatever you bind on earth shall be bound in heaven, and whatever you loose on earth shall be loosed in heaven." (Matthew 16:15–19)

In the name of the Father and of the ✠ Son and of the Holy Spirit. Amen.

My dear brothers on the council, brother pastors, church workers, friends: What a joy to look out upon you and see so many, many familiar faces. And this week we will see many, many more who will become familiar faces.

Martin Luther had been into the controversy four years, almost five hundred years ago, when he was called to confess at Worms. On April 17, 1521, imperial marshal (*Erbmarschall*) Ulrich von Pappenheim knocked on Luther's door and told him that the diet was waiting—the German meeting of all the emperor's people, the emperor, the kings, the princes, the nobles, they were all waiting to hear from him. They brought him over to the building next door and told him they would hear from him at 4:00 p.m. Four p.m. came. He was called to wait below for a few minutes, and then he was called upstairs.

There on a table before him was a pile of twenty-five books that he had written. One of the books, *The Freedom of the Christian Man,* said, "A Christian is a perfectly free lord of all, subject to none. A Christian is a perfectly dutiful servant of all, subject to all" (AE 31:344). He is subject to all out of love.

Johann Eck pointed to the pile. "Luther, are you ready to admit that you wrote these books, and that they contain heresy?"

"Yes, they are mine," Luther said. "But as to whether they contain heresy, that is a matter of faith and salvation of the soul and it cannot be affirmed or rejected without affecting the Word of God."

Luther asked for more time. He was granted a day. We still have the very notes he scribbled that night as he got ready for the next day.

He was brought back at 4:00 p.m., left waiting until 6:00 p.m., and then called in front of the emperor and the whole crowd again. And they told him, "We want to hear one word from you, Luther: *revoco*." *Revoco*. I recant.

Luther was nervous the day before, but he was very confident that day. He apologized. He said, "I'm sorry, I was not brought up in the court. If I used the wrong title for some of you, it is not meant to be rude." You could hear a pin drop. He said, "Some of my books deal with simple Christian matters and simple morality based on the central teaching of the Gospel, and even my enemies would concede they are right. Some of my writings are against the pope." Then Luther went on a rant against the pope, and it was so intense that the emperor told him to stop. A third part of his writings, Luther said, were against the enemies of the faith. Though he had overdone it sometimes in his invective, he would not say the word *revoco*.

The emperor and his advisers left the room for a few minutes. When they returned, they asked Luther one more time, "Are you prepared to answer without evasion and without horns, Luther? Say the word *revoco*."

Luther responded with one sentence. And at this moment in the history of the Church, in the Western world particularly, it was a very consequential sentence. He said it both in Latin and German. "Unless I am convinced by the testimony of the Scriptures or by clear reason (for I do not trust either in the pope or in councils alone, since it is well known that they have often erred and contradicted themselves), I am bound by the Scriptures I have quoted and my conscience is captive to the Word of God. I cannot and I will not retract anything, since it is neither safe nor right to go against conscience. I cannot do otherwise, here I stand, may God help me, Amen" (AE 32:112–13).

To the great frustration of his opponents, he quickly left. He was taken outside, and he held up his arms in front of the crowd, saying, "I'm through. I'm through." There were thousands waiting. And from that point on almost, he had a death sentence hanging over his head.

It was Luther's moment. And it was the moment of the birth of our church, really. A great moment of confession. "You, who do you say that I am?" And Luther responded, "You are the Christ, the Christ of Holy Scripture. The Christ of the Gospel. You are the Christ who teaches aright about natural law and conscience. And a conscience bound by the Word of God."

Luther refused to recant Christ's teaching. Christ is the rock. If we lose the Rock, what do we have left? And he also asserted, and this is important for us today, that the conscience is free from external coercion by anything but the Word of God.

And Luther held forth, even though our culture today does not recognize the fact. Luther, in a big way, for the first time, held forth the idea that the government has no right to coerce the religious conscience. None. And that teaching is a teaching of the Lutheran Church.

"Who do you say that I am?" The first thing we do is confess, like John the Baptizer, "I am not the Christ." Every one of us, from me to the last person in this hall, should get up right now and confess, "I am not the Christ." It says that in John 1:20. John the Baptizer confessed, "I am not the Christ."

How often in your life would you be the Christ, the know-it-all, the religious expert, the one who doesn't need to repent? You are the redeemer; you're the savior of your congregation—if it doesn't do what you want it to do.

I've got news for you. You are not Jesus. And neither am I. And the Missouri Synod and the future of the Missouri Synod doesn't depend on you or me or anybody else. It depends on Christ, the rock. As Luther would say, "I am a maggot sack. It's the doctrine. It's the doctrine."

And we confess not only our sins, but we confess also the strong content of the faith. "You are the Christ, the Messiah." This Jesus has died on the cross for your sins and the sins of the world. "There is no other name under heaven given among men by which we must be saved" (Acts 4:12). Your sins are covered. Your sins are but a drop in the ocean. Your sins are covered by Christ's blood. You are baptized and covered with His free, wonderful righteousness. No matter how troubled your conscience is at times; no matter how terrified you are of your sins or past deeds; no matter if you are sluggish in the faith. Only believe. Christ is yours. He is all yours. You are forgiven. And your conscience is captive to the Word of God. Flesh and blood doesn't reveal this. It's your Father in heaven who has grabbed hold of you. And He's not going to let you out of His hand.

And notice also what this text teaches us. All of us have the Keys. Now this text says the Keys are given to Peter on behalf of all the apostles. We note in Matthew 18:17 that the Keys belong to the whole Church, "Tell it to the church." And we know from today's epistle that you are all, all of us, spiritual priests, and all of us are called to proclaim and speak the Word of God as the royal priesthood.

And it is precisely this speaking, this message of Christ, that is the rock. That's what the Smalcald Articles say. The rock here really means the ministry, this speaking of the rock of Christ. We are called to remind the world that it is Luther and the Lutheran Reformation that asserted the free religious conscience. It went from Luther to Magdeburg, to Beza of the Reformed, to Robinson of the Anglicans, to John Locke, and even to Thomas Jefferson.

The pressure is mounting, my friends. The world and its empires and emperors are saying to us: "*Revoca.* Give it up." Obergefell. "*Revoca.* Your idea of marriage is antiquated." The HHS mandates. "*Revoca.* Nothing must impede choice." "*Revoca.* Accommodate, Concordias, accommodate." "*Revoca.*" Our chaplains are increasingly harassed in the military. "*Revoca.* Your view of marriage and sexuality is ridiculous."

We are at a point now where what the Bible calls good, the government calls evil, and what the Bible calls evil, the government calls good. "*Revoca,*" they all cry out. We must reject exclusivity, the message of Christ. "For there is no other name under heaven given among men by which we must be saved." "*Revoca.* There is no one truth. There are many truths."

Here's the truth. Whether you are L, G, B, T, Q, or just a common farmer from Nebraska or a guy who lives in a St. Louis suburb, this is true: "Christ Jesus came into the world to save sinners, of whom I am the foremost" (1 Timothy 1:15). And this Jesus Christ is for all, whether you are the shooter or the shot. Christ is for all. And so with Luther, we say, "I cannot. My conscience is held captive by the Word. I cannot, I will not, recant. God help me. Amen."

"Who do you say that I am?" "You are the Christ." And we will confess. And we will do it joyously. And the world will snarl at us. And they will hate us the more. They will belittle us and say we are a bunch of kooks and idiots and antiquated fools. And we, like the apostles punished for speaking the name of Jesus in Jerusalem, will suffer with joy, and we will shout it all the louder. "There is no other name under heaven given among men by which we must be saved."

And you know what? "The gates of hell shall not prevail."

And we will say, "*Revoco*, sin. Recant, sin. Your penalty has been suffered, sin. In Christ. You are dead, sin. You are dead to me. I know only Christ and His righteousness."

And we shall say, "*Revoco,* death. Death, you are dead to me. Death, you have died to me. My death is dead in Christ, and I am alive. *Revoco*, death. *Revoco.* Recant."

And I shall say, finally, "*Revoco*, devil. You have become a devil to yourself. You are condemned. You have no more power over me. And I shall live eternally."

"And the gates of hell shall not prevail."

In the name of the Father and of the ✠ Son and of the Holy Spirit. Amen.

2

"Saying What God Says"

1 John 1:8–2:2, Sermon

Rev. Dr. Herbert C. Mueller Jr., LCMS First Vice-President

66th Regular Convention of The Lutheran Church—Missouri Synod

JULY 11, 2016

Dear fellow sinners, washed in the blood! What a great opportunity to be here! To confess Christ, yes! But also, what a great opportunity to *sin*—against God and against one another.

Does that surprise you? Or did we all check our sinful natures at the door? Perhaps the devil will stay home from the convention. Not that we need the devil's help to sin against one another. We are quite capable of that all by ourselves. In the church postils, Martin Luther writes:

> When self-conceit gains the upper hand, so that someone wants to be more learned, wiser, better, and holier than another, he then begins to despise the others. Thus he draws people to himself away from the united understanding and mind which makes us all equal in Christ, so that they are supposed to praise and exalt his teaching, preaching, and doing over others. Then harm has already been done, faith has been abolished, and the Church has been torn. (AE 78:189)

It's almost as though Luther is walking these halls, listening to our side comments. He certainly knows the sinful heart.

Hear again our text: "If we say we have no sin, we deceive ourselves, and the truth is not in us. If we confess our sins . . ." (1 John 1:8–9). To confess is to "say the same thing," to say what God says. There is no escaping the searchlight of God's Law. So, "If we say we have not sinned, we make Him a liar, and His word is not in us" (v. 10). But tell me, who is the Word of God in the flesh? Who is the truth of God incarnate? Jesus is. So if we say we have not sinned, then we are saying Jesus is not in us.

The truth is, we *are* sinners, through and through. When we confess our sins, we are simply saying what God says. *Homologeo*. Yes, God, Your Word tells the truth about me. But if that's the truth about us, we confess an even greater truth about *God*. If we confess our sins, God is faithful—God keeps His promise. God is righteous in Jesus, to forgive us our sins and to cleanse us from all unrighteousness. That's because in Jesus, God Himself did what we could never do. The Book of Hebrews says Jesus was like us "in every respect, so that He might become a merciful and faithful high priest in the service of God, to make propitiation for the sins of the people. For because He Himself has suffered when tempted, He is able to help those who are being tempted" (Hebrews 2:17–18).

Saying that Jesus made propitiation means that Jesus took all our sins. They were ALL heaped on Him, the full lot. On the cross, Jesus absorbed the full blast of God's wrath for all sins; He took it all for us. It's all gone. That's what *propitiation* means. The wrath of God was all poured out on Jesus. There's none left for us.

Therefore, John pleads with us, "My little children, I am writing these things to you so that you may not sin. But if anyone does sin, we have an advocate with the Father, Jesus Christ the righteous" (1 John 2:1). As our advocate, Jesus speaks for us: "Yes, Father, this one is a sinner, like all the rest, but . . . " Then Jesus steps between us. Who does the Father see now? Only Jesus, in our place. And the Father's verdict? Not guilty, but righteous; washed clean in the blood. John continues: Jesus "is the propitiation for our sins, and not for ours only but also for the sins of the whole world." Jesus is the place of atonement, the mercy seat. He is the one Sin-bearer, so that now, as the Scriptures say, we are all "justified by His grace as a gift, through the redemption that is in Christ Jesus, whom God put forward as a propitiation by His blood, to be received by faith" (Romans 3:24–25).

When we confess, we say what God says. We are sinners, yes! But we also confess Jesus, for *in Jesus*, God is faithful and righteous to forgive us our sins and to cleanse us from all unrighteousness. When we assure one another, "Your sin is forgiven you, for Jesus' sake," there is nothing more certain in all the universe, for we are simply saying what God says.

In just a minute, we will hear once more the Absolution. When we say, "Amen," it is the sign that we believe, as the catechism tells us, "*This* is as valid and certain, in heaven also, as if Christ our dear Lord dealt with us Himself" (SC Confession).

In the name of the Father and of the ✠ Son and of the Holy Spirit. Amen.

3

"Held Fast to Hold Fast"

Hebrews 10:23, Sermon

Rev. Dr. John C. Wohlrabe Jr., LCMS Fourth Vice-President

66th Regular Convention of The Lutheran Church—Missouri Synod

JULY 12, 2016

In the name of the Father and of the ✠ Son and of the Holy Spirit. The text for our message is Hebrews 10:23, "Let us hold fast the confession of our hope without wavering, for He who promised is faithful."

Friends of Jesus and friends of mine, fellow shipmates on the good ship we call the Missouri Synod: So much in life is *quid pro quo*—"this for that."

If you do this, **then** you get that. Sadly, some twist the Gospel into "this for that," which is no gospel at all. But God doesn't work in this way. His Gospel is truly Good News for all people. It is not an "if-then" gospel, but rather a "since-then" Gospel, or even more a "because-therefore" Gospel!

The author of the Letter to the Hebrews was addressing Jewish Christians who wanted to return to a *quid pro quo* religion. As Christians, they were facing persecution in the Roman Empire, so they wanted to go back to their old Jewish ways. **If** you follow the regulations of the Torah and trust the sacrifices of the Jewish high priest at the temple in Jerusalem, **then** you will supposedly be right with God. There are many today who present Christianity as an "if-then" religion. If you make a decision for Jesus, then Jesus will come into your heart. If you trust hard enough, then God will deliver you from whatever trouble you are facing or give you whatever you want. If you confess the faith before others, then you are a good Christian and can be confident that God is happy with you.

There is, however, an insurmountable problem with this type of glory gospel. Because it depends on what we do, therefore it is in no way good news. Because we are from birth dead in trespasses and sin (Ephesians 2:1; Psalm 51:5), therefore there is nothing we can do to please God.

Think of it as attempting to scale 3,000-foot El Capitan at Yosemite National Park on your own, without even a belaying rope. One slip—whether at 50 feet or 2,950 feet—and you fall to your death, no "ifs," "thens," or "therefores" about it! If your relationship with God depends on *quid pro quo*, then you would be forever lost!

But thanks be to God that this is not the case at all. **Because** God does all good things for us in Christ Jesus, **therefore** those good things are ours and we can hold fast to that confession. We can hold fast in faith, and we can boldly say the same thing before the world. The author of the Letter to the Hebrews doesn't use this exact grammatical formula. He uses an exhortation to encourage his readers, which biblical scholars refer to as a hortatory subjunctive: "Let us hold fast the confession of our hope."

However, each case of encouragement is tied to the good news of what God does for us. **Because** Jesus is our great High Priest, who gave His flesh and blood for us on the cross, **therefore** we will confidently enter God's presence now and for eternity. **Because** our hearts and bodies were washed clean by the pure waters of Holy Baptism, **therefore** we can draw near with a true heart to God our Father. **Because** the Day of the Lord is drawing near when Christ will return and we will be raised bodily unto eternal life in heaven, **therefore** we won't want to forsake the gathering together with other Christians, as is the habit of some. **Because** God is faithful in all His promises to you, **therefore** you can hold fast to the confession of your hope without wavering.

Over thirty years ago, I served as chaplain for the 3/24 Marines, a reserve infantry battalion, and we were sent to Bridgeport, California, for mountain warfare training. This is fairly close to Yosemite National Park in the High Sierras. I had never done any rock climbing before, and neither had many of the Marines in our battalion. To build our confidence in the belaying ropes, the training gunny had each of us repel halfway down a one-hundred-foot cliff, tie off, and hang upside down. Then we were to do ten sit-ups with our head hanging fifty feet above rather sharp rocks. After that, we practiced climbing up the cliff with the belaying rope attached. We could confidently hold fast because we were securely held fast.

The author of Hebrews exhorts and encourages us to "hold fast the confession." He is using the Greek word *homologian*, which literally translates as "same words"—the same words of our hope in Jesus Christ. These are the same words by which God has faithfully promised our forgiveness and salvation through Jesus' death and resurrection, the same words by which God has faithfully provided our purification in Holy Baptism, the same words by which God has faithfully promised our deliverance and eternal life in heaven. We can hold fast in faith without bending or wavering because God holds us fast through His Word and Sacraments. We can hold fast in boldly confessing this faith before a fallen world because God so faithfully holds us fast through Jesus Christ, our solid rock. Amen.

Soli Deo Gloria

4

"Joy in Jesus"

1 John 1:1–4, Sermon

Rev. Dr. Scott R. Murray, LCMS Second Vice-President

66th Regular Convention of The Lutheran Church—Missouri Synod

JULY 14, 2016

I. **Joy in another.**
II. **Joy in the face of hatred.**
III. **Jesus has joy in us.**
IV. **Complete joy in heavenly fellowship.**

Our joy is in Jesus. Because it is in another, our joy does not depend on us, our mood, the company we keep, the pressures we feel in our daily life, or the anxiety we experience because of our sin and spiritual weakness. It cannot be taken from us. There are many opportunities for us to feel anxiety in the presence of a holy and righteous God. This anxiety so easily cheats us of the joy that we have in Christ. As the psalmist says, "In Your presence there is fullness of joy" (Psalm 16:11). There is fullness of joy in Jesus (1 John 1:4).

I.

Our joy is in another. It is not in ourselves. John the apostle was writing of his experience with the Lord Christ, whom he heard, saw, experienced, and even touched. What was written about Christ joined John's readers in the divine fellowship with the Father and with His Son, Jesus Christ. The apostolic Word unites John's readers with the God who manifested Himself to His people in the person of His Son. Jesus says, "These things I have spoken to you, that My joy may be in you, and that your joy may be full" (John 15:11). Our joy is in Him, not ourselves, and because it is in Him, it is full and complete. Jesus found His joy in others too. His joy is to seek and save the lost. His joy is in His mission to save the world. His joy was to endure the cross for sinners like us (Hebrews 12:2). And our joy is in Him!

II.

The world hates us because our joy is not settled in the things of this world. The sacrilege of the world is to love itself, rather than to find joy as the beloved of Jesus. This is why the world must hate those who find joy in Jesus. We Christians know who we are because we have fellowship with the God who reveals Himself to us in Christ. The world is lost and always has been, but its wandering has gotten clearer recently. We know who we are, while those who love the world are trying to create an identity out of thin air. We know who we are because we have fellowship with the God who names us at the font: as a child of God who is named by the Father and the Son and the Holy Spirit. When I was a young man, my mother would always say to me as I went off with my friends, "Don't forget who you belong to!" She did not mean herself and my father. She meant my heavenly Father. When we know who our God is, then we know who we are. What joy there is in that knowledge, a knowledge delivered to us by the Word of God!

III.

The joyous fellowship that we have with God through the Word of His chosen apostles is a matter for wonderment! He seeks fellowship with sinners like us! I had the joy of sharing our holy faith with a Kurdish man who was suspicious of Islam and had questions about Christianity. He asked good questions about the faith of Christ. I had such joy to say that Jesus is our way to the Father. "Christianity is not a path, at least not in the way in which a road map charts a path. No, Christianity's way is a person: Christ Himself. Christianity is not a way of living. No, it is a life that is Christ's own life. He is your life and you are hidden in Him, as St. Paul says (Colossians 3:4). Christianity is not a truth. No, it is the truth in the flesh of God's own Son." This Kurdish man heard these words with tears in his eyes. He said wonderingly, "Is this your God?" What joy we share with those who hear of Christ's enfleshment of Mary and His suffering and death for the sins of the world! Jesus finds His joy in us that He might be our joy. His joy is not mere feeling or experience. His very joy is made complete only in His suffering and death because it is the joy He has in another. This is the joy He has in us, whom He has redeemed.

IV.

We have joy in Him even when death takes one of our loved ones. When his daughter Magdalena died, Martin Luther said, "I am joyful in spirit but I am sad according to the flesh. The flesh doesn't take kindly to this. . . . She is surely at peace and [she] is well off there, very well off, and yet to grieve so much!" (AE 54:432). Our blessed dead are very well off indeed in the full fellowship of the Church in heaven. They have fullness of joy. In that sharing, our joy is made complete because we have joy in Jesus.

5

"It's All about Love"

Leviticus 19:15–18, Sermon

Rev. Nabil S. Nour, LCMS Third Vice-President

66th Regular Convention of The Lutheran Church—Missouri Synod

JULY 10, 2016

Faithful followers of the Savior: Christ is risen! He is risen indeed! Alleluia!

The text is a portion of the Old Testament Reading: "You shall not take vengeance or bear a grudge against the sons of your own people, but you shall love your neighbor as yourself: I am the LORD" (Leviticus 19:18).

Precious children of the heavenly Father, you who are loved more than the human mind can comprehend, God's love is real, and it's undeserved, unearned, unmerited. It comes from outside of us. It comes from the One who loved us enough to go to the cross, to die for us, and to rise again on the third day.

Today, as the Holy Spirit has brought us to this place under the theme "Upon This Rock," we give thanks to the Holy Spirit for gathering us here to be comforted and to hear once more the great message of salvation from the lips of Moses, who tells us that God is love. It is for this reason I have titled my message "It's All about Love." It is God's love that motivates us to be the men and women who we ought to be. It is God's love that calls us out of darkness into His marvelous light. It is God's love from the start to the finish of all of Scripture, both Old and New Testaments, that speaks about Him who is love and who loved us in spite of ourselves so that He might make us beloved people of God.

Chosen people of God, loved beyond what the human mind can comprehend, the command in Leviticus is this: "Love your neighbor as yourself." This is not only a command but also a privilege and a blessing. To love others in the name of Christ is the greatest honor we have, and, as His beloved people, we have no room in our hearts for grudges, vengeance, or hatred for our brother.

Does that mean it's easy? No, because you and I know that some people say things and do things that make us angry, and then what we want to do is to give them a knuckle sandwich fast, furious, and forever. That's the old nature in us, but we aren't called to be vengeful or resentful. We are to reflect the love of God.

If you read Deuteronomy 7, the Lord God spoke with Moses to tell the Israelites, "I did not choose you because you were the greatest. Oh, no! It's because I have loved you. I have saved you by *water*, by *word*, by *Baptism*, by *Sacrament*." By Jesus, we know the true love of God that motivates us to love even when we are not loved. It is God's love that moves us to forgive when it's hard for us to forgive. It is God's love that motivates us to be kind when somebody is not that kind. It is indeed a challenge to live in this world today, because the world hates us. But we are to be, as Luther said, "little Christs" as we reflect the love of Jesus to the world."

Do you remember when the massacre happened in Florida? A man was so unfriendly that he killed many people in the name of the false god Allah. Shortly after, in an effort to raise money for the victims, Broadway brought out their best to sing "What the World Needs Now Is Love." Boy, how right they are! But how misconstrued they are because they think it is the world's kind of love, that funny feeling inside of you.

How often in the English language we misuse the word *love*! We say, "I love pizza," "I love the Vikings," or, like my buddy John would say, "I love the Green Bay Packers." Do they really love us back? Does pizza love you back? Do the Vikings even know that you love them? What does Moses tell us in the words "love your neighbor as yourself"? It is a privilege to be a neighbor. A neighbor is someone who cares, someone who goes out of his way to reach another person. The apostle Paul touches on that also in the great and wonderful chapter, 1 Corinthians 13. He calls love "a still more excellent way" (1 Corinthians 12:31). My beloved brothers and sisters in Christ, you who are sons of Adam and daughters of Eve, it is God's love that helps us to confess our faults, to repent, rejoice, and stand secure on the solid eternal Rock—Jesus, the Christ. Because of Him, we are able to love and share that love with others.

In the 1960s, a young lady grew up in a very well-to-do home. She got pregnant out of wedlock, and her parents forced her to give the baby up for adoption. Fast forward fifty years, the son that she had given up is a minister of the Gospel. After his adoptive parents went to be with Jesus, he sought out his biological mother. He found her in Canada and called her and said, "This is your son. I would love to meet you." She welcomed him. It was a cold blustery day in January. She put on a light coat and waited outside by the garage for her son. They had a wonderful visit.

As he said good-bye and headed to the car, he opened the door, then turned around and said, "Mom, is there anything that I can do for you?" She said, "Son, love me. Son, love me."

Brothers and sisters, I want you to do something for me. Will you turn to the right and look at the person next to you? Now do the same and turn the other way. Please know this is not a head exercise; it's a heart exercise. The person to your right and the person to your left are your brothers and sisters who need to know that they are loved.

You are God's instruments of grace. You reflect that love to those around you in the way you communicate the Gospel clearly, not because of your profession, but because you are the baptized, redeemed, forgiven, blood-bought child of God. That's who you are.

Loved people of God, people who are loved do nothing but love in return. You see, it's not about my position. It's not about my prosperity. It's not about my prestige. It isn't about the amount of money I have or my station in life. It is about God, who in His mercy, sent His only Son to be the missionary, the greatest neighbor, the greatest lover of humankind to die for scum like me and rise again so that I may be loved more than I can ever comprehend. It really is about the love that God has for me, a sinner, so that I may know I am forgiven. I am made holy, and one day I will stand in the presence of God the Father, the Son, and the Holy Spirit. There with all the saints, I will bow down with gladness, confessing that He is the Lamb, He is our Savior, and He is our Lord.

Beautiful children of the heavenly Father, you who are loved more than you can comprehend, remember this and take it to heart: God loves you more than you can understand, more than you can comprehend. And I want you to know with certainty that it's not because you are so good, because I don't see anybody here who's that good, not even President Harrison. But what I do see are men and women who have been wrapped with the righteousness of Christ, who have been baptized, whose sins have been removed; and now they stand loved beyond measure so that they in return can share that love with a world that desperately needs to know of the real love, the love that cannot be purchased except by the blood of Jesus.

Therefore, today may God grant to you and to me the joy of repentance, of confession, and of rejoicing as we stand upon the eternal Rock, Jesus Christ, our true neighbor, who loved us because we needed to be loved. Thank God for what He has accomplished in our lives so that we will stand with Him some day in paradise. God grant it all for Jesus' sake. Amen.

Soli Deo Gloria

6

"Saints and Faithful Brothers"

Colossians 1:1–14, Sermon

Rev. Christopher S. Esget, LCMS Sixth Vice-President

66th Regular Convention of The Lutheran Church—Missouri Synod

JULY 10, 2016

Our Lord Jesus Christ, on the night when He was betrayed, took bread and gave it to the disciples. And the disciples argued.

How quickly we can go from the Lord's Table to the devil's business! St. Luke tells us that they received Christ's blood, then immediately quarreled about "which of them was to be regarded as the greatest" (Luke 22:24).

These men were brothers twice. Sons of our first father, Adam, they were now by His Supper blood brothers with Jesus. Yet they fought.

The history of the world is the history of feuding brothers: Cain and Abel, Jacob and Esau, Joseph and his eleven brothers. "But not so with you," says the Lord Jesus (Luke 22:26). His Father is our Father; He is our Brother, making us all brothers and sisters of one another, not by blood alone, but by forgiveness. How then is it that you murmur and grumble about those whom Jesus has joined to Himself?

This morning's remarkable reading has words easy to gloss over, a standard sermon opening we've heard a thousand times: "Grace to you and peace from God our Father" (Colossians 1:2). *Boring!* Yet that greeting is the good news!

To whom are these words spoken? To saints. And not saints alone, but "saints and faithful brothers."

That is who you are: holy ones, brothers and sisters of the Lord Jesus, and so brothers and sisters with one another.

How, then, can we argue with and grumble about one another? St. Paul says in Romans, "Whether we live or whether we die, we are the Lord's" (Romans 14:8). Together, we belong to Jesus. So, the apostle asks, "Why do you pass judgment on your brother? Or you, why do you despise your brother? For we will all stand before the judgment seat of God" (Romans 14:10). Whom Christ has joined as brothers, dare we put asunder?

Sometimes brothers can be united in the wrong way. James and John, the sons of thunder, were eager to call down fire on those who did not receive Jesus.

Jesus told them, "You do not know what manner of spirit you are of" (see Luke 9:55). Will the Lord Jesus say this of us at our convention?

There must be divisions, the Scriptures say, to show who is approved. But arguing in the church is like arguing in marriage: if you're trying to win, you'll lose even when you win.

A wise pastor said to a young seminary student eager to bring change to the church, "Beware of loving the fight." Conventions and debates are necessary; but the moment we love winning more than we love one another as saints and faithful brothers, we've lost even if we win.

This is what St. Paul wants for us: "May you be strengthened with all power, according to His glorious might, for all endurance and patience with joy, giving thanks to the Father, who has qualified you to share in the inheritance of the saints in light" (Colossians 1:11–12).

Compare that with the man who said to Jesus, "Teacher, tell my brother to divide the inheritance with me" (Luke 12:13). The inheritance is shared; it is not mine or yours, something we can divide up or hoard for ourselves. It is the inheritance of the saints—and that only by virtue of being in Christ, the true Saint, the true Holy One. Jesus said to Peter in the Upper Room, "Unless I wash you, you have no share—no part, no portion of the inheritance—with Me" (see John 13:8). Jesus does this, Jesus acts, Jesus performs, Jesus gives us the share of His inheritance.

Which is to say, our congregations, our districts, our Synod, our families, our own calling as disciples of Jesus—none of it is our own doing. The Father has qualified us, delivered us, transferred us to the Son's kingdom, for He has redeemed us.

St. Paul continues this theme in the next chapter of Colossians, where everything is grounded in our new identity in Jesus:

> In Him also you were circumcised with a circumcision made without hands, by putting off the body of the flesh, by the circumcision of Christ, having been buried with Him in baptism, in which you were also raised with Him through faith in the powerful working of God, who raised Him from the dead. And you, who were dead in your trespasses and the uncircumcision of your flesh, God made alive together with Him, having forgiven us all our trespasses. (Colossians 2:11–13)

"In Him," "with Him," "with Him," "with Him": Circumcised in Him, buried with Him, raised with Him, made alive with Him—all things are with Him and in Him and through Him.

The Father has delivered us from wars, strife, and contention. He has transferred us to Christ's kingdom, where forgiven brothers and sisters forgive one another.

This is why St. Paul can call us saints, holy ones, because Jesus takes sinners and calls them saints. We are faithful brothers, loyal to one another, for we have one Brother from whom we derive our brotherhood.

"We know that we have passed out of death into life," St. John says, "because we love the brothers" (1 John 3:14). Over this week, we may disagree on some things. May it not be as sons of thunder, calling down fire or jockeying for positions of greatness. We are saints, made holy by the blood of the Lamb. We are faithful brothers because we have a Brother who was faithful unto death. In Him will we live, in Him will we die, and His will we be forever.

✠INJ✠

7

"Built on the Rock—Confess"

Convention Essay

Rev. Dr. Daniel O. S. Preus, LCMS Fifth Vice-President

66th Regular Convention of The Lutheran Church—Missouri Synod

JULY 12, 2016

Built on the Rock the Church shall stand
　　Even when steeples are falling.
Crumbled have spires in every land;
　　Bells still are chiming and calling,
Calling the young and old to rest,
But above all the souls distressed,
　　Longing for rest everlasting. (*LSB* 645:1)

These words are true. Spires have crumbled and fallen in our land—many of them, but bells are still chiming and calling. They're calling to you and to me and to all who are looking for rest from their labors. And what do the bells stand for? They stand for the confession. They stand for the rock on which our Church is built. "You are the Christ, the Son of the living God" (Matthew 16:16), Peter confessed. This is the confession and the rock on which you and I are built. The theme I have been given today to talk to you about is confession.

A person could go in more than one direction with this theme. We could talk about the confession of sin—and there would certainly be a great deal to talk about. In fact, if we spent our time together actually confessing our sins, we would never get out of here. There is far too much to confess.

We could talk about the fifth chief part of Luther's Small Catechism, I suppose—the Office of the Keys and Confession. But the Confession spoken of in this part of the Small Catechism also deals with the confession of sin and then, of course, Absolution. But, as Luther says, "Confession has two parts. First, that we confess our sins, and second, that we receive absolution, that is, forgiveness, from the pastor as from God Himself, not doubting, but firmly believing that by it our sins are forgiven before God in heaven." Actually, it is this message of absolution, that is, forgiveness, which leads us into the kind of confession we are talking about here. Peter's confession is actually a confession about the forgiveness of sins, a confession about the Gospel, a confession that Jesus is the Christ, the Son of the living God. In other words, God the Son took on human flesh in the person of Jesus and came to save us from our sins by forgiving them. This is what Peter's confession means. This is the rock, this message of the Gospel about Jesus, this is the confession upon which you and I and the entire Church are built.

As we consider this confession, I would like to do it under the subtheme espoused by Jesus in the Gospel of Matthew. He says, "So everyone who acknowledges Me before men, I also will acknowledge before My Father who is in heaven" (Matthew 10:32). A key word here is translated from the Greek word ὁμολογέω. Literally, it means "to speak the same word." It could be translated "to speak together, to speak the same language or to agree." In the New Testament, the translation I favor most frequently is the word *confess*. But however it is translated, it should be remembered that the Greek word ὁμολογέω begins with the prefix ὁμο, which is short for ὁμός, which means "same or together." So it is that the confessing we do is the confession of the same thing, the same doctrine, the same faith, and we do it together. Together, we confess the same faith the Church has always confessed since God established the first congregation of believers, Adam and Eve, when He gave them the promise of the Savior, created faith in their hearts, and founded the Church.

"Whoever confesses Me before men." Just think—when the pastor opens the service in the name of the Father and of the Son and of the Holy Spirit, you hear the same name of the triune God that has been heard by the members of the Church universal since the time of Jesus; and to that name you add your

"Amen," and you confess thereby your faith in the same gracious God in whom they believed. When you speak the words of the Apostles' Creed or of the Nicene Creed, you confess with your mouth, together with those around you, precisely the same convictions the Church has been expressing for the past seventeen hundred years. And just think—every Christian since the time of Jesus has prayed using the same words you pray every time you pray the Lord's Prayer, and in so praying, you are united in faith with every Christian who has gone before you, and you are confessing your reliance on the same God in whom they believed and to whom they prayed. Whenever your pastor concludes the Divine Service with the Benediction given to Aaron and used among God's people for over thirty-five hundred years, you hear these words, "The Lord bless you and keep you, the Lord make His face shine on you and be gracious unto you, the Lord look upon you with favor and give you peace." And when you hear those words, you realize again that the faith that lived in the hearts of Moses and Aaron and the children of Israel is the same faith that God has given to you and those around you. You sing "Amen," and you confess your unity in the faith with the Church universal.

Nor is this common confession of the faith confined to earth. We sing the same song as the 144,000 who even at this moment stand around the throne of the Lamb. Isn't that what we confess every time we receive the Lord's Supper and the pastor prays, "Therefore with angels and archangels and with all the company of heaven we laud and magnify Your glorious name, evermore praising You and saying, 'Holy, holy, holy Lord, God of Sabaoth; heav'n and earth are full of Thy glory'"? (See *LSB Altar Book*, p. 264.) Our voices are joined together with those of the saints and angels in heaven as one Church, one choir. Together, we confess the Lamb and sing His praises.

"Whoever confesses Me before men." It is important in this day of individualism and of the selfie, an age of hedonism and narcissism and the deification of the self, that we emphasize the importance of corporate confession. And I'm talking here not about the confession of sins—we need to do that, too, of course. But I'm talking about the common confession of the faith.

Although we certainly confess individually, we also confess together, and because our confession is based not on our own thoughts or the ideas of brilliant people but on the Word of God, we all can confess with the same words. And we do. So don't ever imagine, even for a moment, that you are not a confessor.

"Whoever confesses Me before men." From the time of Baptism until the time of death, the life of the Christian is a life of confession. In the Rite of Holy Baptism, the person to be baptized is asked, "Do you renounce the devil?" "Yes, I renounce him," is the answer given. "Do you renounce all his works and all his ways?" "Yes," is the response, "I renounce them" (*LSB*, p. 270). It is a confession. And if you participate in the commendation of the dying, before you breathe your last, you will again confess the words of the Apostles' Creed, and together with Simeon, you will pray, "Lord, now You are letting Your servant depart in peace, according to Your word; for my eyes have seen Your salvation that You have prepared in the presence of all peoples" (Luke 2:29–31).

"Whoever confesses Me before men." The life of a Christian is a life of confession, and we who are Lutherans are particularly aware of this truth. In the Lutheran Church today, we are accustomed to celebrating the Festival of the Reformation on October 31, the day in 1517 when Martin Luther posted his Ninety-Five Theses on the door of the Castle Church in Wittenberg. What was Luther's response to the false teaching of his day? Confession. It started with the very first of the Ninety-Five Theses, and it has continued for five hundred years. The Lutheran Church began as a confessing church. And as you know well, Martin Luther was not the only confessor.

On June 25, 1530, the Augsburg Confession was presented to Charles V, emperor of the Holy Roman Empire. This was the first public confession produced by the Lutherans and subscribed to by all Lutheran congregations. It was written by Philip Melanchthon, who had depended extensively on the writings of Martin Luther for its content. It was written to demonstrate that the Lutheran teaching was, simply put, the teaching of the Bible and of historic Christianity. And although it was a confession embraced only by the Lutherans at that time, it was nevertheless a confession for all Christians. Because in all its teachings, in everything it says, it is in complete agreement with the Scriptures, and it faithfully teaches the pure Gospel of our Lord Jesus Christ. But the Augsburg Confession was in many parts rejected by the Church of Rome. So, the Lutherans produced another confession, the Apology of the Augsburg Confession. The Apology expanded upon the teachings of the Augsburg Confession, laying out at great length and with extreme clarity the scriptural teaching of justification by grace through faith in Jesus Christ. These two initial confessions were followed by the Smalcald Articles, further clarifying the Lutheran teaching over and against the false teachings of the Roman Church. Eventually, the Formula of Concord was written to clear up disagreements that arose after the death of Luther, and all these confessions, together with Luther's two catechisms and the three Ecumenical Creeds, were gathered together in 1580 into what we call the Book of Concord.

"Whoever confesses Me before men." Every congregation of The Lutheran Church—Missouri Synod and every pastor and every commissioned minister subscribes to the Book of Concord and says on the day of ordination or commissioning, "This is my confession." What a wondrous treasure we have in this unity of confession!

This treasure is even greater than at first might be imagined. In The Lutheran Church—Missouri Synod, we subscribe to the Lutheran Confessions in a very specific way. There are two ways in which one can state support for these Lutheran Confessions. We have historically described these ways with two Latin words, *quia* and *quatenus*. *Quia* means "because"; *quatenus* means "insofar as." Over the years, there have been liberal Lutherans who have claimed that they subscribe to the Lutheran Confessions *insofar* as they agree with the Scriptures. At first glance, this might sound rather pious. After all, we certainly would not want to confess anything as true that is in disagreement with the Scriptures. Unfortunately, this kind of approach strongly implies that there are statements, maybe many statements, in the Lutheran Confessions that are not in agreement with the Bible. To these statements, a person with a so-called *quatenus* subscription would not want to agree. But a *quatenus* subscription is really no subscription at all. After all, I can subscribe to the Book of Mormon insofar as it agrees with the Scriptures. I can subscribe to the Yellow Pages insofar as they agree with the Scriptures. I suppose I could even subscribe to the Qur'an insofar as it agrees with the Scriptures! To say, "I subscribe to the Lutheran Confessions insofar as they agree with the Scriptures" is actually to say, "I do not subscribe to the Lutheran Confessions."

In all faithful Lutheran churches, a *quia* subscription to the Lutheran Confessions has always been the practice—by pastors, by teachers, by congregations. The service of ordination in our *LSB Agenda* gives a good example of how faithful Lutherans subscribe to the Book of Concord. The following question is asked of a man who is seeking ordination as a pastor. This is not the only question, of course, but one of many, and it is a very important question. It follows immediately after questions about the pastor's commitment to the Scriptures and the Ecumenical Creeds.

> **Here's the question:**
>
> Do you confess the Unaltered Augsburg Confession to be a true exposition of Holy Scripture and a correct exhibition of the doctrine of the Evangelical Lutheran Church? And do you confess that the Apology of the Augsburg Confession, the Small and Large Catechisms of Martin Luther; The Smalcald Articles; The Treatise on the Power and Primacy of the Pope; and The Formula of Concord—as these are contained in The Book of Concord—are also in agreement with this one scriptural faith?
>
> **The answer:**
>
> Yes, I make these Confessions my own **because** they are in accord with the Word of God. (*LSB Agenda*, p. 166)

"Whoever confesses Me before men." What a wonderful gift the Holy Spirit has given us in the unity of our confession! We are in agreement on the scriptural teaching of the Trinity. We are in agreement on the two natures in Christ, the human and the divine. We are in agreement on infant Baptism and on the blessings that Baptism brings, namely, the gift of the Holy Spirit and the forgiveness of sins. We are in agreement in our teaching on the Lord's Supper, namely, that the bread and the wine are the body and blood of Jesus, the Son of God, and that with them we receive the forgiveness of sins, and where there is forgiveness of sins, there is also life and salvation. And we are in agreement that salvation is a gift of God received through faith in Jesus Christ without any merit or worthiness on our part. What a gift we have in this unity and in many other teachings contained in our Lutheran Confessions to which all our pastors and church workers and congregations subscribe. And we do not subscribe to these confessions because their teachings happen to coincide with ours. We subscribe to them because their teachings are the teachings of the Bible.

Five hundred years ago, this Lutheran confessing began with the nailing of a document to the door of a church in Wittenberg. That's a half millennium of confessing. And in this confessing, our Lutheran forebears were following the example of the martyrs and saints who went before them, men and women who confessed the truth—often in the face of severe persecution and even death. At times, their confession was a bold and powerful one, at times it may have been rather quiet, but in one way or another, they gave an answer concerning the hope that was in them.

And it is especially as we consider the death of the martyrs that we realize this confessing we do is not just something we do together; nor does this joy and this right of confessing the faith and confessing our trust in Jesus belong just to the Church as a whole. Rather, it belongs to every individual Christian. It belongs to you. You see, there is an intimate connection between faith and confession. The apostle Paul says, "If you confess with your mouth that Jesus is Lord and believe in your heart that God has raised Him from the dead, you will be saved. For with the heart one believes and is justified, and with the mouth one confesses and is saved" (Romans 10:9–10). This is not to suggest that confession is a good work that in and of itself saves. No, faith justifies, Paul says, and out of this faith the mouth sends out a confession. The Holy Spirit, through His Word, breathes in faith, and the one who is a Christian breathes out a confession of that faith. Christians confess the faith, whether together with other Christians in the Divine Service or individually, as they go about their daily lives. Do they confess at every single opportunity? Sadly, no. But Christians do confess the faith. There is an intimate connection between faith and confession. Martin Franzmann put it this way in stanza 3 of his hymn "Thy Strong Word," where we sing, "And our lives our hopes confess" (*LSB* 578). Our lives our hopes confess. I think, therefore, it is entirely appropriate that the Office of National Mission has adopted the theme "Every One His Witness"™ for its outreach program.

When I used to teach a confirmation class, I would have a true/false section on the tests I gave. One of the questions that would generate a lot of discussion was this one: "True or false? Christians go to church." Now some of the students would mark "False," because they wanted to avoid the idea that if you missed church for one or two Sundays, you were not a Christian. On the other hand, the statement "Christians do not go to church" is obviously false.

So it is with the confessing of the faith. True or false? Christians confess their faith in church and in the world. You cannot respond to this statement with the word *False*. At the same time, we admit that we do not always do what we should. We are sinful, and although it ought to be as natural as breathing to confess this faith that is in us, we are often reluctant or timid or afraid or embarrassed. Yes, it is true. We don't treat our spouse the way we should; we don't treat our children the way we should; we don't treat our neighbors the way we should; we don't confess our Lord the way we should.

But Paul says, "If you confess with your mouth that Jesus is Lord and believe in your heart that God has raised Him from the dead, you will be saved. For with the heart one believes and is justified, and with the mouth one confesses and is saved." And Peter says, "In your hearts honor Christ the Lord as holy, always being prepared to make a defense to anyone who asks you for a reason for the hope that is in you; yet do it with gentleness and respect" (1 Peter 3:15). And Jesus says, "So everyone who acknowledges Me before men, I also will acknowledge before My Father who is in heaven" (Matthew 10:32).

Now if Peter and Paul and Jesus tell us this is something we should be doing as we live out our lives as Christians, then shouldn't we be looking for every opportunity to confess with confidence and with joy the hope that is in us? But perhaps, like Moses, you don't think you are eloquent enough. Let me tell you a story.

When I was a pastor in Colorado Springs back in the early '90s, one of my members, a seventeen-year-old man named Matthew, contracted leukemia. The good news was that one of the most qualified doctors in the nation for the treatment of leukemia practiced in Colorado Springs. The bad news was that Matthew's leukemia was spreading rapidly, and he was allergic to penicillin and all penicillin-related drugs. The doctor told Matthew there was an experimental treatment he could try. The doctor could make no promises, but Matthew didn't know what else to do. Matthew agreed, and the treatment began. I would visit Matthew quite frequently, as he deteriorated, every day. One day, Matthew had an interesting story to tell me. The previous day, his doctor had stopped by and said to him, "Matthew, I want to give you something. I have given this to many of my other patients, and they have all survived. It is a Buddhist stone. If you hold it tightly in your hand and pray, I believe it can help you." What do you think Matthew did? This doctor held Matthew's life in his hands.

The day after the doctor had given him the Buddhist stone, when he came to see Matthew again, Matthew said to him, "Doctor, I appreciate everything you are doing for me, but I need to give you this stone back. I have my God and my Savior; I don't need a stone."

Matthew didn't need a stone. He was built on the Rock.

You know, Matthew's confession, although it was a courageous one made to a person responsible for his survival, was not a particularly eloquent confession.

When Jerome of Prague (1379–1416) was about to be burned at the stake for his faith, his confession was eloquent, "This soul, I offer, Christ, in flames to thee."[1] Matthew's confession was much simpler. But it said what needed to be said. Our confession of the faith doesn't need to be eloquent. What does the familiar hymn say?

> If you cannot speak like angels,
> If you cannot preach like Paul,
> You can tell the love of Jesus,
> You can say He died for all.
> If you cannot rouse the wicked
> With the judgment's dread alarms,
> You can lead the little children
> To the Savior's waiting arms.[2]

Our testimony doesn't need to be eloquent. But there is one thing that it must do. When I was twenty years old, I was living in Germany attending the *Lutherische Theologische Hochschule*, a school and seminary of our partner church in Germany, the *Selbständige Evangelische—Lutherische Kirche*. All of the classes for the year had ended, and all the students had gone home. My flight home to the United States would leave the evening of the next day, and I was packing. But I was also a bit lonely. Nobody was on campus, and I was bored, so I thought I would visit the American military base in town. I walked down the hill to Camp King, showed them my passport, and they told me where I was allowed to go. I discovered a bowling alley and for lack of anything better to do, decided to bowl a few games. A young man was there watching me bowl, and since I was bowling pretty well that day, he continued to watch. Eventually, we struck up a conversation, and I learned that he had just enlisted in the military and was at his first posting. His name was Steve, and he was Jewish. He was away from home for the first time in his life, and he was lonely. He discovered that I was studying to be a pastor and thought he would take advantage of this budding theologian in front of him and ask me some questions. Now I am usually ready for questions, but his first one almost stumped me. "I have been seeing a lot of dead birds lately. What does this mean?" I was tempted to answer, "Pesticides?" but I didn't know him well, so I avoided what may have been cute but also

1 *Fox's Book of Martyrs*, ed. John Malham and T. Pratt (Philadelphia: J. & J. L. Gihon, 1813), 750.

2 *The Lutheran Hymnal* (St. Louis: Concordia, 1941), 496:2.

might have offended him. At any rate, I answered his question in a way I can't remember and spent the next four hours answering other questions about God, eternal life, heaven, the resurrection, and a number of other topics. As it grew late in the afternoon, I decided to go back to my dorm and pack for my flight home. As I prepared to leave, he said, "Daniel, I want you to know how much this conversation has meant to me. I think when I am done in the military, I'm going to become a rabbi."

It took me a moment to register what I had omitted in my conversation with Steve. And I was ashamed when I realized that in four hours of conversation, I had not talked about Jesus. I changed my plans on the spot. I would just go to bed late. I spent another four hours with Steve, and I spent all of it talking about Jesus. The next morning, I took him to a Lutheran service done in English in Frankfurt, and the pastor had the best sermon I ever heard him preach—and he preached about Jesus. I then took Steve to the Frankfurt Zoo and continued our conversation, all the while directing his attention to the person and work of Jesus. And then I really had to leave, or I would have missed my flight back to the States. But before I left, Steve said to me, "Daniel, I believe everything you have told me."

The point is that when we make our confession to others, in whatever form we make it, it is absolutely essential that we remember to keep the person and work of Jesus at the center of our confession. As the hymn declares:

> Christ alone is our salvation,
> Christ the Rock on which we stand;
> Other than this sure foundation
> Will be found but sinking sand.
> Christ, His cross and resurrection,
> Is alone the sinner's plea;
> At the throne of God's perfection
> Nothing else can set him free.[3]

Nothing else! There is no access to the Father, there is no salvation, there is no hope apart from the person of Jesus. That's why we sing, "My hope is built on nothing less Than Jesus' blood and righteousness" (*LSB* 575:1). That's why St. Paul says, "For no one can lay a foundation other than that which is laid,

3 *The Lutheran Hymnary* (Minneapolis: Augsburg Publishing House, 1913), 81:1.

which is Jesus Christ" (1 Corinthians 3:11). That's why St. Peter says, "There is no other name under heaven given among men by which we must be saved" (Acts 4:12). That's why we sing, "On Christ, the solid rock, I stand; All other ground is sinking sand" (*LSB* 575:Refrain). It is about Him that we speak when asked about the hope that is in us. You see, in Jesus, and only in Jesus, God's grace was poured out upon us and is always offered to us. For He alone is the Lamb of God who takes away the sins of the world. Mohammed never did that. Christ alone has kept the Law for us perfectly. Buddha never did that. Jesus alone was our substitute, punished in our place. He alone bore the full wrath of God at sin and died for every sinner who ever lived. No Hindu god has ever done that. Christ alone has, by His own power, risen from the dead, proving that He alone has the power to save all who trust in Him. No one else has ever raised himself from the dead. Salvation comes through Jesus alone. In Him alone is grace. For this reason, President Harrison has identified the phrase "It's *still* all about Jesus" as the theme for the Missouri Synod's celebration of the five-hundredth anniversary of the Reformation. Indeed, it is still all about Jesus!

There is one more aspect of this topic of our confession that I need to address before I conclude. Jesus says, "Whoever confesses Me before men, him will I confess before My Father who is in heaven." As I was preparing a sermon about six months ago, I was reading these words of Jesus, and they hit me with great impact. "Him will I confess." One day, I will stand before the judgment seat of God, and my Savior Jesus is going to confess me before the Father. He is going to point to me and say, "Father, this is one of Your dear children. He confessed Me before men; I confess him now before You. Receive him into the kingdom, which You prepared for him before the world began." And the Father will look at me, and He will say, "Come. I cannot refuse him whom My Son confesses. So, come, enter the place My Son has prepared for you. Come, receive your inheritance." This is what you and I look forward to as the Last Day approaches. It will be the day on which Jesus confesses you and me to the Father.

What joy to know, when life is past,
The Lord we love is first and last,
    The end and the beginning!
He will one day, oh, glorious grace,
Transport us to that happy place
    Beyond all tears and sinning!
    Amen! Amen!

Come, Lord Jesus!
Crown of gladness!
We are yearning
For the day of Your returning! (*LSB* 395:6)

And on that day, He will confess you before the Father. Luther writes about this text in Matthew:

> Who would not be afire and for joy desire not only to confess but even to die confessing Christ? These things which Christ here speaks to comfort His own are priceless, for He knows our infirmity and the intensity of persecution in the world from our flesh and from the devil. Against this distress, therefore, He sets Himself in all His majesty and boasts that He Himself is the one who preaches us, that His Father and the angels are the audience, and that heaven is the place, or church, where He preaches. (AE 67:110)

What a marvelous explanation of the text Luther gives us. We preach Jesus to everyone on earth, and He preaches us to everyone in heaven. On the Last Day, Jesus will confess you and me to the Father in heaven and to the angels. But He confesses us even now. He is a mediator. This is what He does. "Father, forgive them, for they know not what they do" (Luke 23:34). He pleads from the cross for those who have sinned against Him. He pleads also for us who have sinned against Him. The Book of Hebrews says, "He is able to save to the uttermost those who draw near to God through Him, since He always lives to make intercession for them" (Hebrews 7:25).

My brothers and sisters, The Lutheran Church—Missouri Synod is a confessional church. And it is not only because we subscribe to the Lutheran Confessions. That is one reason. But it is also because we believe in confessing. And now is the time for confessing! The apostle Paul says in 2 Corinthians, "For He says, 'In a favorable time I listened to you, and in a day of salvation I have helped you.' Behold, now is the favorable time; behold, now is the day of salvation" (2 Corinthians 6:2). Well, if now is the day of salvation, it is then irrefutable that now is also the day for confession! Because now is the day of salvation, Jesus is even now confessing you and me to the Father. Therefore, it is the time for us to confess—and we want to confess—as individuals in our daily lives and vocations, as congregations when we gather together around Word and Sacrament, and as a church body to the world around us. It is the time for us to confess that Jesus is Lord to the glory of God the Father and to proclaim to all that everyone who calls upon Him will be saved. It is the time for us to confess, for the day of His return is drawing near. Bo Giertz describes the significance of that day for us who are built upon Jesus:

> Now another storm is raging, the breath from the four winds that breathes upon these slain, that they may live (Ezekiel 37:9). Everything that does not belong to Christ is swept away. However, everything that is born of the Spirit will rise up and sing and rejoice in the coming of the Lord. It turns out there is a dwelling-place that isn't made by hand, a building that comes from God. It rests on the Rock, Jesus, and not even the gates of hell are too much for it.[4]

May God lead us always to confess the One who confesses us. Amen.

By the way, Matthew survived his struggle with leukemia. God heard his prayer and answered him and restored him. Today he is married and lives in Ohio with his wife and children.

---

4 Bo Giertz, *To Live with Christ* (St. Louis: Concordia, 2008), 595.

The Gates of Hell and the Religion of Sex

Rev. Dr. Scott R. Murray

An old-line Protestant seminary rescinds a prestigious prize to a pastor of its own denomination who does not share its new-line sex-driven theology.

Sermons and other communications of pastors in Houston are subpoenaed by the city attorney when the mayor is enraged by their opposition to her bathroom ordinance requiring that public restrooms in the city be opened to people according to their personal gender assumptions, irrespective of their biological sex.

The livelihood of a pious Christian florist in Washington State is threatened when she declines to provide flowers for a same-sex wedding and pleads that she could not participate in the event by providing floral arrangements because it violated her Christian moral principle that marriage be between one man and one woman.

The Religion of Sex

What is going on? How did we get here? We are amid a societal shift of epic proportions; and make no mistake, this shift will have dramatic effects on the Church. Each of these scenarios, in which Christianity is being attacked, have in common one thing: sex. Christians must face the fact that we are being challenged by another aggressive religion.

The elites[1] would like us to think that Christianity's most dangerous enemy is Islamic extremism. As dangerous as Islamism might be to our Western society, we are far more endangered by the religion that is growing up in our midst. The enemy within is much more dangerous than external enemies, because it is a harbinger of Western society's suicide. This new religion endangers all in its path and threatens Christianity with persecution.

Rev. Timothy Keller had the 2017 Kuyper Prize rescinded after some hemming and hawing by the Princeton Theological Seminary leadership, because the seminary community objected so vociferously. When the prize was originally announced, Princeton Seminary cited Keller's effort in bringing mission work back to the inner cities, publishing religious books, and helping start many mission churches as the supporting reasons why they would so honor Keller.

Within days, the Princeton Seminary community exploded with rage against Keller. What had Tim Keller done to raise the ire of that community and cause the seminary to rescind the Kuyper Prize? Keller, who founded the burgeoning Redeemer Presbyterian Church in Manhattan, had the prize rescinded for the sins of (gasp!) opposing the ordination of women and the sexual practice of LGBTQ+ individuals, while supporting marriage as the lifelong union of one man and one woman. Keller's congregation is committed to these positions, because the Bible actually has something to say about sexual practice, marriage, and the sexual roles of men and women.

However, what could be the position of a historically Christian seminary, like Princeton, on these issues? How could Princeton Seminary be opposed to Keller's views? Most people presume that such seminaries are faithfully passing on the Christian tradition as they remember its being taught to them in church and Sunday School in the past. Unfortunately, old-line seminaries like Princeton long ago abandoned the traditional depiction of the Christian truth.

Case Thorp, himself a Presbyterian pastor, points out that progressive Christianity, which has completely hijacked Princeton Seminary, has rejected the idea that the Church and her children find their identity in Christ and has turned to a foreign identity cult in which the Christian finds his or her meaning in sexual experience or orientation. "Entire theologies have developed from one's self orientation in an attempt to denounce patriarchy, sexism, racism and homophobia. . . . Now queer theology asks, in the words of Marcella Althaus-Reid [died 2009], 'What can sexual stories from fetishism and sadomasochism

1 See Victor Davis Hanson's definition of the word *elite* in the Introduction above.

tell us about our relationship with God, Jesus and Mary?'"[2] Sexually perverted stories are now defining our relationship with our God. In such a theology, sex trumps Christ every time; in other words, sex has become God.

In 2014, Houston's then mayor, Annise Parker, rammed through the city council a so-called "bathroom ordinance," opening women's restrooms to biological males who claimed to be feminine in gender (and vice versa), placing women and children at risk. The people of Houston, where I am a pastor, did not take kindly to this imposition and immediately agitated for a referendum to repeal the measure, for which there is provision in the city charter.

Mayor Parker was particularly angry with the Christian pastors who campaigned to procure enough signatures on the petition to put the issue on the next election ballot in an effort to overturn the measure. The mayor's administration tried to silence five pastors, whose sermons and personal communications were subpoenaed by the city attorney. This caused a fair amount of anger in Houston, because Houstonians expect to be free to speak and write about their moral convictions without any threat from political authorities.

The effort to silence the pastors, known as "The Houston Five," became a national media circus. As a Christian pastor and as a citizen living under the protections of the First Amendment of the United States Constitution, I joined the fray in an editorial carried by *Religion News Service* entitled, "Why I Stand with the Houston Five." If there is a First Amendment right to the free exercise of religion, our pastors ought to be free to say whatever they want about moral issues in the public square without fear of government coercion.

Unfortunately, that expectation is not supported by many people in our country and especially most of the activist class. Already in 1993, declining freedom for religious practice and speech gave rise to the so-called "Religious Freedom Restoration Act" (RFRA) introduced by New York Senator Chuck Schumer, passed by the United States Congress, and signed into law by President Bill Clinton. How amazing the precipitous decline in religious freedoms that has occurred since then! Now there is rage and spite against the very ideas of free speech and religious freedom.

---

2 Case Thorp, "A Seminary Snubs a Presbyterian Pastor," *The Wall Street Journal*, March 24, 2017.

What Happened to the Free Exercise of Religion?

Twenty states have passed RFRA laws and other similar religious protections, including one passed by the Texas legislature to grant pastors the right to practice in accordance with their consciences: the "Pastor Protection Act." Theoretically, this law would keep Christian pastors from being forced by law to perform a wedding of two men. About it, Governor Greg Abbott said, "Religious leaders in the state of Texas must be absolutely secure in the knowledge that religious freedom is beyond the reach of government or coercion by the courts."[3] What is troubling about laws of this sort, including RFRAs, is that they are an admission that the First Amendment of the Constitution is no longer able to defend the right of Christians (let alone Christian pastors!) to exercise their religion freely. Why would such a law be necessary in Texas if, as stated in the First Amendment, "Congress shall make no law . . . prohibiting the free exercise [of religion]"?[4] Wouldn't the First Amendment free pastors and other Christians from coercion and enable them to practice in accordance with their conscience? The answer is that the animus against the Christian Church and her leaders has grown exponentially over the last twenty years. State legislators are attempting to provide a rearguard action protecting the speech and practice of the religious in our culture. Despite this, and perhaps even because of this, the hatred of Christianity, its adherents, and its values continues to grow.

Normally, Christians have attempted to live at peace with all people. St. Paul admonished his Roman readers, "If possible, so far as it depends on you, live peaceably with all" (Romans 12:18). Yet, despite that (albeit imperfect) effort to live at peace with all, we continue to attract the hatred of the world. Christians do wonder, "Why do they hate us?"

Consider these words from the progressive website Salon, describing religious instruction as "child abuse": "Religion as child abuse has, of course, always formed the mainstay of faith. A desire to indoctrinate the unsuspecting young in faith's dark, lurid dogmas before science, reason, and the enlightening joys of secularism take over and help them mature into healthy adults."[5] Christians are

3 Liz Crampton, "Abbott Signs 'Pastor Protection Act' into Law," *The Texas Tribune*, June 11, 2015, https://www.texastribune.org/2015/06/11/gov-abbott-signs-pastor-protection-act.

4 The author recognizes that some constitutional scholars do not believe that the federal Constitution constrains the states. However, the text of the Fourteenth Amendment reads in part: "No State shall make or enforce any law which shall abridge the privileges or immunities of citizens of the United States; nor shall any State deprive any person of life, liberty, or property, without due process of law; nor deny to any person within its jurisdiction the equal protection of the laws."

5 Jeffrey Tayler, "The Religious Have Gone Insane: The Separation of Church and State—and Scalia from His Mind," Salon, July 26, 2015, http://www.salon.com/2015/07/26/the_religious_have_gone_insane_the_separation_of_church_and_state_and_scalia_from_his_mind.

a drag on the progressive betterment of Western society, stuck as they are in a medieval, flat-earth religious worldview. Secularists want to free us Christians from our dogmatic darkness.

Of course, secularism itself has its own dogmatic convictions incapable of falsification, rendering it for many of its adherents a religious commitment, whose mainstay faith is sex *über alles*. The effort to catechize our children into the faith of Christ is flatly described as child abuse, because it leads children into a false faith. And remember, child abuse is punishable by law. This is an ominous warning.

The Myth of Secularity

Progressives in our culture presume that "secularity" is the neutral non-religious position. However, we Christians must argue that secularity is itself a religious presupposition. It is a presupposition as easily defended as our traditional religious position. Secular materialism is no less religious than a spiritualist position. By spiritualism, I mean a theistic worldview in which there is presumed to be something beyond the measurable world, whatever that something might be. Materialism is the philosophy that there can be nothing beyond this visible, externally measurable world. The materialist believes that we live in a closed system. Materialism denies there is anything beyond what can be seen, measured, or quantified.

Most moderns are materialists. They believe that materialistic secularity is the intellectual default position. They won't believe anything they can't see. This way, religion is ruled out of bounds tout court. No truly rational person could believe the prejudices peddled by the religious as truth. J. Budziszewski, government and philosophy professor at the University of Texas, points out, however, that that which is religious is not merely a prejudice for the existence of God, but rather a religion is that which is of ultimate concern to the believer, whether secular or otherwise.

> In the first place, even a secularism may be the practice of an ultimate concern. We acknowledge this, for instance, by calling Leninism a religion; similarly we say of a greedy man that "his God is money" and call misplaced devotion "idolatry." In the second place, even among those secularisms that do not go so far as to identify ultimate concerns, none is without implications as to what could, or could not,

> count as an ultimate concern. [British philosopher] John Stuart Mill could never decide which, if any, of the "permanent interests of man as a progressive being" was deserving of unconditional loyalty. But one thing he was sure of, that Messiah was not among them.[6]

What makes this secular position religious is that it is held against all other evidence. Ask a materialist if there is any evidence that could be offered to him that would lead him to reject his materialism, and he will likely answer, "No, there can be none." We would answer the same about giving up faith in Christ. Both are equally religious positions, because falsification is unacceptable in both.

It is both increasingly clear and increasingly opaque that progressives in our culture are claiming that their position is both secular and objectively rational, when in fact it represents a belief of ultimate concern and is therefore as much a religious commitment as one centered on Jesus as the Messiah. On the one hand, it is increasingly clear, in that we can see how progressivism will not tolerate any views divergent from its own. This intolerance of any other views is indicative of an ultimate concern, admitting no discussion and brooking no opposition.

On the other hand, it is increasingly opaque to the average person that this is the case because of the brainwashing to which the media industrial complex is committed. A great deal of effort is expended to hide the religious nature of secularism's presuppositions. "What all this tells us is that 'religious' and 'secular' constitute a false dichotomy."[7] Both are fundamentally religious in their nature.

This dichotomy runs completely counter to the claims of the Christian revelation of God's intervention into the world; and especially in His incarnate Son. Christianity's "other-worldly" claims are made in the world and are themselves events in the world. For instance, John the apostle writes of his face-to-face experience of Jesus in his first epistle: "That which was from the beginning, which we have heard, which we have seen with our eyes, which we looked upon and have touched with our hands, concerning the word of life—the life was made manifest, and we have seen it, and testify to it and proclaim to you the eternal life, which was with the Father and was made manifest to us" (1 John 1:1–2).

The events he experienced are the life, death, and resurrection of Christ. They remain evidence that demands a verdict. Unfortunately, many Christians in America

6 J. Budziszewski, "The Illusion of Moral Neutrality," *First Things*, August 1993, https://www.firstthings.com/article/1993/08/the-illusion-of-moral-neutrality.

7 Budziszewski, "The Illusion of Moral Neutrality."

are themselves implicit materialists. They reflexively accept the presuppositions of materialism that they have not examined but that is fed to them from their mother's breast by the media industrial complex. They assume that secularism is neutral, rational, and defensible on its own terms, while Christianity or other religions are full of unproven ideas and indefensible prejudices.

Government is susceptible to being influenced by both secularity and religiosity, because neither position is absolutely defensible in a rationalistic way. However, if this is true, how would the constitutional government of the United States be kept from being taken hostage by a particular sectarian religious view, if there is no barrier to keep religion from influencing government? In other words, how do we keep religion from meddling in the government's affairs where it has no competence? The answer to this problem pivots on the way Christianity views the specific religious teachings of the Bible.

Christians believe that the sum and essence of the Christian religion is the life, death, and resurrection of Jesus. These acts of Jesus are the way in which God, through the preaching of His Word in the world, converts, saves, forgives sins, and brings to heaven those who believe in Jesus Christ. None of these things are susceptible to worldly wisdom. They are, as Paul says in 1 Corinthians 1, foolishness to human reason itself. Tragically, in an attempt to co-opt worldly thinking, many churches have reduced their teaching to a set of moral precepts, sometimes as insipid as the gospel according to Rodney King: "Why can't we all just get along?" This is often what secularists are rejecting—the moral meanderings of liberal churches and their people.

For Gospel-centered Christians, the government can never have the competence to establish a religion of any kind or to offer religious instruction to the people. In other words, the Gospel is what makes the Church different from every other institution, including, and especially, government. The Gospel is not the government's bailiwick. Law is. That competence God has given to the government.

God has given government power over right and wrong. Moral authority is precisely the government's gift from God. I am amazed by the number of people who say that government must not impose morals on people! What else is the authority to punish evildoers? When a murderer is sent to prison for life, how else could this be done, but by moral authority? If it is not a moral authority that demands we do this, then we ought to open all the prisons and let out those poor souls upon whom the government has imposed its morals.

Government is God's creature to punish immorality and keep external order (Romans 13). But government may not tell you what you are to believe about Christ, forgiveness, and eternal life. The government's competence is only in law, mere reason, right and wrong, do and don't do. This is the competence of moral law or what we might call natural law.

Thus, when government privileges the secular view of sex, as it did in the Obergefell decision,[8] it makes a fundamentally religious choice, for which it has neither the competence nor the right. It is coercing Christians (and other religious people) to acquiesce to a religion for which there is no basis in our law or tradition. Government in such a move becomes totalitarian; that is, the state becomes the omni-competent authority in all matters, including religious matters, and it attempts to crush all competition. Mediating social institutions are in the crosshairs, especially those that make their own religious claims like the church.

As we Christians fight for our right to exist and to exercise our religion within our country, I believe we need to more forcefully make the point that secularism is not a religiously neutral point of view, but rather an ultimate concern demanding faith on the part of its adherents. Secularists must be treated just as the churches are treated by government.[9]

Unfortunately, there will be a great deal of brainwashing to overcome as we try to make this point with our secularist/materialist friends. If we are to recover an understanding of the First Amendment that gives Christians and Christian institutions equal protection under the law, this is a case that we must make, and I don't mean just before the Supreme Court, but also with our neighbors, friends, and fellow citizens. If we don't, we may soon lose our schools and then our churches.

So-called secularity is now being imposed on Christian colleges and universities. This is beginning to be seen in legislation such as the 2016 California bill (SB 1146) that would have forbidden Christian universities from using religious criteria in hiring professors, a bill that was withdrawn by its sponsor in the California State Senate to an audible sigh of relief from Christian universities in California.

We cannot let our schools and churches have "secular" hiring practices imposed on them. They would cease to be Christian in any recognizable way. This

---

8 *Obergefell v. Hodges*, 135 S. Ct. 2584 (2015). In a 5–4 decision, the United States Supreme Court held that the fundamental right to marry is guaranteed to same-sex couples.

9 This is the point of the case *Trinity Lutheran Church of Columbia, Inc. v. Comer*, 582 US __ (2017), in which the state of Missouri refused to give the church's day care free tire rubber for its playground specifically because it was a Christian institution. The case was decided by the US Supreme Court in favor of Trinity Lutheran Church on June 26, 2017.

would enable the syncretistic secular religion to be imposed on them, including in particular the concomitant religion of sex so avidly supported by secularists. Such a law would make our Christian universities subject to the secular religion and all its dicta enforced by an all-powerful government. Already, our colleges are being held hostage to the secular sexual religion by thinly-veiled threats of Title IX[10] violations.

Government Coercion

The order of battle against Christianity has begun with private business. The enemies of the Church are now testing the waters to attack Christian universities. Once those dominoes fall, the churches themselves will be targeted.

Increasingly, the secularists are employing the coercion of government and the courts to enforce their ideas of enlightenment on religious believers, who are exercising their sincere religious beliefs in the forum of commerce. Take the renowned case of the Christian florist, Barronelle Stutzman, owner of Arlene's Flowers in Richland, Washington. She was sued by the American Civil Liberties Union (ACLU) because she declined to create flower arrangements for the wedding of two men to each other, citing her religious objection to same-sex marriage, despite referring the men to other florists willing to serve them.

Barronelle has consistently served and employed people who identify as homosexual. Yet, the ACLU and the Washington State Attorney General claim that she was guilty of unlawful discrimination when she acted according to her faith by declining to beautify with her floral arrangements the same-sex ceremony of a long-time customer. Stutzman even expressed love and appreciation for this customer. This was to no avail where preference for sexual acts over all other principles is operative.

Unfortunately for Stutzman, her freedom of religion has been deemed to have stopped at the point where her Christian convictions conflicted with the sexual practice of her business clients. The sexual practice of others has overruled in law the Christian convictions of this pious woman.[11]

Would that this case were an anomaly. However, there are several similar cases wending their way through the courts, in which sexual practice limits the religious freedoms of business owners, and in at least one case, a state court has

10 Title IX of the Education Amendments Act of 1972 prohibits discrimination on the basis of sex in any education program or activity that receives federal funding.

11 The oral arguments in this case were presented before the Washington State Supreme Court on November 15, 2016.

said that the limitation of free religious expression is simply the price of doing business in this country. So much for the First Amendment! The chief and primary expression of our constitutional rights is being trampled by a "right" that the framers of the Constitution failed even to enumerate, the right to untrammeled sexual practice.

What do rescinding the Kuyper Prize, subpoenaing church leaders, and suing a Christian florist all have in common? They all involve the issue of sex, especially sexual practice. The West has made a religious commitment to sex. The fact is that sex and sexual practice is fast becoming the ruling religion of the progressive West.

Mary Eberstadt's recent book, *It's Dangerous to Believe: Religious Freedom and Its Enemies,*[12] was deeply clarifying for me. In it, Eberstadt argues that the sexual revolution has generated a secular Western faith, complete with religious ritual and theology as a rival to Christianity. This sexual theology is presently seeking to rule out of bounds the rival faith of traditional Christianity with its acceptance of specific sexual taboos (see the Sixth Commandment).

Eberstadt pleads with the adherents of this new religion (it is perhaps as old as the Garden of Eden) for the toleration of Christianity. I certainly agree with Eberstadt's diagnosis of the problem, but I think that toleration for Christianity is an unlikely outcome. It is unlikely because the views of sexual theology and Christian theology are simply mutually exclusive.

Because it is a new religion, the sexual religion is aggressively militant and persecutes those who are not true believers or who cast doubt on its verities. And in an ultimate irony, there is nothing more intolerant than tolerationism, the creed of the new religion. It will tolerate anyone who agrees with its dicta. If that's toleration, I would hate to experience intolerance!

How Can Sex Be Religion?

By now, you may be asking, "How can sex be considered a religion?" Let's consider the meaning of the word *religion*. Religion implies being unconditionally bound to a set of spiritual or moral principles. According to the French sociologist Émile Durkheim, those who belong to a religion accept a set of behaviors and attitudes that lead to their being identifiably distinguished from others.

12 New York: Harper, 2016.

These beliefs and attitudes set adherents apart from others and imply that there are moral and ceremonial taboos. These things unite the adherents into one community. A religion is held against all possible contradictions; it does not admit of falsification. For example, we Lutheran Christians would say that there would never be any conditions under which we would give up the teaching that Jesus is God.

In our modern context, those who think they have escaped the divine and restrictive impositions of traditional religions, including Christianity, have fallen for a religion that stands for untrammeled sexual freedom against all possible contradictions. Ask one of its adherents, "Is there any argument that would lead you to reject absolute sexual freedom and to require others to tolerate, accept, and even celebrate this way of living?" The answer, in most cases, would be "No." A commitment to behaviors that cannot be subject to contrary arguments is a religious commitment.

I am amazed that when those who are adherents of the religion of sex are asked who they are, they will often answer, "I am homosexual, bi-, lesbian," and so on. When Christians are asked who they are, they will answer, "I am a child of God." How different those two stories of identity are! This difference is an unbridgeable chasm. And the animosity it engenders will be religious in its fury; including shaming, witch hunts, and the demand that the civil government extirpate adherents of the rival religion. In many cases, Western old-line denominations that claim to be Christian actually long ago became adherents of the religion of sex; sexual practice has become the most important issue in their teaching, trumping everything, including and especially the Bible—as is obvious, for example, at Princeton Seminary.

Even the Church Is a Convert

Isn't the language of shaming, witch hunts, and extirpation somewhat extreme? Yet, there are plenty of examples of extremism in the cause of the sexual religion. Some years ago, Western church bodies approached a Lutheran church body in Africa offering large sums of desperately needed money to its theological seminaries, but only under the condition that the African Lutheran Church admit females as candidates to its pastoral office. Of course, the Westerners were encouraging female ordination and were using blackmail to do it.

The wily Africans took the financial support and admitted women to their seminaries with the intent of educating a cadre of deaconesses. These faithful

Africans avoided the ordination of women because they held that the Bible strictly forbids the ordination of women to the Office of the Ministry (1 Corinthians 14:33–34, 37; 1 Timothy 2:11–12; 3:1–2; Titus 1:5–6).

The Westerners, primarily North Americans and Europeans, were quite sure that the sexual differences between men and women should have no effect on actual church practice, under the presumption that the Bible's views about sexuality were outmoded and oppressive toward women ("We've come a long way, baby!"). The Bible was considered to be just plain wrong about the distinction between men and women.

When I pointed to the passages in the apostle Paul's epistles forbidding female leadership in the church's worship life, a progressive woman simply replied, "Oh, yes, Paul. He was a misogynist." The Bible must be wrong when it is found to contradict our views.

The African Christians, however, were not convinced by Western prejudices and refused to be blackmailed into Western sexual heresies. When their African brothers went their own way, the Western churches shamefully treated them as ignorant little brothers, unable to understand correctly, even though these faithful African brothers shared the view of the Church over the previous twenty centuries. Sex defeated every Christian virtue, including genuine respect for Christian fellowship. The sexual verities of the West had become more important to the progressive churches than the biblical truth. For this defection from the divine truth, we Western Christians must heartily repent.

Sex Is Not Far from Spiritual Adultery

The Old Testament warns against the worship of foreign gods, not only to defend the exclusive monotheism of Israel, but also because the foreign gods of the ancient Near East almost always had a strong sexual tendency; they were often worshiped sexually, indeed in orgiastic sexuality. Yahweh warned against this throughout the time of the prophets.

The prophets commonly described acceptance of these deities as spiritual adultery against Yahweh, the true husband of Israel, as for example in Jeremiah 3:6–10, where participation in the pagan cult is described as whoring. (See also Leviticus 17:7.) There is a strong link between a faulty faith and faulty sexual practice.

Rebellion against Yahweh was often explicitly sexual. As Matthew Rueger points out in his timely book *Sexual Morality in a Christless World,*[13] the Early Church likewise confronted an overtly sexualized religious culture among the ancient Romans. The sex cult that is new to us perhaps isn't so new; it was confronted by Jeremiah, Jesus, and John. The Early Church fought this battle long ago, with the martyrs' blood poured out in the work of the Church.

The early Christians themselves constantly battled against the sexual perversion of the Roman world around them. We sometimes accept one particular aspect of the secular myth, that is, that of constant, continual improvement in humanity. This myth, long ago junked by responsible historians, has had long coattails in the Western consciousness, when in fact the world has been better or worse at different times and in different places.

There's no straight-line progression in history. For example, nineteenth-century Germany was one of the best-educated and most genteel countries in the world, and yet Germany became a totalitarian bringer of death in both the first and second world wars in the twentieth century. While both Kaiser Wilhelm and Adolf Hitler would have called this progress, the rest of the world would hardly agree.

World history has always traveled over peaks and through valleys; for example, women have at times been well-treated as persons and raised their families together with respectful and loving husbands, and at other times they have been treated as mere property by their husbands and fathers.

We could be on the verge of falling into exactly that pattern in our day in which women are seen primarily as sexual objects by our culture. There is absolutely no guarantee that human culture would continue in a positive and helpful trajectory. What is called progress has some risk of being detrimental to society and its structure—and every chance of being a regression.

The New Testament: Always Countercultural

Christians battled against a cultural low point in the first three centuries of the Church's era, and they were viciously persecuted for it. The New Testament's forbidding of sexual immorality and the demand for sexual purity within the bounds of the marriage of one man and one woman for life was deeply countercultural in the Roman world. So much so, that the Romans considered it part of the rebellion against Roman government.

13 St. Louis: Concordia, 2016.

Rueger pointed out how deeply sexualized pagan Roman culture was, in which the Romans sexually abused slaves and vulnerable young people, if they had the power to do so. For the Romans, sexuality was often merely an imposition of power, not an act of love as it was conceived by the Christians on the basis of the text of the New Testament. Christianity was a decisive protest against this misuse of humanity and the abuse of the sexual nature of humans.

The pervasive problem of sexual trafficking is an example of the objectification of sexuality in our culture. Rueger encourages Christians: "There are many in our society, as there were in Roman society, who have been victimized by sexual hedonism. Genuine concern for them, joined with a message of sexual chastity, can point them to the Savior whose love stands ready to forgive and restore those broken by sin."[14]

The Church's true love for the needs of the neighbor and her high view of humanity as a gift of a creator God opens the door for Christians to reach out to those who have been used up by the religion of sex and are in need of refuge and a statement of their true identity and value in Christ, who has loved them completely.

The Disappearing Other

The reinterpretation of other humans as sexual objects in our culture leads to a deep and lonely self-centeredness. Others are no longer in pursuit of deep interpersonal relationships, including love and marriage with all of its struggles and difficulties. Instead, others seek only self-gratification. The Christian definition of love, which is a matter of self-giving to the other, has been replaced by a self-love that ignores the benefit of the other entirely. In fact, we are so completely focused on our own pleasure, that the other's reaction is irrelevant. The other is a sexual object who doesn't even need to exist unless he or she gives pleasure.

Religious skeptics used to ask, "Does God really exist?" Sadly, this is a moot question today. The question that should be posed today is "Do others really exist?" Others are unimportant in themselves, except as they give pleasure. This solipsistic dehumanization grows out of a denial of God's existence. Without God to define humanity, I can begin to doubt; first, I doubt the reality of other persons, and finally, I begin to doubt my own existence, leading to a culture of death and suicide.

---

14 Rueger, *Sexual Immorality in a Christless World*, 35.

How can we look on the sexual ethics of our time as anything other than a dehumanization of others, in which they are merely objects for bestowal of pleasure of whatever kind, not persons in their own right to be honored, loved, respected, and sacrificed for? What does the assisted-suicide culture mean, in which others are encouraged to "off" themselves so we don't have to deal with the burden of their suffering? The other is no longer human, but an object. That's all.

Western society has increasingly hated the God who wanted to be "for us" in Christ. With that God dead and gone to our culture, we have now demanded that all others be reduced to "for me." This is a horrifying irony. Other persons only exist for my purposes and my good. But God wants to be "for us." That is the purpose of His sending Jesus to us: "Not to be served but to serve, and to give His life as a ransom for many" (Matthew 20:28). How could true humanity flourish under such conditions where others are not given to and treasured, but used and discarded?

The Christian desire to treat others as better than ourselves will increasingly cause us to run afoul of the sexual religion of our culture and will perhaps land us in prison or before those who are the judges of our laws. We will be seen as haters of humanity, because our views about sexual discipline, which honor the other as worthy of respect, will lead us to clash with the Western sexual religion. The leading edges of these legal challenges are now being seen in the lawsuits against business people like Barronelle Stutzman. We aren't very far from witch trials against Christian morals.

Witch Trials! Are You Kidding?

This is not as far-fetched as it sounds. Witch trials have broken out, as Mary Eberstadt points out, not only in seventeenth-century Salem, Massachusetts, but also more recently in the 1983 trial of the McMartin family, owners of a Los Angeles day care whose teachers were accused of "chopping up animals, sacrificing a baby in a church, making children drink blood, and flying in the air dressed like witches";[15] claims that would have given the Salem Puritans a run for their witch-trial money.

These ridiculous claims did not keep the McMartins from being arrested and brought to trial on the flimsiest of evidence. The capacity of otherwise rational

---

15 Eberstadt, *It's Dangerous to Believe*, 19.

persons to believe these claims against the McMartins is clear evidence of the human desire to identify and punish what we categorize as evil in our midst.

The modern mania for sex is increasingly looking for victims to call out and marginalize, including the naysayers in the confessing Christian churches. Churches' unwillingness to accede to the narrative that aberrant sexual practice is merely a variation of racial tolerance has earned Christians increasingly strident accusations of "hater" or "bigot."

Isn't Sexual Freedom a Civil Right?

This argument, which I heard more than ten years ago from a young homosexual man attempting to justify his lifestyle to me over a pleasant lunch at a local restaurant, presumes that the demand to tolerate all and any sexual activity is the next step beyond the civil rights battle for a color-blind society. And who could be against civil rights? Those who are are accused of wanting to return us to Jim Crow laws and their implication of second-class citizenship. Sexual practice is considered the same as skin color, a morally neutral and an irreformable human characteristic, and therefore no more able to be disapproved of than the color of a person's skin.

This is one of the narratives that was employed by the Supreme Court majority that gave us the Obergefell ruling, requiring that marriage be defined and recognized by the government as any human relationship between two (for now) consenting adults. The court presumed that because race was not constitutive of marriage, as was rightfully argued in the anti-miscegenation case of *Loving v. Virginia,*[16] sex also could not be considered constitutive of marriage.

The point of *Loving v. Virginia* is that race is not constitutive of marriage. However, sex is precisely constitutive of marriage, because man and woman have a sexual complementarity leading to childbearing and child-rearing. This is one of the arguments by which Justice Kennedy, writing for the majority, weakened his defense of same-sex marriage. The arguments of *Loving* are against the goal of same-sex marriage, because *Loving* dealt with matters not having to do with sexual differences. So-called racial differences do not render childbearing and child-rearing or marriage impossible.

---

16 *Loving v. Virginia*, 388 US 1 (1967), is a landmark civil rights decision of the United States Supreme Court, which invalidated laws prohibiting interracial marriage. The case was brought by Mildred Loving, a black woman, and Richard Loving, a white man, who had been sentenced to a year in prison in Virginia for marrying each other. Their marriage violated the state's anti-miscegenation statute, the Racial Integrity Act of 1924, which prohibited marriage between people classified as "white" and people classified as "colored." The Supreme Court's unanimous decision determined that this prohibition was unconstitutional, overruling *Pace v. Alabama*, 106 US 583 (1883), and ending all race-based legal restrictions on marriage in the United States.

Therefore, the Church, with its longstanding ideal that marriage is between one man and one woman, is not hateful and bigoted. And despite whatever sins the Church's children may have perpetrated in the defense of Jim Crow laws, she does not now hate those whose sexual proclivities she considers immoral. She is calling them to repentance that they, too, could be saved sinners, like us. She wants such sinners in the Church and embraces those whose repentant tears require Holy Absolution to wipe them away.

At this point, it would be easy to throw up our hands in despair at the hopelessness of properly defending ourselves against the onslaught of the sexual religion in our culture. And unfortunately, many so-called Christians already capitulated on this issue long ago. If we are not going to capitulate, what shall we do? The Church and her children need to act and respond in faithful, biblical, Gospel-centered ways to this aggressive new religion in our culture. What would that look like? What resources are at our disposal?

What Is There to Be Afraid Of?

I am deeply concerned about being able to defend our faith in the face of mounting cultural and governmental pressure. It has been a long time since government was an overt enemy of the Church and her confession. We are out of practice for defending ourselves from this increasingly powerful onslaught.

There are some things to be learned from the faithful confession of Middle Eastern Christians who are being attacked by radical Islam. They are refusing to let such pressure break up their communities and their church meetings. It should remind us of the encouragement in the Letter to the Hebrews: "Let us consider how to stir up one another to love and good works, not neglecting to meet together, as is the habit of some, but encouraging one another, and all the more as you see the Day drawing near" (Hebrews 10:24–25). Gathering at the Divine Services of our churches will reinforce our love for our neighbor and our desire to share Christ with a dying world.

The Early Church bore up under great persecutions because she had the New Testament gifts of Word and Sacraments always on the lips of her children. Sometimes the people of the Church fled, failed to confess, or capitulated by handing over the sacred books to the Roman authorities; but on the whole, the Lord led the community to confess Him in spite of ridicule, financial pressure, torture, jail time, and slaughter.

We needn't fear what humans can do to us, because we trust a God who is our almighty and living Lord. How comforting this assurance of Jesus remains:

> Do not fear those who kill the body but cannot kill the soul. Rather fear Him who can destroy both soul and body in hell. Are not two sparrows sold for a penny? And not one of them will fall to the ground apart from your Father. But even the hairs of your head are all numbered. Fear not, therefore; you are of more value than many sparrows. So everyone who acknowledges Me before men, I also will acknowledge before My Father who is in heaven, but whoever denies Me before men, I also will deny before My Father who is in heaven. (Matthew 10:28–33)

I have a Father who acknowledges me, even when no one else will. We have nothing to fear. He promises.

Franklin D. Roosevelt said in his first inaugural address, "The only thing we have to fear is fear itself—nameless, unreasoning, unjustified terror which paralyzes needed efforts to convert retreat into advance."[17] We must not freeze like the mouse cornered by a ravening cat. The Church must not be paralyzed by the unreasoning hatred we experience when our enemies attack us, because we have a God; and it is evident, because of that hatred, that we have the truth. The world would not hate us otherwise.

The world has much more to fear than we do. We should not respond to their hatred with unreasoning fear, but far deeper love and concern for God's precious world and every person in it. How many times have we faced a fearful crisis in life and then afterward wondered why we were so afraid? So it is for the Church. We must not let ourselves be frightened into inaction and unfaithfulness. We have nothing to fear. Not even the gates of hell.

Perhaps you know someone who thinks they can win any argument by lambasting you with so many arguments that you finally capitulate, even if those arguments are not compelling for his point. Sometimes people like that will even stoop to personal attacks, calling you names instead of making rational arguments. Many proponents for the sexual religion argue like this. They simply shout down the opposition and attempt to verbally bludgeon them into submission.

---

17 Franklin D. Roosevelt, Inaugural Address, March 4, 1933, as published in Samuel Rosenman, ed., *The Public Papers of Franklin D. Roosevelt, Volume Two: The Year of Crisis, 1933* (New York: Random House, 1938), 11–16.

Defenders of traditional marriage such as Anthony Esolen, Sherif Girgis, and Ryan Anderson have testified to these brown-shirt tactics against them. For example, when Esolen protested against the secularization of the Catholic Providence College, where he was an esteemed professor, students retaliated with a protest march and his faculty "colleagues" circulated a petition that castigated his articles because they contained "racist, xenophobic, misogynist, homophobic, and religiously chauvinist statements." That's quite a mouthful. In response, Esolen said of the petition, "I find the whole thing disgusting."[18] Quite so.

Yet, as common as these tactics are, we should not despair but rather be encouraged. Those who shout the loudest usually have the weakest arguments. Many proponents of the union of one man and one woman in marriage have been attacked this way: "Haters, bigots, racists!" It is ironic that such hateful accusations are leveled against those who are attempting to defend their faith and share the truth. This rage and spite (Psalm 2:1) should only comfort us that we are on the side of truth, where the gates of hell cannot prevail.

Remember How God Has Always Responded to Sin

We have the same resources at our disposal in our battle with the sexual religion as the Early Church had: the truth, Christ, and the Word of God. The victory remains with our Lord Jesus as it did in the first three centuries of Christian history.

We may not, however, expect a quick victory. God seldom works as quickly as we want. The Lord remained with the Church through three hundred years of sporadic persecution, ridicule, hatred, torture, and death. He didn't abandon her in her suffering. He was with her at every moment, and especially in her suffering.

Christ's own suffering shaped the Church's response to her suffering. St. Peter encourages Christians just like us to receive suffering with Christ in mind:

> If when you do good and suffer for it you endure, this is a gracious thing in the sight of God. For to this you have been called, because Christ also suffered for you, leaving you an example, so that you might follow in His steps. He committed no sin, neither was deceit found in His mouth. When He was reviled, He did not revile in return; when

---

18 Brian Fraga, "The Esolen Affair: Esteemed Providence College Professor Attacked Over 'Diversity,'" *National Catholic Register*, December 15, 2016, http://www.ncregister.com/daily-news/the-esolen-affair-esteemed-providence-college-professor-attacked-over-diver.

> He suffered, He did not threaten, but continued entrusting Himself to Him who judges justly. He Himself bore our sins in His body on the tree, that we might die to sin and live to righteousness. By His wounds you have been healed. For you were straying like sheep, but have now returned to the Shepherd and Overseer of your souls. (1 Peter 2:20–25)

The Church of the twenty-first century is increasingly like the Church to which St. Peter wrote; a church under pressure trying to find its way in the world while not being of the world. She would be shaped by suffering; first, because the Lord Himself shaped her in His suffering, and second, because the Lord permitted suffering in the world to shape her into a cruciform shape through that suffering.

We must learn to rejoice in the suffering that the Lord permits to come to us through a world much more hostile to our faith and to our Lord than we have been accustomed until now. We will find ourselves suffering unjustly as justice is redefined in such a way that the law is used against the faith of Christ. Like Christ, we will be faced by unjust justice. Those who confess the Christian faith will increasingly find that they are not admitted to the best schools, or they will find themselves deprived of their businesses or good jobs on purely religious grounds. About this we must rejoice (Matthew 5:11–12). We must not reciprocate this hatred, but should instead pray for those who have made themselves our enemies.

While our moral indignation can get the best of us, it will be no help to vent against the world and its aberrant practices, whether in person or on social media. We must remember that we ourselves have received grace, although we have in no way deserved it. We, too, should heartily forgive and readily do good to those who hate us.

The parable of the unforgiving servant (Matthew 18:23–35) certainly reinforces the need for us to generously share God's grace with those in our culture who hate the Law and the Gospel. Those who hate us should not find any reason to accuse us of hating them. We Christians are in no way narrow-minded bigots; we love those who sin against our God by their lifestyle. We pity those caught in the web of lies and deceit that leads to undisciplined sexual practice.

We love them enough to want to lead them to repentance that they might believe the Gospel (Mark 1:15), even if this causes them to hate us all the more. Our love is not reciprocal; that's why it is Christian love. We give it freely for Christ's sake, not because it is earned. We give it freely and without hope of its being returned by those whom we love. This is especially true of those who are living sexually aberrant lifestyles.

We must remember that many of these people have themselves been abused sexually or have experienced very low self-regard and are seeking affirmation through the degrading means offered by our culture and its religion of sex. They know nothing of the divine gift of spiritual regard given to sinners for the sake of another. They are slaves to the regard of the world and for that reason are willing to give themselves over to its abuse in the hope of gaining the world's esteem.

What a life-changing revelation it is for such a person to come face-to-face with the living God who loves for His own sake and gives Himself away completely, even to His enemies! He forgives those who have sinned against Him and have hurt themselves by their self-destructive actions, and He clears away the wreckage left by their hedonistic lives. Such a God needs to be reflected in the mirror of the Church's children; not to earn good works "points" with God, but to provide rescue to our broken and lost neighbor.

While people who live a sexually depraved life are hurting themselves, offending God, and causing the fabric of our culture to fray badly, at one level we have no reason to be angry with them. We should only be sorry for them and express compassion toward them. They are not hurting us directly (although they are indirectly). We have nothing personally at stake for which we should take offense. It is not up to us to defend God's Law. As they say in Texas, "We have no dog in this hunt."

Yes, we should testify to the Word of God. But God is fully capable of defending His own Law. This enables us to share Christ's Law and Gospel with the person trapped in the religion of sex in a dispassionate way, which may get us a hearing where histrionics will instantly get us shouted down.

Remember, Peter exhorts us to always be "prepared to make a defense to anyone who asks you for a reason for the hope that is in you; yet do it with gentleness and respect, having a good conscience, so that, when you are slandered, those who revile your good behavior in Christ may be put to shame" (1 Peter 3:15–16).

A dear pastor friend of mine lived in an AIDS-blighted neighborhood of New Orleans in the days of the 1990s AIDS epidemic. At the request of a concerned mother, he met with her son, a man who was dying of AIDS. After getting to know the man, he ministered to his physical needs while he lay dying. And in the course of this service, the man confessed to my friend his sexually promiscuous lifestyle and how deeply sorry he was for it.

My friend hadn't even asked how the man had contracted AIDS. But now he was able to share the Gospel with him, and the man was reconverted to his faith before his death. My friend proclaimed the Good News of Christ's defeat of our sin and death at this man's funeral. Although there's no way to know for sure, I don't think he would have been as successful bringing this man the ministry of Law and Gospel had he not also provided sacrificial physical service to the man on his deathbed.

After the world has used up and spit out those who have accepted the sexual religion, we can still bring life and salvation to the broken and discarded because we have an other-worldly faith in which God mends the broken (Matthew 12:20). Our life of mercy given to such persons will be a powerful witness to this other-worldly faith. Our sacrificial service will lead those who are suffering and in need of our help to wonder what kind of Lord leads people to give themselves this way. Those who recognize that they have been abused by the world will be delighted to discover the love of the One who accepted the world's abuse. Through us, God will be snatching Satan's prey from the very gates of his domain and returning them to the kingdom of the Son whom God loves.

Faithfulness in the Face of Wreckage

Adherence to the sexual religion and its rejection of God's Law cannot go on without serious consequences in the world. Families are coming apart because the partners, who think they create family by their choices, abandon each other for a better sexual deal elsewhere. As a result, the most basic building block of human society is crumbling. Children are being neglected and left with the clear message that their parents' pleasure is far more important than their needs, which undergirds the opinion of the Supreme Court majority in *Obergefell.*

The crumbling foundation of the family will have enormous, detrimental effects in society. The lie of complete sexual freedom will also wreak its own wreckages and the god of sexuality will be seen for the empty and useless deity it is. When comes the time prayed for by the psalmist, "Render them their due reward. Because they do not regard the works of the Lord or the work of His hands, He will tear them down and build them up no more" (Psalm 28:4–5), we must have ready the divine Word, which alone can stave off this disaster and resolve for people the aching needs that they themselves will recognize as the world crumbles around them.

We needn't fear this eventuality for two reasons. First, our Lord has predicted the failure of the world and its ultimate consummation at His second coming. The present devolving of this groaning world, burdened as it is under sin, only points to that final judgment for which we eagerly look (Romans 8:22–23), because it includes the fullness of our redemption and our rescue from this present evil age (Galatians 1:4).

Second, the crumbling world is not ultimate. If, in its death throes, the world can serve unto the salvation of my neighbor, then its crumbling will be for a good purpose. Of course, we don't pray for such collapse. We pray for the world to be brought to repentance in a way that is less painful; and all the more because we shall all suffer together, just as those sitting in the front and in the back of the plane all die when it crashes.

If the Church has made common cause with the world by buying into the sexual religion through a slow, but inexorable, worldliness, then the Church will have no resources with which to fight off the new religion or to help those betrayed by it recover themselves. If the worldly churches are lost, they shall never be any good to those who are also lost. It will be the blind leading the blind into a deeper darkness.

We always have a good reason to properly teach our faith to both children and adults in our parishes, to encourage faithful Bible reading and devotional life in the homes of our families; however, this becomes much more urgent in the face of the present descent into religious darkness that will be prevalent in our culture. In the face of such darkness, it is absolutely necessary that we know who we are and who has redeemed us and who is the light of the world.

The institutional church used to depend on the weight of culture to push people toward it in the time when joining a church was seen as "the right thing to do." Now that it has become a positive evil to confess Christ, that complacency will no longer work. Positive catechesis is the only antidote. Faithful confession of the truth on the lips of God's people who have been properly taught in the Church is absolutely critical to this moment in the Church's life.

This has always been the case. In Luther's time, the Reformation was built and buttressed on catechesis. When he saw the miserable religious conditions of the Saxon parishes, he wrote his Small Catechism, a book that has had more impact on the world than any book other than the Bible itself.

A return to a faithful catechetical instruction in difficult days enables us to confess rightly when called to account and to have something meaty and faithful to hand over when the spiritual starvation diet offered by the world leaves us with the famished seeking a little food for the soul. If we can't be distinguished from the world, we will not be a city set on a hill, nor a shining beacon for those dying in the dark.

Catechism instruction and confirmation will no longer be able to be confused with graduation, coming of age, or an escape from the drudgeries of Sunday School. We must see to it that our children know and can confess the faith of the Bible, so they can respond with love and faithfulness to the sexual religion being practiced around them. Adults will have to model this for our children by reciting the catechism with them as they recite it. This is not a torture imposed on children by adults, but the implantation of the divine truth on the hearts of all children, young and old alike.

Everyone is being catechized by someone. Now-aged relatives of mine catechized their children in the modern presumptions about the overpopulation of the world and the low value of human life, convinced as they were by Paul R. Ehrlich's *Population Bomb* (even if they hadn't actually read it). They are now lamenting their lack of grandchildren, because their children have avoided childbearing. The world's catechesis works.

Ours will too, if we are willing to be faithful to our task in this generation. We are catechizing our children with the truth! We are delivering to their hearts the beautiful teaching of Scripture about the inestimably great value of humans and the huge cost at which the Lord redeemed us from our sin and our fallen way of life.

Every family that has properly catechized its children will be a fortress of faithfulness and sanity in an age of false belief and confusion. Out of those children will arise some who will become leaders in thought, art, public affairs, and the church. They will provide a backbone to the future that God has charted for His world. What we teach leads to life. Why wouldn't we teach it as aggressively as we can? There is nothing to fear.

The Deep Humility of the Churches

There is much for which the churches must be humble. First, they have a humiliated Lord. Why should they, too, not wear that mantle? Luther said that the cross is our theology.[19] The cross is the life of the Church, and therefore, the

19 See the Heidelberg Disputation, thesis 20 in AE 31:40ff.

cross shadows the Church in humility. The cross triumphs through weakness and letting be. She receives the divine visitation when and where God is pleased to send it. She lives the Marian faith, "Let it be to me according to your word" (Luke 1:38).

The Church certainly has nothing of her own about which to be proud. Her boast, if she has one, is in a Lord marked by humiliation. Humiliation comes naturally to the Church and her children. Her theology of humiliation, then, should lead us to receive gladly those occasions when we are humbled by the world. We become an instantiation of Christ in His humility when we are humbled.

When we make common cause with those who the world considers to be morally retrograde and weak, those who refuse to bow to the sex god of our culture, the outcome will be obvious. We will be reviled and shouted down by the world. We should, however, wear the badge of such revilement as a sign of who we are in Christ as we share His love for the world.

The Church is often ignored because she appears to be putting on airs, acting puffed up about her authority, and demanding a place at the world's negotiating table. This will no longer be able to be sustained. The Church will have to appear as a penitent, although she may not bow down to the government (Luke 20:25). What's so wrong with appearing as a penitent? Has not our Lord told us that the whole Christian life is a life of repentance? Our power is not in our power, but in our weakness. The humility of the Church before the world is more likely to get us the hearing the world needs.

The old so-called Moral Majority attempted to enforce its will on the world, but it is now dead and perhaps is also a partial cause of our present travail. We are not able to force the world to do anything and shouldn't try in our role as Church (our responsibility to our community as citizens is quite a different thing!).

The human care ministry programs being carried out by the churches show us to be a humble community serving those in need, rather than ourselves. We don't ask questions about whom we are serving; we just do it. We come not to be served, but to serve and give ourselves up. Hasn't our Lord done precisely that (Matthew 20:28)? Humility in the sight of the world has a long theological pedigree.

Our Christian schools are an open door to serve the community with sacrificial service and gain us a hearing. This is why many of our schools are eschewing progressivism for classical methods, fleeing indoctrination for content-rich teaching, giving students the capacity to sort through the emotional appeals of postmodern arguments with carefully constructed logical arguments that hold up under the canons of Aristotelian logic.

These schools will teach that there is truth, beauty, and a morally coherent universe, preparing the next generation to husband these gifts until they can again be shared with a truth-starved world. Admittedly, Christian schools will appeal to a niche market, but if they are successful, they will have an outsized impact.

One of my children graduated from Hillsdale College, a small liberal arts college that uses classical methods. When its president, Dr. Larry Arnn, was asked at a parent weekend event why Hillsdale did not admit more than thirteen hundred students, he answered, "We don't want any more students in the college for two reasons. First, it would make it impossible for us to be a college, that is truly collegial, where parents, students, administrators, and faculty members all work together educating your children. If there were more students we couldn't carry out our mission. Second, if we graduated and let loose on the world any more than 450 graduates per year, the rest of the world wouldn't have a chance!" Well-educated students from the classical schools founded, supported, and maintained by Christians could have a huge impact on the world because they will be well equipped with the recovered gifts of classical learning.

Let's Try!

We should be seen fighting. God should be seen winning. God does not guarantee the results we expect. Often, the Church appears to be losing. The persecutions of the Early Church certainly had that aspect.

As we attempt to reach out to those who are suffering the depredations of the sexual religion, what we do may not work, it may get us animosity, and even persecution. But we should still try. We have God's Word. It does what it says. However, there are no guarantees that an outreach to sexually compromised people would succeed, as the world defines success. But if we have the opportunity, why not try? If invited to speak about Christian views on sexuality, why not try? Of course, the words will have to emphasize Christ's open-hearted desire to recover the broken and hurting, calling them to repentance.

When we see the agony of those who have become the victims of the lies of our culture, we will desire to show mercy, forgiveness, and acceptance. We will want to meet the needs of those who are broken. Let's remind them what Isaiah said about our God: "A bruised reed He will not break, and a faintly burning wick He will not quench" (Isaiah 42:3). This is especially helpful to those who have abandoned the Church for a hedonistic lifestyle. They believe there is no way back, that what they have done is too heinous for God to be reconciled to them.

I am told that military commanders will never leave a defeated battlefield enemy without an avenue of retreat, so that they do not fight to the death. Instead, when they realize that they are defeated, they will still have hope of escape and will take it. We need to assure those who realize they have been defeated that their means of escape remains Christ, who is waiting with open arms for sinners. We don't want them to battle to death in their despair.

How comforting for them to hear the invitation of James that they will be lifted up by God. "Draw near to God, and He will draw near to you. Cleanse your hands, you sinners, and purify your hearts, you double-minded. Be wretched and mourn and weep. Let your laughter be turned to mourning and your joy to gloom. Humble yourselves before the Lord, and He will exalt you" (James 4:8–10). Christ is their avenue of escape. They need us to show them that avenue. We can try, knowing that success is not in our hands, but in the hands of Him who loves sinners and dies for them. It is this Lord against whom hell cannot prevail.

Constancy in Prayer

We have the privilege of praying for those who are trapped by the legalistic impositions of the sexual religion. We have a God who hears our prayers and loves to hear His children making requests of Him. James places the exhortation to constancy in prayer (James 5:13–18) near the missionary conclusion to his letter, where he says, "My brothers, if anyone among you wanders from the truth and someone brings him back, let him know that whoever brings back a sinner from his wandering will save his soul from death and will cover a multitude of sins" (James 5:19–20).

Prayer is the prelude to saving those who have wandered from the faith so that they might be saved as a burning brand is snatched from the fire (Jude 23). Monica, the mother of Augustine of Hippo (died 430) prayed her whole life for her pagan son who had been sexually compromised by living with a concubine. She wouldn't stop praying. Only just before her death did her Lord see fit to fulfill her constant request.

Let us never stop begging the God of all grace to bring to repentance and faith those who are dying under the burdens of the world's faulty religion. Maybe we won't ever see the fruit of our petitions, but we can leave the fruit in the hands of God. The One against whom hell's gates cannot prevail can manage to answer our prayers without our seeing the result.

The Formation of Christian Clergy at Our Seminaries

Seminary students and other church leaders will have to be trained much more directly and intentionally to respond to the world's sexual religion, both to counter it and also so as not to be drawn into its candied web of death. The threats closing in on us will demand that we keep a close eye on the teaching and practice delivered by our theological seminaries to students.

It will require more intensive and intentional formation of seminary students to prepare them for the onslaughts of Satan. We will not be able to allow pet academic theories to be indulged, no matter how attractive they may be to theological dilettantes. We will need to require that the meat and potatoes of clear biblical and confessionally adequate teaching is the regular substance delivered by teachers to students.

Perhaps the threat we face demands formation that takes place in residential seminaries. Many seminaries are attempting to educate on the cheap by packaging some major portion of the instruction on electronic platforms. Part-time instruction over the information media will be inadequate to the challenge with which we are faced. It would be like the Marine Corps switching to online training instead of sending recruits to boot camp. Their foes would make mincemeat of them. Let us not send into the fray against Satan church leaders inadequately prepared for the fight.

The cohesion of church leaders as the shock troops of the Lord in this battle will also be facilitated by common formation together in a residential seminary. I have a great deal of confidence in the men who were trained around the same time that I was at the same seminary. I know they are well-trained, and I can reliably predict what they are going to teach and do in the face of a crisis. When I need their help, I can depend on them. They "have my back" as men trained together will. This will become increasingly crucial as our crisis deepens.

The quality of students seems to be improving and will continue to improve as those whom we recruit for seminary training become increasingly aware that the clergy stole is a bull's-eye for the adherents of the sexual religion. Our clergy will be obvious targets of persecution.

No one should choose the Office of the Ministry with the idea that it is a cushy, respected position. However, when culture supported the Church and her aims, this was sometimes the result of the Church's efforts to recruit candidates for the ministry. Ministry was thought of as easy, honorable, and generally helpful. I once saw a low-capability colleague recruit high-school men by saying, "You know I am not very smart and I got through seminary. So can you."

This kind of recruiting will no longer suffice, because of the inherent and growing danger of being a Christian leader. This will result in improving the aggregate quality of seminary students. They will be passionately committed to the Gospel ministry of Christ, because none of the old cultural trappings will support church service and make it outwardly attractive.

We will be asking students to proclaim a message that will get them the suffering that brings the capstone of salvation in Christ. Peter says,

> In this you rejoice, though now for a little while, if necessary, you have been grieved by various trials, so that the tested genuineness of your faith—more precious than gold that perishes though it is tested by fire—may be found to result in praise and glory and honor at the revelation of Jesus Christ. Though you have not seen Him, you love Him. Though you do not now see Him, you believe in Him and rejoice with joy that is inexpressible and filled with glory, obtaining the outcome of your faith, the salvation of your souls. (1 Peter 1:6–9)

Christ is the ultimate victor in this battle. The gates of hell can never prevail against His precious Church.

The Person of Christ and Sexual Reality

Although not everyone is capable of articulating this connection, except perhaps implicitly, we must work to tie clearly the person and work of Christ with sexual reality. Our Christian sexual ethics are not pulled out of thin air. They are given as a gift from God, who has revealed Himself in His Son.

Christ is the proto-human being. He is the recovery of the full image of God in man. Because of His divinity, He is certainly different from us mere humans; however, by reason of His incarnation, He is the Second Adam. He is humanity made new.

Notice that the Bible doesn't breathe a single syllable about His sexual practice. This is a far cry from the demand of our modern world that everyone define themselves by their sexual practice. Sexuality in our modern sense is plainly irrelevant to the New Testament's picture of the person of Christ. His work cannot be encompassed by sexual terms. Because we are remade in Him, we also are not defined in terms of sexual practice.

Christ is like the angels in heaven in not marrying. This, then, also becomes the paradigm for the risen humanity. While we will be sexually distinguishable as male and female (as Jesus, too, was male sexually), yet sexuality will be so far from defining humanity because humanity is much bigger than sexual preferences. There will be no sexual union in heaven, because there will be no need for reproduction, which is the purpose of sexuality. Christ's reproduction of Himself occurs at the font, where we are "born of water and the Spirit" (John 3:5). This is asexual reproduction. The truth of who we are is intimately tied to who Christ is. I am God's child in Him.

Christ has promised that the gates of hell can never prevail against His Church (Matthew 16:18). This promise alone will support us in the daily strife that the Church will face as she contradicts the sexual religion. We have nothing to be afraid of as we confess Christ before the world. He has promised to bring us the final victory, even if in the midst of that victory, we appear to be dying. The fight has been won by Christ; we are just gaining the blessings of that victory by confessing His truth in the world. Satan cannot win, because Christ has won. His victory is ours. No matter what.

Study Questions

1. Can you think of examples of sex trumping religious freedom other than those listed above? How could we best respond to this?

2. Do you ever fear persecution, and how you might answer if called to account for our Christian hope? What are the best ways to be properly equipped to confess the truth when it is difficult to do so?

3. List some ways in which Christ's mercy to you changes how you would respond to others trapped in the religion of sex.

4. Discuss ways in which you could support your church leaders' confession of the truth about marriage and family in the face of the sexual religion.

5. What tools should we use to prepare our children and families to be faithful to Christ and His confession?

6. List ways in which we could avoid arrogance as we seek to save those who have fallen under the spell of the sexual religion.

7. Is there someone for whom you should pray, because they have been put under the spell of this evil plague?

8. How can you support the proper formation of pastors for the future life of your church?

9

The Gates of Hell: Luther and the Two Kingdoms

What to Do When Government Attacks the Church

Rev. Dr. Matthew C. Harrison

The famous Lutheran historian Hermann Sasse wrote in the crucible of German Nazism in 1935 that "the correct ordering of the relationship between state and church is one of those great problems which throughout the history of the church must always be solved anew." The problem "is always one of the greatest tasks of an era." I must agree with Sasse that because of diversity and fluctuation of church and state through the ages, "There finally is no one answer, valid for all time."[1] Luther himself nuanced his position to meet evolving circumstances of the relationship between church and state. However, there are constants, and Luther got hold of them as he wrestled with his contemporaries under the guidance of the New Testament.

What does the Church do in the face of government suppression and harassment? Jesus promised His apostles from the beginning that their confession of Him would meet with opposition from authorities. "Blessed are those who are persecuted" (Matthew 5:10; see vv. 11–12). "When they bring you before the synagogues and the rulers and the authorities, do not be anxious about how you should defend yourself or what you should say" (Luke 12:11). It happened

1 Hermann Sasse, "Church Government and Secular Authority," in *The Lonely Way*, vol. 1, trans. Matthew C. Harrison (St. Louis: Concordia, 2001), 175.

to St. Paul (Acts 23–25; "I appeal to Caesar" [Acts 25:11]). It occurred through the early Roman persecutions. It transpired after the empire officially adopted Christianity in the fourth century. And it has continued unabated under various "Christian," secular, Muslim, and anti-Christian governments to the present.

The Lutheran Doctrine of the Two Kingdoms

The participation or non-participation of Christians in government in all its manifestations, over the better part of two millennia, has been the source of bad governance in state and church, confusion, consternation, crisis of conscience, and martyrdom. States have meddled in the church's affairs and churches have meddled in state affairs, all to the detriment of the Gospel of free forgiveness in the sacrificial death of Christ for the sins of the world, the benefits of which are obtained by faith alone. Of course, there have been a plethora of blessings from Christians honorably participating in government.

From the beginning of the Reformation, Luther and his compatriots struggled with these issues. His contemporaries gave varying answers to fundamental questions involving interpretation of New Testament teaching. While Luther himself and those who followed in his theological footsteps were not always consistent in applying the New Testament's teaching and consequent application to contemporary circumstances, Luther's basic insights were enormously beneficial to state, church, and especially individual Christians, when applied consistently. Luther and the teaching of the Lutheran Confessional writings provide us with guidance when states overstep their legitimate bounds, reject divine Law, or inhibit the Gospel and religious freedom. They also provide limits to the church's activity with respect to the state.

Today, not many Lutherans have a proper understanding of the unique gift of the Lutheran approach to state and church. It has been my experience to find very few Lutherans elected to public office who can begin to articulate the Lutheran position, or who know much of anything of Luther's groundbreaking and unique contribution to questions of government, church, and individual participation in governmental structures.

That's a pity, because the Lutheran teaching gets the New Testament teaching correct and provides direction in all manner of issues that challenge Christians living in their respective governmental jurisdictions. It is the particular greatness of Luther's teaching that it frees the conscience, and stiffens the backbone when needed, in the context of life's manifold and frequent challenges.

The Lutheran teaching rejects government coercion of religious conscience and ecclesiastical meddling in matters of government that are not of fundamental concern to the church as such. The Lutheran teaching also provides direction on where and when Christians must "draw the line" against government coercion or interference. Furthermore, the Lutheran teaching recognizes that individuals—faithful to Christ and His Word—may respond differently to the same circumstances. Finally, the Lutheran teaching opposes the conservative American Protestant propensity to Christianize government.

I shall touch on these hallmarks of Lutheran doctrine as I unfold Luther's developing views from the Diet of Worms (1521) through the Diet of Augsburg and the Augsburg Confession (1530).

Jesus, Caesar, and God

Jesus' response to religious leaders who were trying to trick Him and stir up trouble for Him with the Roman government that had occupied Israel was, of course, divine genius.

> And they sent to Him some of the Pharisees and some of the Herodians, to trap Him in His talk. And they came and said to Him, "Teacher, we know that You are true and do not care about anyone's opinion. For You are not swayed by appearances, but truly teach the way of God. Is it lawful to pay taxes to Caesar, or not? Should we pay them, or should we not?" But, knowing their hypocrisy, He said to them, "Why put Me to the test? Bring Me a denarius and let Me look at it." And they brought one. And He said to them, "Whose likeness and inscription is this?" They said to Him, "Caesar's." Jesus said to them, "Render to Caesar the things that are Caesar's, and to God the things that are God's." And they marveled at Him. (Mark 12:13–17)

At the time of Jesus, "The Jewish establishment represented by the high priest and Sanhedrin was supposed to maintain good relations with the Roman establishment represented by the prefect in Caesarea and the governor in Antioch, and indirectly with the *princeps* [Ruler] and senate of the empire."[2] The Jewish authorities accused Jesus of two crimes: First, before the Council, He was counted

2 Bo Reicke, *Re-examining Paul's Letters: The History of the Pauline Correspondence*, eds. David P. Moessner and Ingalisa Reicke (Harrisburg, PA: Trinity Press International, 2001), 9.

guilty of blasphemy or false teaching; "Then the high priest tore his robes and said, 'He has uttered blasphemy. What further witnesses do we need? You have now heard His blasphemy. What is your judgment?'" (Matthew 26:65–66). Second, before Pilate, the Roman prefect, He was counted guilty of insurrection (rebellion): "We found this man misleading our nation and forbidding us to give tribute to Caesar, and saying that He Himself is Christ, a king" (Luke 23:2).[3]

Jesus threaded the needle on the tax question. To deny the obligation to pay taxes would have given grounds for the false accusation of Luke 23:2 (rebellion). To simply affirm taxation without qualification would have landed Him in hot water with zealots and other nationalists found among His own supporters. The zealots were "Jewish nationalists, who, during the period in question, fought desperately against Greek influence and Roman sovereignty."[4] The zealots committed acts of terror, even assassinating Jews who collaborated with the occupying Roman government. Religious expectation of an earthly messiah king who would bring Israel once again to independence animated the movement. Similar to Islam, the zealots had a rigorous "one kingdom dogma." Church and state were to be one.

Jesus' response, "Render to Caesar the things that are Caesar's, and to God the things that are God's" (Matthew 22:21), makes a careful but fundamental distinction. He does not deny the legitimacy of the ruling government, though it is not Jewish or Christian. He does not excuse Christians from obligation to the state. He does not enter upon an extended treatment on whether Christians may in good conscience pay taxes to a regime that uses that money for nefarious purposes. He does not tell Christians to separate from participation in a society where government mints coinage, establishes monetary policy, and so on. His simple teaching establishes the fact that there are two realms in which the Christian lives.

The Christian has obligations to God via the state in the realms of law and reason (here Jesus grants taxation). The Christian also has (higher) obligations to God, based upon the Gospel and the Word of God. The obligations to God via the state are temporal. The obligations to God with respect to faith are eternal. "Do not fear those who kill the body but cannot kill the soul. Rather fear Him who can destroy both soul and body in hell" (Matthew 10:28).

---

3 Reicke provides a concise explanation of the political context from the time of Christ through the completion of Paul's correspondence.

4 Reicke, *Re-examining Paul's Letters*, 10.

This distinction of realms or kingdoms can be seen in the encounters of John the Baptizer and Jesus with Roman soldiers, and even tax collectors. "Tax collectors also came to be baptized and said to him [John], 'Teacher, what shall we do?' And he said to them, 'Collect no more than you are authorized to do'" (Luke 3:12–13). The Baptizer does not delegitimize government. He does not vilify taxation. He does not instruct a repentant man to leave the profession and government service. He urges the man to act honorably in the service of the state. As radical as the Christian message and movement were, it did not nor does it now delegitimize temporal authority and its functions. "For he [the ruler] is God's servant for your good" (Romans 13:4).

Soldiering On?

After the Sermon on the Mount, when Jesus entered Capernaum, a centurion approached Him about his ailing servant. Jesus said He would come to the man's home and heal the person. The soldier gave his famous response of faith. "Lord, I am not worthy to have You come under my roof, but only say the word and my servant will be healed. For I too am a man under authority, with soldiers under me. And I say to one, 'Go,' and he goes, and to another, 'Come,' and he comes, and to my servant, 'Do this,' and he does it." Jesus "marveled" at his answer and responded, "Go; let it be done for you as you have believed" (Matthew 8:8–10, 13). Jesus gives no direction to the man to leave his profession. In fact, no soldier in the New Testament is ever told to leave his vocation of government service.

But how in the world could such service of government like tax collection (which is coercive even under the best of circumstances) or, even more so, a soldier's use of force (even killing) be reconciled to Jesus' ethical teaching in the Sermon on the Mount? "Do not resist the one who is evil. But if anyone slaps you on the right cheek, turn to him the other also. And if anyone would sue you and take your tunic, let him have your cloak as well" (Matthew 5:39–40). How could a soldier be a follower of Jesus?

Two Wrong Answers

Luther in his time complained of two wrong answers to this question. Both had ancient precedent. Medieval Catholicism had come to teach that Christ's instruction in the Sermon on the Mount does not apply to all. "Twelve evangelical counsels," including "Do not avenge yourself! Offer the other cheek! Do not resist evil" were "advice to those who want to become perfect" (AE 21:4). Thus, it was believed that the difficult commands of Christ, particularly in Matthew 5, applied to the religious professionals, not the average person. The religious professional could work toward perfection, seriously reducing time in purgatory by paying for "temporal" punishments. Christ had taken care only of the "eternal" punishment for sins.

As Luther began to understand the Gospel, he was horrified. It was nothing less than the "wicked devil" who "has managed so cleverly to twist and pervert especially the fifth chapter [of Matthew], making it teach the exact opposite of what it means" (AE 21:3). After all, Jesus states in this very chapter, "I have not come to abolish [the Law]" (Matthew 5:17). Interpreting Matthew 5 according to the distinction between the professional religious and the laity was a horrid confusion caused by a failure to understand the Gospel of free forgiveness in Christ. It was a confusion of Law and Gospel. That is, if certain people did "extra stuff," they would get extra spiritual goodies from God (less time in purgatory). Meanwhile, the unyielding Law preached by Jesus—they asserted—did not apply to regular folks.

There was a second approach current at Luther's time, and it came from radicals who initially welcomed the Lutheran Reformation. He laid it at the feet of "the new jurists and sophists, the schismatic spirits and Anabaptists. From their crazy heads they are making new trouble out of this fifth chapter. . . . They teach miserable stuff like this: that it is wrong to own private property, to swear, to hold office as a ruler or judge, to protect or defend oneself, to stay with wife and children" (AE 21:5). What the Roman Catholics demanded from the professionals, some Anabaptists were demanding of all "genuine" Christians, as though these texts prohibit the owning of property, service in government, military service, and so on. Both were wrong.

Law and Gospel—Left- and Right-Hand Kingdoms

In both cases, the problem has a similar cause. "Thus the devil blows and brews on both sides so that they do not recognize any difference between the secular and the divine realm, much less what should be the distinctive doctrine and action in each realm" (AE 21:5). There are two "realms." One is "secular," the other "divine." "Secular" is not used in a pejorative sense here, like the way we often speak of "secularist" in a negative way today. In fact, quite the opposite. God Himself has provided all the blessings of the "kingdom of the left hand." The list under the First Article of the Creed, and particularly that of the explanation of the Fourth Petition of the Lord's Prayer in Luther's Small Catechism, comes readily to mind.

> *What is meant by daily bread?* Daily bread includes everything that has to do with the support and needs of the body, such as food, drink, clothing, shoes, house, home, land, animals, money, goods, a devout husband or wife, devout children, devout workers, devout and faithful rulers, good government, good weather, peace, health, self-control, good reputation, good friends, faithful neighbors, and the like. (SC Lord's Prayer, Fourth Petition)

Luther says that "the Gospel does not trouble itself" with matters of secular law, punishment, rank, management, and distribution of property. "It teaches the right relation of the heart to God" (AE 21:108). To be sure, we must "learn the difference between the two persons that a Christian must carry simultaneously on earth, because he lives in human society and has to make use of secular and imperial things, the same way the heathen do" (AE 21:110). "There is no getting around it, a Christian has to be a secular person of some sort" (AE 21:109).

Matthew 5: It's about the Heart!

Luther concludes that the commands of Matthew 5 (indeed the Beatitudes and the whole Sermon on the Mount) apply to every Christian and have to do with the fundamental attitude of the heart. Jesus does not forbid property, government, nor the punishment of evildoers. He does not forbid Christians to hold vocations in these and other secular realms. Neither are secular courts or other avenues closed to Christians. "It is permissible for you to use orderly procedure in demanding and obtaining your rights, but be careful not to have a vindictive heart" (AE 21:111).

> As regards his own person, according to his life as a Christian, he is in subjection to no one but Christ, without any obligation either to the emperor or to any other man. But at least outwardly, according to his body and property, he is related by subjection and obligation to the emperor, inasmuch as he occupies some office or station in life or has a house and home, a wife and children; for all these are things

> that pertain to the emperor. . . . If he has a house or a wife and children or servants and refuses to support them, or if need be, to protect them, he does wrong. (AE 21:109)

Christ is not "tampering with the responsibility and authority of the government, but He is teaching His individual Christians how to live personally, apart from their official position and authority. . . . What He wants is a heart that will neither be impatient nor wreak vengeance nor disturb the peace" (AE 21:106). The purpose of the law in the left-hand (secular) kingdom is order, safety, peace, and justice (Romans 13:1–7; Titus 3:1). The purpose of the Law in the right-hand kingdom (of the Gospel/Church) is repentance toward faith and consequent un-coerced love of neighbor (Matthew 3:8; 4:17).

Luther: "Thoughts Are Tax-Free" (AE 45:108).

The Lutheran Reformation was many things. It was the beginning of the Lutheran Church (the purified Catholic Church). It was the beginning of Protestantism. It was above all a religious event in which the question "How am I righteous before God?" swept like wildfire through Europe for an amazing couple of decades. It brought advances in science, education, knowledge, and art. It was also a move toward disentangling church and state (though hardly successful, as the medieval pattern of monarch ruling his local church persisted with a vengeance). As Sasse points out, "The idea that the secular prince could also govern the church is precisely a medieval idea. It presupposes a medieval society which is both state and church, in which all members are so bound by the unity of faith that the heretic cannot be guaranteed any civil or even physical existence."[5] The Reformation—and Luther—definitely moved the Western world toward the idea of religious freedom for the individual conscience.

Conscience

Luther's reformation was a matter of conscience. It was not his intent that conscience be unhinged from reason and the Word of God. Note Luther's reference to a conscience "captive" in his famous "Here I stand" speech, before Emperor Charles V and the assembled dignitaries of the empire. At that decisive moment in history, in the city of Worms on April 16, 1521, he mentioned

5 Sasse, "Church Government and Secular Authority," 183.

conscience informed by both reason and the Word of God (of course, reason itself is trumped by the Word of God for Luther).

> Since then your serene majesty and your lordships seek a simple answer, I will give it in this manner, neither horned nor toothed: Unless I am convinced by the testimony of the Scriptures or by clear reason (for I do not trust either in the pope or in councils alone, since it is well known that they have often erred and contradicted themselves), I am bound by the Scriptures I have quoted and my conscience is captive to the Word of God. I cannot and will not retract anything, since it is neither safe nor right to go against conscience. (AE 32:112)

When Luther spoke these words, it was getting late. The hall was dark. As the assembly was exiting, "A large group of Spaniards followed Luther, the man of God, with jeers, derisive gestures, and much loud noise" (AE 32:114). Just a day later, the emperor sent a note to the gathered "princes, electors, dukes and nobles."

> Our ancestors who were also Christian princes, were nevertheless obedient to the Roman Church which Dr. Martin now attacks. And because he is determined to move not even a hair's breadth from his errors, we are not able with propriety to depart from the example of our ancestors in defending the ancient faith, and giving aid to the Roman see [the pope]. Therefore, we shall pursue Martin himself and his adherents with excommunication, and use other methods available for their liquidation. (AE 32:115)

The most powerful man in the Western world, perhaps on earth at the time, noted, "I am determined to proceed against him as a notorious heretic" (AE 32:115). That was indeed a heavy "tax" on Luther's thoughts!

Faith, Freedom, and Conscience

Before he confessed at Worms, Luther had written (1520) a brilliant little pamphlet on the Christian life: *The Freedom of a Christian* (AE 31:333). It helps explain the nexus between faith, freedom, and conscience and why Luther was so adamant in the face of all opposition (papal or governmental). He explicated two propositions:

> A Christian is perfectly free lord of all, subject to none.
> A Christian is a perfectly dutiful servant of all, subject to all.

A Christian has an inner, spiritual nature. "He is called a spiritual, inner, or new man" (AE 31:344). And a Christian has a "bodily nature, which men refer to as flesh." "He is called a carnal, outward, or old man, of whom the Apostle writes in II Corinthians 4[:16], 'Though our outer nature is wasting away, our inner nature is being renewed every day'" (AE 31:344). Luther asserted that only one thing is needed for the Christian life, "righteousness and freedom" (AE 31:345). The Word of God consists of "commandments and promises" (AE 31:348). The Law condemns and damns. "Commandments show us what we ought to do but do not give us the power to do it" (AE 31:348). God's gracious promises of mercy in Christ "give what the commandments of God demand" (AE 31:349). Faith makes Christians kings and priests with Christ. By faith in Christ, the Christian is forgiven, "Free lord of all, subject to none." The result is a free and joyous conscience.

Luther knew the hellish torture of a conscience under the condemnation of the Law, without Christ's Gospel of free forgiveness. "The believing soul by means of the pledge of its faith is free in Christ, its bridegroom, free from all sins, secure against death and hell, and is endowed with the eternal righteousness, life, and salvation of Christ its bridegroom" (AE 31:352). The conscience is at the heart of the Christian's existence, the secondary (subjective) focus of the Christian life, comforted only by the primary (objective) focus, Christ and His Gospel. "Faith redeems, corrects, and preserves our consciences so that we know that righteousness does not consist in works" (AE 31:373).

A Christian "Lives in His Neighbor"

With such divine righteousness by faith, and freed consciences, "As priests we are worthy to appear before God to pray for others and to teach one another divine things" (AE 31:355). Good works don't make the Christian; the Christian makes good works! As Christ "put on" our flesh and acted for us in His incarnation, we "put on" our neighbors' "flesh." I "cover and intercede for the sins of my neighbor" (AE 31:371). "Love is true and genuine where there is true and genuine faith." "Therefore . . . a Christian lives not in himself, but in Christ and in his neighbor. Otherwise he is not a Christian. He lives in Christ through faith, in his neighbor through love. By faith he is caught up beyond himself into God. By love he descends beneath himself into his neighbor" (AE 31:371).

All good works of the Christian serve the neighbor, including subjection to governing authorities, and secular (everyday) vocations of service:

> Christians should be subject to the governing authorities and be ready to do every good work, not that they shall in this way be justified, since they already are righteous through faith, but that in the liberty of the Spirit they shall by so doing serve others and the authorities themselves and obey their will freely and out of love. (AE 31:369)

To What Extent Is the Government to Be Obeyed?

As the Reformation advanced, things were heating up. City and state governments around Germany and beyond were aligning for and against Luther and his cadre. A year and a half after Worms (in October 1522), Luther visited Weimar and preached a series of six sermons, the last two of which became an outline for a book he soon wrote: *Temporal Authority: To What Extent It Should Be Obeyed* (1523, AE 45:75). The reformer elucidated the matter of the conscience. It is true that Paul stated, "Let every person be subject to the governing authorities" (Romans 13:1). And Peter asserted that we should "be subject . . . to every human institution" (1 Peter 2:13). Luther, however, responded that these passages give government authority over temporal matters only. The apostle Paul "is not speaking of faith, to the effect that temporal authority should have the right to command faith. He is speaking rather of external things, that they should be ordered and governed on earth" (AE 45:110). That is why Paul also says, "Pay to all what is owed to them: taxes to whom taxes are owed, revenue to whom revenue is owed, respect to whom respect is owed, honor to whom honor is owed" (Romans 13:7). These are matters of the law and temporal obedience. Thus "rulers are not a terror to good conduct, but to bad" (Romans 13:3).

"Governing authority," asserts Luther, "is not to have the mastery over faith or the Word of God, but over evil works. . . . A human ordinance cannot possibly extend its authority into heaven over souls; it is limited to the earth, to external dealings men have with one another. . . . Christ Himself made this distinction, and summed it all up very nicely when He said in Matthew 22[:21], 'Render unto Caesar the things that are Caesar's and unto God the things that are God's'" (AE

45:110). When Peter says in Acts 5:29 that "We must obey God rather than men," "He clearly sets a limit to the temporal authority" (AE 45:111).

And this brings Luther to speak of the inherent freedom of the conscience (here soul) from government coercion.

> The soul is not under the authority of Caesar; he can neither teach it nor guide it, neither kill it nor give it life, neither bind it nor loose it, neither judge it nor condemn it, neither hold it fast nor release it. All this he would have to do, had he the authority to command it and to impose laws upon it. But with respect to body, property, and honor he has indeed to do these things, for such matters are under his authority. (AE 45:111)

Temporal authority is to be obeyed, so long as it stays within its limits. "Command me within the limits of your authority on earth, and I will obey. But if you command me to believe or to get rid of certain books,[6] I will not obey; for then you are a tyrant and overreach yourself, commanding where you have neither the right nor the authority" (AE 45:112).

A wise prince has always been a "rare bird," according to Luther. In fact, "They are generally the biggest fools or the worst scoundrels on earth; therefore, one must constantly expect the worst from them and look for little good, especially in divine matters which concern the salvation of souls." Nevertheless, rulers are "God's executioners and hangmen" to punish wickedness. Luther is quite happy to have people "fall at their [rulers'] feet . . . so long as they do not ply their trade and try to become shepherds [i.e., get involved in religion] instead of hangmen" (AE 45:113).

So what about heresy? Shouldn't the government stop heresy and restrain false doctrine? Luther responded: "This the bishops should do; it is a function entrusted to them and not to the princes. Heresy can never be restrained by force. . . . Here God's word must do the fighting. . . . Heresy is a spiritual matter which you cannot hack to pieces with iron, consume with fire, or drown in water" (AE 45:114). In fact, says the reformer, heresy is never so strong as when it is opposed by force, and not the Word of God.

6 After the Diet of Worms, various princes were making laws that Luther's books were to be burned.

So What Does Good Government Look Like?

In the final section of his book on temporal authority, Luther changes course from writing about the limits of temporal authority to suggesting how that authority should be wielded. "Now that we know the limits of temporal authority, it is time to inquire also how a prince should use it" (AE 45:118). Jesus described how princes act in Luke 22:25, "The princes of this world exercise lordship, and those that are in authority proceed with force" (Luther's translation). Luther curses such rule by force when aimed at self-aggrandizement. "Cursed are all works not done in love" (AE 45:118). As for civil laws, as usual, Luther says there are too many such books and too many lawyers as well. "A prince who lacks understanding will oppress many with injustice" (Proverbs 28:16, translated from the Vulgate). There are many exceptions, and laws cannot always be strictly enforced by princes. The prince should have the law firmly in mind but apply it strictly or with moderation depending on the circumstance, as needed and dictated by reason (cf. AE 45:120).

> The natural law precedes all written and positive laws [according to Luther], and takes precedence over them. It determines all positive statues—or at least it ought to determine them. For all of them have their source in this natural law and are to be critically evaluated on the basis of it.[7]

Natural law was originally written on man's heart, but since the fall, it has been obscured by sin. The Ten Commandments mirror natural law, according to Luther. Mankind does not need the Ten Commandments to recognize its responsibilities to God in the realm of religion or ethics.[8] The Law of Moses is only applicable for Christians so far as it reflects natural law, which was before it. The golden rule, "Do unto others as you would have them do unto you" (see Matthew 7:12), is the content of the law. All Ten Commandments were written on man's heart. The content of the commandments is simply love.[9]

7 Paul Althaus, *The Ethics of Martin Luther* (Philadelphia: Fortress Press, 1972), 26. I know of no better or more lucid presentation of Luther's two kingdoms dogma than this work.

8 Althaus, *The Ethics of Martin Luther*, 27.

9 Althaus, *The Ethics of Martin Luther*, 29.

Luther's Advice for the Christian Prince

Luther proceeds with three brief points of advice for the Christian ruler. First, the prince "must give consideration and attention to his subjects, and really devote himself to it. This he does when he directs his every thought to making himself useful and beneficial to them" (AE 45:121). A Christian prince will consider how he has been served by Christ. Christ did not seek power and kingdom from the prince, but humbly served him. So, the prince should take note and humbly serve his subjects. "I will use my office to serve and protect them, listen to their problems and defend them, and govern to the sole end that they, not I, may benefit and profit from my rule." To the opponents who claim this would make the princely estate "full of trouble, labor, and sorrow," Luther responds, "We are not here teaching how a temporal prince is to live, but how a temporal prince is to be a Christian, such that he may also reach heaven" (AE 45:120). Thus, princes who are Christians are informed by God's Word. "God's Word will neither turn nor bend for princes, but princes must bend themselves to God's Word" (AE 45:121). The Word of God Luther referred to was the great self-humiliation of Christ in Philippians 2, as the great example for a prince in service to his subjects! Luther is quite happy to let the princes have their "dancing and hunting and racing," but if they gave their subjects the attention necessary, there'd be less of it to be sure (AE 45:121)!

Second, the prince should be careful not to despise anyone, or leave all decisions in the hands of one or a few. "Beware of the high and mighty." He should allow competent people to act, but also "keep the reins of government in his own hands" (AE 45:121). Flatterers will come, asking for more control of this or that, but the prince must be careful. "He wants to be lord in the land and make a monkey of you" (AE 45:122).

Third, "He must take care to deal justly with evildoers" (AE 45:123). The prince should not be overcome with retribution or listen to "fire-eaters who would stir and incite him to start a war. . . . He is a mighty poor Christian who for the sake of a single castle would put the whole land in jeopardy. . . . Where wrong cannot be punished without greater wrong, there let him waive his rights, however just they may be" (AE 45:124).

Luther summarizes:

> A [Christian] prince's duty is fourfold: First, toward God there must be true confidence and earnest prayer; second, toward his subjects

> there must be love and Christian service; third, with respect to his counselors and officials he must maintain an untrammeled reason and unfettered judgment; fourth, with respect to evildoers he must manifest a restrained severity and firmness. Then the prince's job will be done right, both outwardly and inwardly; it will be pleasing to God and to the people. But he will have to expect much envy and sorrow on account of it; the cross will soon rest on the shoulders of such a prince. (AE 45:126)

Is Rebellion against the Government Ever Justified?

The question of rebellion against governing authority came up early in the course of the Reformation. Already while Luther was in hiding in the Wartburg castle (1521–22) after his great stand at Worms, his colleague in Wittenberg, Karlstadt (a Luther wannabe), was fomenting reforms by popular uprising and force (particularly among university students). They were causing violence and destruction. Luther was well-informed about what was happening back in his hometown, and before he paid a surprise visit disguised as Knight George, with beard and appropriate dress, he had written *A Sincere Admonition to All Christians to Guard against Insurrection and Rebellion* (AE 45:67–69).

Luther was convinced the "papacy and the clerical estate will not be destroyed by the hand of men, or by insurrection. Their wickedness is so horrible that no punishment is adequate except the wrath of God itself, without any intermediary" (AE 45:61).[10]

The "duly constituted authority" must handle matters of disruption. "For what is done by duly constituted authority cannot be regarded as insurrection" (AE 45:61). But the princes in that day were doing little to help. They should have done what they could to suppress violence and insurrection, but they themselves were not united and God was thereby using this whole mess as punishment. "Even if insurrection were a practical possibility," it is still "an unprofitable method of procedure. It never brings about the desired improvement" (AE

10 Today, we are prone to smirk at such negative comments by Luther about the papacy. He wrote much worse in the course of his long career. It must be remembered that in Luther's day, the corruption of the Roman Church and the papacy itself was beyond profound. The papal state had a standing army and navy. It had been involved in numerous wars with the emperor and with other states of the empire. The year before Luther's death, the pope sent a legate to the 1545 Diet at Worms (meeting of all the estates of the empire to deal with all things political) to promise Emperor Charles V large amounts of cash, church property in Spain, twelve thousand troops, and three thousand horsemen if only he finally attacked the Lutheran princes in Germany. Suffice it to say, the popes of Luther's day were no John Paul II.

45:62). "Insurrection lacks discernment; it generally harms the innocent more than the guilty. . . . Hence no insurrection is ever right, no matter how right the cause it seeks to promote" (AE 45:62–63).

Such as it was, Luther preferred leaving the matter of dealing with disturbance in the hands of the governing authorities. Government has been established to "punish the wicked and protect the upright." "When Sir Mob breaks loose he cannot tell the wicked from the upright, or keep them apart; he lays about him at random, and a great and horrible injustice is inevitable" (AE 45:63). Christians are to follow the lead of the authorities and "keep hand, mouth, and heart quiet, and assume no responsibility" (AE 45:63). If the authorities can be moved to act by Christian citizens to resolve matters, then well and good. Luther states his position with intensity. "I am and always will be on the side of those against whom insurrection is directed. . . . I am opposed to those who rise in insurrection, no matter how just their cause, because there can be no insurrection without hurting the innocent and shedding their blood. . . . God has forbidden insurrection. . . . [The Lord Himself says,] 'Revenge is mine; I will repay'" (AE 45:63).

Not by Force

From the beginning, it was Luther's deepest conviction that the cause of the Gospel is advanced not by force, but by proclamation. Christians should never participate in insurrection, but should first acknowledge their own sins (repent), pray "against the papal regime," and "let your mouth become such a mouth of the Spirit of Christ." "For [the pope and papists] must first be slain with words; the mouth of Christ must do it" (AE 45:66–67). Luther was convinced that suffering is always the lot of the Christian and is always salutary. As what became the Peasants' War of 1525 began to take shape, Luther admonished them: "Matthew 6 [5:39], 'Do not resist one who is evil.' . . . How does your program stand in light of this law?" (AE 46:28). "Suffering! suffering! Cross! cross! This and nothing else is the Christian law!" (AE 46:29).

For Luther, good works and suffering are what faith brings. Faith pervades life. Faith confesses in word and deed, and suffering results. Faith is thus strengthened.[11]

> Luther does not think of faith as existing in and of itself and thus separate from the activity of life; he thinks of it only in terms of the

11 Althaus, *The Ethics of Martin Luther*, 17.

> concrete acts of life in specific existential situations. . . . "Works" are nothing but the concrete realization of faith itself. Faith needs works—that is, concrete specific acts of life—in order to be itself at any point. Faith always needs secular life—just as secular life in turn always needs faith. Believing is not something I do alongside my life in this world but rather in it—in each and every act of living. . . . Faith lives in works, just as works are done in faith.[12]

Collapsing the Two Kingdoms into One

The Peasants' War rocked German lands in the first six months of 1525. It started out more like a "general strike than an outright rebellion."[13] But it soon turned bloody. The lot of peasants in the sixteenth century was quite appalling. They rallied around "Twelve Articles" written in the spring of 1525. The document was written to quell the accusation that by revolting they had given up the Gospel.[14] It expressed a mix of religious, social, and economic concerns, and was produced to try to align the peasants' concerns with Luther's Reformation, quoting the Bible frequently.

The driving force for the revolt in Thuringia was Thomas Müntzer, new pastor in the city of Mühlhausen. Müntzer and his supporters pushed for and achieved government reforms in the city. The "Gospel" was to be advanced by force. "Whereas Luther attempted to distinguish church from state, Müntzer agitated for the community to embody the doctrine of election by patterning its political life after biblical norms. For Müntzer, those who rejected this concept of the kingdom of God belong to the kingdom of Satan."[15] Thus, Müntzer fomented rebellion. He ranted:

> But what is one to do with the sword? Exactly this: sweep aside those evil men who obstruct the Gospel! Take them out of circulation! Otherwise you will be Devils not the servants of God which Paul calls you to be in Romans 13. . . . Drive His enemies away from the

12 Althaus, *The Ethics of Martin Luther*, 17.

13 Peter Bickle quoted in David M. Whitford, *Tyranny and Resistance: The Magdeburg Confession and the Lutheran Tradition* (St. Louis: Concordia, 2001), 39. This is an extraordinary book exploring the Lutheran response to bad government in the sixteenth century. It is required reading.

14 Whitford, *Tyranny and Resistance*, 40. I am dependent on Whitford for this section.

15 Whitford, *Tyranny and Resistance*, 48.

> elect; you are the instruments to do this. My friend, don't let us have any of these hackneyed posturings about the power of God achieving everything without any resort to your sword;[16] otherwise it may rust in its scabbard. . . . Christ speaks clearly enough in Matthew 7, John 15 . . . do not therefore, allow the evil-doers, who turn us away from God to continue living, Deut. 13, for a godless man has no right to live if he is hindering the pious. In Exodus 22 God says, "you shall not let the evil-doer live."[17]

Such words could have come from a contemporary Muslim extremist. Why? As David Whitford notes, in Müntzer "the two kingdoms collapse into one." Church and state are one. Verses like Matthew 7:19, "Every tree that does not bear good fruit is cut down and thrown into the fire," are referenced by Müntzer, as though Christ advocates violence to bring about His kingdom on earth. And whenever the kingdoms "collapse" or even begin to be mixed or confused, the theocratic stories and actions of God and His people from the Old Testament are quickly but wrongly applied to government. "Jesus said to him [Peter], 'Put your sword back into its place. For all who take the sword will perish by the sword'" (Matthew 26:52). Jesus did not establish a theocracy, nor shall there be one until after the resurrection of all flesh.

After a murderous rampage of rebellion and destruction of church and state property, Müntzer was beheaded on May 27, 1525. The princes struck back with intensity. One hundred thousand peasants died before it was over.

Indeed, Luther had pointed out to the peasants, commenting on the Twelve Articles, well before the blood flowed, "'All who take the sword will perish by the sword' [Matt. 26:52]. That means nothing else than that no one, by his own violence, shall arrogate authority to himself; but as Paul says, 'Let every person be subject to the governing authorities with fear and reverence' (Romans 13:1)." Suffering wrong is part of being a Christian. "You are quite unwilling to suffer any wrong. That is contrary not only to Christian law and the gospel, but also to natural law and all equity" (AE 46:25).

But the reformer was not toady. Luther blasted the princes for their maltreatment of the peasants, who had just grievances. He admonished the rulers to "stop

16 Author's note: This is a direct criticism of Luther.

17 Whitford, *Tyranny and Resistance*, 48, quoting *The Collected Works of Thomas Müntzer*, ed. and trans. Peter Matheson (Edinburgh: T. & T. Clark, 1988), 248.

being so stubborn" and "stop being such oppressive tyrants!" "You lords, stop being so stubborn! . . . Give these poor people room in which to live and air to breath" (AE 46:43). "It is not my intention to justify or defend the rulers in the intolerable injustices which you suffer from them. They are unjust, and commit heinous wrongs against you, that I admit. . . . I hope that God will, as is usual in these situations, use one rascal to punish the other" (AE 46:32).

Luther viewed rebellion as the complete collapse of all order and law in society (AE 46:27). Mob rule is contrary to all law. "Now in all this I have been speaking of the common, divine, and natural law which even the heathen, Turks, and Jews have to keep if there is to be any peace or order in the world. . . . You are much worse than these, because you rage and struggle against the divine and natural law, which all the heathen keep" (AE 46:27). Luther rightly feared, "Some prophets of murder have come among you" (AE 46:28). And the reformer countered by quoting relevant passages of Scripture:

> If, now, you really want to keep the divine law, as you boast, then do it. There it stands! God says, "Vengeance is mine; I will repay" [Rom. 12:19], and, "Be subject not only to the good lords, but also to the wicked" [I Pet. 2:18]. (AE 46:28)

> Matthew 6 [5:39], "Do not resist one who is evil." . . . How does your program stand in light of this law? (AE 46:28)

> To Peter after he cuts off Malchus' ear: Take the sword, perish by the sword. (cf. AE 46:30)

> [Christ] prayed . . . "Father, forgive them, for they know not what they do" [Luke 23:34]. (AE 46:30)

Christ triumphed by suffering and resurrection, not by taking up the sword. The Gospel is not a matter of force and sword.

> Suffering! suffering! Cross! cross! This and nothing else is the Christian law! (AE 46:29)

Not one of your articles deals with the Gospel. It's all about temporal and worldly matters. (cf. AE 46:35)

Christians do not fight for themselves with sword and musket, but with the cross and with suffering, just as Christ, our leader, does not bear a sword, but hangs on the cross. (AE 46:32)

Like with Christ, if you truly follow His law, you will see what happens. The Word of God will rise among you. "He will help you as he helped Christ, whom he avenged after the completion of his passion in such a way that his gospel and his kingdom won a powerful victory and gained the upper hand, in spite of all his enemies." (AE 46:30)

Because you do not want to triumph by suffering, but by your fists, you are interfering with God's vengeance and you will keep neither the gospel nor your fists. (AE 46:31)

Luther offered himself as an example:

I have never drawn a sword or desired revenge. I began neither conspiracy nor rebellion, but so far as I was able, I have helped the worldly rulers—even those who persecuted the gospel and me—to preserve their power and honor. I stopped with committing the matter to God and relying confidently at all times upon his hand. This is why God has not only preserved my life in spite of the pope and all the tyrants . . . but He has made my gospel grow and spread. (AE 46:31)

About the other eight articles, Luther says,

The other articles, which discuss the freedom to hunt game animals and birds, to catch fish, to use wood from the forest, their obligation to provide free labor, the amount of their rents and taxes, the death tax, etc. are all matters for the lawyers to discuss. It is not fitting that I, an evangelist, should judge or make decisions in such matters. I am to instruct and teach men's consciences in things that concern divine and Christian matters. (AE 46:39–40)

> For because both of you are wrong, and both of you want to avenge and defend yourselves, both of you will destroy yourselves and God will use one rascal to flog another. (AE 46:40–41)

Rebellion Revisited: Can Governing Authority Be Opposed by Force?

Five years after the Peasants' Revolt, the prospect of an imperial attack upon the Lutherans was increasing. So much so, that the Lutheran princes were contemplating a defensive military alliance. Luther never did anything but oppose rebellion up to 1530. He had, however, been in a state of civil disobedience (along with his prince who protected him) since the Edict of Worms in 1521 called for his apprehension, as well as the punishment of any of his supporters. The edict issued by Charles V reads in part:

> For this reason we forbid anyone from this time forward to dare, either by words or by deeds, to receive, defend, sustain, or favor the said Martin Luther. On the contrary, we want him to be apprehended and punished as a notorious heretic, as he deserves, to be brought personally before us, or to be securely guarded until those who have captured him inform us, whereupon we will order the appropriate manner of proceeding against the said Luther. Those who will help in his capture will be rewarded generously for their good work.
>
> As for his accomplices, those who help or favor the said Martin in whatever manner or who show obstinacy in their perversity, not receiving absolution from the pope for the evils they have committed, we will also proceed against them and will take all of their goods and belongings, movable and fixed, with the help either of the judges in the area in which they reside or of our parliaments and councils at Malines or in other cities in which these events are made known. Action will be taken according to the desire of the accusers or of our fiscal procurators, but always according to the constitution and the laws, whether canon, civil, or divine, written against those who commit heresy or the crime of *lèse majesté*. These laws will be applied

> regardless of person, degree, or privilege if anyone does not obey our edict in every manner.[18]

Augsburg 1530

By March 6, 1530, Luther was resolutely opposing military action against the imperial government. "According to Scripture, it is in no way proper for anyone who would be a Christian to set himself against his government, whether it acts justly or unjustly." A Christian should suffer "oppression and injustice by his government." Luther tells Elector John of Saxony, even if the emperor were acting contrary to his "duty and oath," "neither his imperial authority nor his subjects' obligation of obedience has thereby been abolished" (AE 47:6). But by the time he had written *Warning to His Dear German People* (probably October 1530), published in April 1531, Luther's view had changed (see AE 47:6–55).

Philip Melanchthon had written the Augsburg Confession for the Diet of Augsburg, which began in June 1530. It is a famously irenic document, seeking peace. The diet accomplished no such religious or civil peace. After the presentation of the Augsburg Confession on June 25, there was an extended period of waiting for the Catholics to respond. Luther was camped out at Coburg Castle, at the edge of the territory within protection of his prince. As usual in such circumstances, he was busy writing commentaries on the Old Testament, and anxiously trying to advise Melanchthon in Augsburg from afar. Melanchthon was typically nervous, worried about military attack, and seeking compromise. He was even willing to back off the statements of the Augsburg Confession! Luther repeatedly tried to gin up Philip's courage, quite rightly convinced that the opposition would not compromise. Luther complained about Melanchthon "stepping softly." "Luther was utterly indignant that Melanchthon could not be dissuaded from his attempts at reaching a compromise."[19] Luther encouraged his compatriots. He wrote Chancellor Gregory Brück about looking at the heavens from his castle window: "I saw the stars in the sky and the whole beautiful vault of heaven, but I saw nowhere any pillars on which the Master had rested this vault; yet the sky did not collapse, and the vault stills stands fast."[20]

---

18 "The Edict of Worms (1521)," The Voice, accessed June 1, 2017, http://www.crivoice.org/creededictworms.html.

19 Martin Brecht, *Martin Luther: Shaping and Defining the Reformation 1521–1532,* trans. James Schaff (Minneapolis: Fortress Press, 1990), 400.

20 Brecht, *Martin Luther,* 401.

The Augsburg Confession, Article XVI on civil government, succinctly asserted the biblical and Lutheran position on left-hand kingdom issues.

> Our churches teach that lawful civil regulations are good works of God. They teach that it is right for Christians to hold political office, to serve as judges, to judge matters by imperial laws and other existing laws, to impose just punishments, to engage in just wars, to serve as soldiers, to make legal contracts, to hold property, to take oaths when required by the magistrates, for a man to marry a wife, or a woman to be given in marriage [Romans 13; 1 Corinthians 7:2].
>
> Our churches condemn the Anabaptists who forbid these political offices to Christians. They also condemn those who do not locate evangelical perfection in the fear of God and in faith, but place it in forsaking political offices. For the Gospel teaches an eternal righteousness of the heart (Romans 10:10). At the same time, it does not require the destruction of the civil state or the family. The Gospel very much requires that they be preserved as God's ordinances and that love be practiced in such ordinances. Therefore, it is necessary for Christians to be obedient to their rulers and laws. The only exception is when they are commanded to sin. Then they ought to obey God rather than men (Acts 5:29). (AC XVI)

Here the Confession presents the consistent Lutheran position. This article was accepted by the Catholics. The Apology elucidated this article a year later, with themes all common to Luther's theology, though the affirmation of the use of courts by Christians went further than Luther, who discouraged Christians to seek redress in the courts particularly for personal individual wrongs.

> Christ's kingdom allows us outwardly to use legitimate political ordinances of every nation in which we live, just as it allows us to use medicine or the art of building, or food, drink, and air. Neither does the Gospel offer new laws about the public state, but commands that we obey present laws, whether they have been framed by heathens or by others. It commands that in this obedience we should exercise

> love. Carlstadt [sic] was crazy to impose on us Moses' judicial laws. (Ap XVI 54–56)
>
> The Gospel does not introduce laws about the public state, but is the forgiveness of sins and the beginning of a new life in the hearts of believers. Besides, the Gospel not only approves outward governments, but also subjects us to them (Romans 13:1). (Ap XVI 58)

The Apology of the Augsburg Confession (1531) notes that governments operate under natural law, or the law of reason. "In a similar way we have been necessarily placed under the laws of seasons, the changes of winter and summer, as divine ordinances" (Ap XVI 58). When Christ speaks about the heart and actions of Christians, He "forbids private remedy," not the use of legitimate laws and courts. "Public remedy, made through the office of the public official, is not condemned, but is commanded and is God's work according to Paul (Romans 13). Now the different kinds of public remedy are legal decisions, capital punishment, wars, and military service" (Ap XVI 59). "Good consciences can never be satisfied about them [contracts] unless they know the rule that it is lawful for a Christian to make use of public ordinances and laws" (Ap XVI 64). "The doctrine we follow does not wreck the authority of magistrates and the dignity of all public ordinances. Rather, they are strengthened even more" (Ap XVI 65).

A Dismal Outcome at Augsburg

Aside from the brilliant Lutheran confession produced at Augsburg, the diet had a dismal outcome. No thanks to Melanchthon (what irony!), the Lutherans maintained an uncompromised confession.[21] The Roman Catholics finally issued the Confutation of the Augsburg Confession, a clear rejection of the Gospel of grace. "For it is entirely contrary to Holy Scripture to deny that our works are meritorious."[22] It did, however, approve of the Lutherans' confession regarding civil authority. "The sixteenth article, concerning civil magistrates, is received with pleasure, as in harmony not only with civil law, but also with canonical law, the Gospel, the Holy Scriptures, and the universal norm of faith" (Romans

---

21 See Brecht's treatment of the topic, *Martin Luther*, 393–404.

22 Michael Reu, *The Augsburg Confession: A Collection of Sources with an Historical Introduction* (Chicago: Wartburg Publishing House, 1930; repr., St. Louis: Concordia, 1983), 351.

13:1–7 is quoted).[23] The emperor ruled on September 7 that a council would decide the religious issue, and in the meantime, the old religious practices were to be restored.[24]

Chancellor Brück, who had read the Augsburg Confession to the assembly, spoke his final words to the emperor before his departure for Wittenberg: "Well, if it cannot be otherwise, we still know that all the gates of hell cannot prevail against this teaching."[25]

Luther's *Warning*

The Lutheran princes were nervous in the wake of the events at Augsburg. Luther, the princes, and the free cities that had adopted the Reformation and protected Luther and his compatriots were guilty of civil disobedience. One must proclaim the Gospel whether the authorities countenance it or not. "We must obey God rather than men" (Acts 5:29). As political circumstances deteriorated, and opposition consolidated, the Lutherans feared the emperor and papal forces would undertake a military campaign against them. Prince Philip of Hesse was particularly advocating that the theologians sanction action against military aggression. Luther had steadfastly refused it on theological grounds since the beginning. Elector John of Saxony proposed a defensive organization (which became the Smalcald League) just after the emperor issued his decision at Augsburg (the Augsburg Recess).[26] The princes decided to resist if Charles's forces attacked, and they needed Luther and the theologians on board.

Luther, Jonas, Melanchthon, and Spalatin (Luther's closest associates) were all called to Elector John's headquarters in Torgau in October. There the princes' lawyers made the legal case for the right of a lesser magistrate to resist an emperor who would attack them. The theologians were cautious and maintained their position, but then began ever so slightly to grant that perhaps there is legal precedent (kingdom of the left hand) to protect oneself from an aggressor. In the Torgau Declaration, they stated,

> We are in receipt of a memorandum from which we learn that the doctors of law have come to an agreement on the question: In what

---

23 Reu, *The Augsburg Confession*, 357.

24 Brecht, *Martin Luther*, 405.

25 Brecht, *Martin Luther*, 407.

26 See Whitford, *Tyranny and Resistance*, 50–53.

> situations may one resist the government? Since this possibility has now been established by these doctors and experts in the law, and since we certainly are in the kind of situation in which, as they know, resistance to the government is permissible, and since, further, we have always taught that one should acknowledge civil laws, submit to them, and respect their authority, inasmuch as the Gospel does not militate against civil laws, we cannot invalidate from Scripture the right of men to defend themselves even against the emperor in person, or anyone acting in his name. And now that the situation everywhere has become so dangerous that events may daily make it necessary for men to take immediate measure to protect themselves, not only on the basis of civil law but on the grounds of duty and distress of conscience, *it is fitting for them to arm themselves and to be prepared to defend themselves against the use of force*; and such may easily occur, to judge by the present pattern and course of events. For previously teaching that resistance to governmental authorities is altogether forbidden, we were unaware that this right has been granted by the government's own laws which we have diligently taught are to be obeyed at all times.[27]

The princes asked Luther immediately to write something popular that granted the possibility of armed resistance (defense "against the use of force"). He produced *Dr. Martin Luther's Warning to His Dear German People* (AE 47:5–55). Here he moved from speaking of "rebellion" and always negatively, to "self-defense." "I will not reprove those who defend themselves against the murderers and bloodthirsty papists, nor let anyone else rebuke them as being seditious, but I will accept their action and let it pass as self-defense" (AE 47:19).

Luther avers that he himself had always taught peace and opposed rebellion. The papists, too, up to that time had supported peace. Luther's followers had let themselves be "challenged, defied, jeered, and mocked at the diet by the papists," yet "they humbled themselves." That was not how Müntzer and his crowd acted (AE 47:14).

The papists refused to publish their "Confutation" of the Augsburg Confession, while Luther's side had been open and transparent about their confession (AE 47:15). Luther declares, "It is not fitting for me, a preacher, vested with the

27 Whitford, *Tyranny and Resistance*, 50–51.

spiritual office, to wage war or to counsel war or incite it, but rather to dissuade from war and to direct to peace, as I have done until now with all diligence" (AE 47:18). If war comes this time, Luther will let his pen rest, and not quell it. "If war breaks out . . . I will not reprove those who defend themselves against the murderous and bloodthirsty papists, nor let anyone else rebuke them as being seditious, but I will accept their action and let it pass as self-defense." Luther directs those who suffer attack "to the law and to the jurists." For Luther—as he says—"make[s] a distinction between sedition and other acts and to deprive the bloodhounds of the pretext of boasting that they are warring against rebellious people and that they are justified according to both human and divine law" (AE 47:19). As Karl Holl wrote, "Luther never reached the point of advocating resistance enthusiastically and with full inner conviction."[28] In 1519, Luther stated that spiritual power must be resisted when it does wrong, for souls are at stake. When temporal power goes wrong, "It improves the soul, though it does inflict hurt to our body and our possessions" (AE 44:92).

Just War

Luther had contemplated and elaborated on the topic of just war before 1530. In 1519, the reformer asserted that when temporal authorities require something contrary to God's commands, "Obedience ends and the obligation ceases." Thus, he states immediately following, "If a prince desired to go to war, and his cause was clearly unrighteous; we should neither follow nor help such a prince, because God had commanded us not to kill our neighbor or do him a wrong." In fact, "In such cases we should indeed give up our property and honor, our life and limb, so that God's commandments remain" (AE 44:100).

In his sermons on the Catholic Epistles (1 Peter 2:13–17) in 1523, Luther stated that government "was instituted for the sake of the unbelievers." "Christians let the Word of God rule them; for themselves they have no need whatever of the secular government" (AE 30:76). This was an early theme that soon gave way to the teaching that government is in fact a gift of God for believers and unbelievers alike. Christians may participate in the "power of the sword" (i.e., serve in the military) "to restrain the wicked with it, in order that the pious may remain in peace among them." Still, a Christian is not to "use [the sword] for himself,"

28 Quoted in Althaus, *The Ethics of Martin Luther*, 130.

or "avenge himself but use it solely for others." And such an act to "protect and defend a whole community" is an act of love (AE 30:76).

Luther clearly has in mind just war as a defensive act, against an aggressive foreign power, threatening life and limb. Circumstances however, forced the contemplation of the unthinkable.

The Emperor Attacked

The Smalcald League was formed in late February 1531 by Luther's prince, John Frederick I, Elector of Saxony, and Philip, Landgrave of Hesse. After Luther's death in 1546, the emperor attacked, and finally routed John Frederick's troops in the Battle of Mühlberg on April 24, 1547. The Lutheran troops had been attacked on Sunday morning during the Divine Service. Five thousand were killed. John Frederick was himself injured, captured, and his life was used as a bargaining tool to force the walled city of Wittenberg to surrender (the Wittenberg Capitulation).[29] Soon after, Charles V rode through the city's open gate. He wanted to see the interior of the City Church where Luther had done so much of his preaching. His entourage stopped at Bugenhagen's parsonage, but the custodian who had the key could not be found! There is a long and probably genuine Wittenberg tradition that the emperor also stopped to view the grave of Luther in the Castle Church. When the fiery Duke of Alba urged him to exhume Luther's body and drag it through the streets as that of a heretic, Charles is said to have responded, "I wage war against the living, not against the dead."[30]

Meanwhile, northern Germans continued to resist the aggression of the emperor, most notably the City of Magdeburg. In 1553, the emperor was defeated at Sievershausen, and in 1555, the Peace of Augsburg was signed by both parties, granting the *cuius region, eius religio* policy of religious freedom, that is, "He who rules determines the religion" of his territory. It was a remarkable advance in religious freedom, until the Peace of Westphalia granted those of a faith different from their ruler the right to live in peace in 1648.

Led by the uncompromising Lutheran theologian, Matthias Flacius Illyricus, Luther's close compatriot, Nikolaus von Amsdorf, and Nicholas Gallus, the Magdeburgers produced *The Confession, Instruction, and Warning of the Pastors*

29 Wieland Held, *1547, Die Schlacht bei Mühlburg/Elbe: Entscheidung auf dem Wege zum albertinischen Kurfürstentum Sachsen* (Leipzig: Sax Verlag Beucha, 1997), 100ff.

30 Helmar Junghans, *Kaiser Karl V am Grabe Martin Luthers in der Schlosskirche zu Wittenberg* in *Lutherjahrbuch* 54 (1987): 101.

and Preachers of the Christian Church in Magdeburg, published in April 1550.[31] Fundamental to their argument was their assertion that Romans 13:3 ("For rulers are not a terror to good conduct, but to bad") commands ruler not to be a "terror to good conduct, but to bad." If in fact a ruler becomes a "terror" to "good conduct," then such a ruler loses his legitimacy.

> The Magistrate is an ordinance of God for honor to good works, and a terror to evil works (Romans 13). Therefore, when he begins to be a terror to good works and honor to evil, there is no longer in him, because he does thus, the ordinance of God, but the ordinance of the devil. And he who resists such works, does not resist the ordinance of God, but the ordinance of the devil.[32]

We cannot pursue the details of the Magdeburg Confession here. The history of "resistance by the lesser magistrate" undertook development from Luther, to Magdeburg to Beza to John Locke and even Thomas Jefferson. Luther and even the Magdeburgers would hardly have supported war against a "tyrant" on grounds of the American doctrine "No taxation without representation." The context of the Magdeburgers was intense. Imperial forces intent upon military subjection and the reinstitution of papal religion attacked their walled city just three months after they published their confession, on July 27, 1550. The unsuccessful siege lasted over a year. Whitford says that "the stalemate of Magdeburg brought to an end the medieval ideal of a *corpus christianorum* or a unified state (in this case the empire) and church."[33] The Magdeburgers carefully defined the circumstances in which subjects may protect themselves against a tyrant. Different levels of severity of attack required carefully measured responses. In the case of the emperor, he was denying natural law and the Ten Commandments by threatening to attack and deny the Magdeburgers their livelihoods and very lives. He was rejecting the Gospel by attempting to force them to give up their confession of Christ, contrary to the Bible and their consciences. Persecution of the church is an abuse of power.

31 *The Magdeburg Confession: 13th of April 1550 AD*, trans. Matthew Colvin (North Charleston, SC: CreateSpace, 2012).

32 *The Magdeburg Confession*, 57.

33 Whitford, *Tyranny and Resistance*, 99.

What Can We Learn?

Luther's doctrine of the two kingdoms (particularly as codified for us in the Augsburg Confession) provides guidance for a biblical approach to totalitarian government, or governments that harass the church directly or indirectly by passing laws that forbid the confession of Christ, force citizens to act contrary to their consciences, or penalize Christians for their unwillingness to bow to laws that are contrary to reason and the Ten Commandments. Governments that do so, and governments that forbid and even attack the Gospel, fail to qualify unconditionally as the legitimate ruling authority described in Romans 13.

Yet, as Luther and the Magdeburgers noted, here 1 Peter 2:18 comes to bear. "Servants, be subject to your masters with all respect, not only to the good and gentle but also the unjust." As Luther repeatedly noted, Christians must act according to conscience informed by Scripture. In matters of government, reason and natural law (which agree with the Ten Commandments) are the plumb line.

The conscience freely believes in Christ. Suffering is the lot of Christians in this life. The conscience that would make of Christianity an earthly kingdom, governed by biblical revelation, or immediate revelation (Müntzer), instead of the Ten Commandments and reason (the Ten Commandments, particularly the Second Table according with reason), errs. The Christian may be subject to bad government up to the point of Acts 5:29 ("We must obey God rather than men").

Luther's time was very different from ours. He could not conceive of the chaos of religions and anti-religions in postmodern Western society. He certainly predicted the loss of the Gospel and the rise of the Turk in Germany! In our time, Christians face a broad range of government-sponsored antagonism, harassment, and even persecution. In the West, Sexual Orientation and Gender Identity (SOGI) laws increasingly batter the consciences of Christians and other rational and religious citizens. Potential adoptive parents in the state of Illinois now have to agree to gender identity training, should their adoptive child desire to change his/her identity. The legalization of gay marriage in the United States affects every aspect of life touched by the government and places Christians and others in constant moral dilemma.

From Luther's insight, we can conclude with the New Testament that legitimate governing authorities "are not a terror to good conduct, but to bad" (Romans 13:3). To the extent that government actually carries out its legitimate functions such as offering protection, the punishment of evil, conducting just/defensive war, providing aid to the most needy, because government flows from the Fourth

Commandment, it is to be obeyed. But governing authorities often go beyond their reasonable limits and prevent and suppress the Gospel. In so doing, the government may cease to qualify as legitimate authority according to Romans 13. "He who does wrong or imposes intolerable measures is not God's servant but God's enemy" (AE 48:256–63).[34] Nevertheless, the Christian will obey such a government to the extent its laws are just. Christians may, for the sake of conscience and confession, make differing decisions in these challenging circumstances.

Christians must expect harassment by authorities. Such suffering is under the theology of the cross, that is, that suffering is divinely willed for the good of the Gospel and Christians. Under such circumstances, Christians pray for their rulers, good and evil alike. Wars are not "Christian" missions. Luther even rejected treating the empire's war against the Turk as such. "The emperor is not the head of Christendom or defender of the gospel or the faith. The church and the faith must have a defender other than emperors and kings" (AE 46:185). The weapons of Christians are repentance, conversion, and prayer.[35]

War is strictly a left-hand kingdom activity, to be ruled just or unjust according to reason and just war theory. A Christian may, on the grounds of conscience, refuse to serve in an unjust war. Christians may, particularly for the sake of others (Luther), and for their own sakes (AC XVI; Ap XVI), seek legal remedy for left-hand kingdom issues, and for issues of religious conscience and state law. Just state laws will not contradict the Ten Commandments or natural law.

It is hard to envision a circumstance parallel to the perils faced by Lutherans in 1530 (Augsburg) and that which came to fruition in 1550 when the emperor was about to attack Magdeburg. Although, there are today large communities of Lutherans in Africa, for instance, who might suffer attack on religious grounds. The just war doctrine, and even the doctrine of the resistance of the lesser magistrate, may well justify defensive action, but only defensive action, and in no way mob war or revolution.

In any case, the matters of the right-hand kingdom involve the Gospel and eternal life, and therefore outweigh matters of temporal authority and its use or abuse. Therefore, the words of Chancellor Brück to Charles V, which echo Jesus' own, remain true, come what may. "Well, if it cannot be otherwise, we still know that all the gates of hell cannot prevail against this teaching."[36]

34 Luther, *Letter to Melanchthon*, July 13, 1521.

35 Althaus, *The Ethics of Martin Luther*, 142.

36 Brecht, *Martin Luther*, 407.

Study Questions

1. How does it benefit members of a society in which the church and state work side by side, each in their own areas of responsibility?

2. Luther said a Christian is a perfectly free lord of all, and at the same time, a perfectly dutiful servant of all. How does your freedom in Christ make it possible for you to more fully serve your family, work, church, and community?

3. How is a congregation's mission affected (for better and/or worse) when it gets involved in social issues?

4. Where are some areas in which you wouldn't be surprised to someday see the state pushing itself into your congregation's matters? How do you think your church should respond?

5. How do you respond to the statement, "Christians must expect harassment by authorities"?

6. Under what circumstances do you think it would be appropriate for congregations and individual Christians to be civilly disobedient? How can we determine which forms of disobedience are most effective and appropriate?

7. Why might some Christians choose to respond to the same government overreach by passively suffering while others would choose active civil disobedience?

8. Under what circumstances might it be appropriate for a group of Christians to mount an armed self-defense against the governing authorities?

10

The Gates of Hell and the Status of the Church in Western Society

Rev. Dr. John C. Wohlrabe Jr.

Introduction

Much is said these days about Western Society having become post-Christian. Other descriptive terms are bandied about as well, like post-Christendom or post-Constantinian. Post-Christian can be identified as the decline and loss of a Christian worldview, particularly within Western society or what is also called the global North. Here, Christianity previously flourished and even served as the dominant worldview.[1] Post-Christendom is defined as the culture that emerged within society as the Christian faith and institutions of Christian denominations declined in influence throughout Europe and now also in North America. Constantinianism is understood as an accommodation between political authority and Christian churches dating back to Roman Emperor Constantine (AD 312). In Constantinianism, Christianity is promoted using state power. Post-Constantinian is when governments, particularly those of

1 Rod Dreher, "Coming to Terms with a Post-Christian World," *Christianity Today*, November 2, 2015, http://www.christianitytoday.com/ct/2015/november/coming-to-terms-with-post-christian-world.html. Russel Moore, "Is America Post-Christian?" RussellMoore.com, May 26, 2015, http://www.russellmoore.com/2015/05/26/is-america-post-christian.

Europe and North America, no longer provide accommodation for Christianity or Christian denominations.

Is it true that we are living in a post-Christian, post-Christendom, and post-Constantinian age? And if so, is this a good thing or a bad thing for the Christian Church and individual Christians? What does all this mean for you and me as Christians in the twenty-first century? How do we cope with the so-called death of the "Constantinian accommodation" (if that is in fact what we are facing)?

Denoting the Decline

Such labels are not new to the twenty-first century. The decline of a Christian influence in Western civilization has been noted since at least the middle of the twentieth century. C. S. Lewis (1898–1963) was a former atheist who became a lay Christian apologist. He described and defended Christianity via radio broadcasts and various forms of literature to a war-torn Britain that considered itself "part of a 'post-Christian' world."[2]

Francis Schaeffer (1912–84), an American Presbyterian pastor who established a Christian community in Switzerland called L'Abri, sought to defend the Christian faith to what he identified as a "post-Christian" culture.[3]

In 1984, then Lutheran pastor Richard John Neuhaus stated that in America, the public square has become hostile to Christianity, something that was significantly intensified after the 1973 *Roe v. Wade* decision of the U.S. Supreme Court legalized abortion on demand.[4]

American Evangelical apologist Charles Colson (1931–2012) maintained that "In the West secularism has aggressively spread irreligion, turning Europe into a post-Christian culture and America into a battleground with orthodox religion in retreat."[5]

Yale Law professor Stephen Carter (born 1954) notes that many in America tolerate only a civil religion that is filled primarily with platitudes: "Since the 1970s, liberals have been shedding religious rhetoric like a useless second skin,

---

2 Kathleen Norris, foreword to *Mere Christianity*, by C. S. Lewis (San Francisco: Harper Collins, 1952), xix.

3 John Stonestreet, "Living Out Your Faith in a 'Post-Christian-and-Darn-Proud-of-It' Culture," cnsnews.com, April 25, 2016, http://www.cnsnews.com/commentary/john-stonestreet/living-out-your-faith-post-christian-and-darn-proud-it-culture; Francis A. Schaeffer, *How Should We Then Live?* in *The Complete Works of Francis A. Schaeffer: A Christian Worldview*, vol. 5 (Westchester, IL: Crossway, 1982), 211–27.

4 Richard John Neuhaus, *The Naked Public Square: Religion and Democracy in America* (Grand Rapids: Eerdmans, 1984).

5 Charles Colson, *Kingdoms in Conflict* (Grand Rapids: William Morrow and Zondervan, 1987), 113.

while conservatives have been turning to it one issue after another,"[6] the result of which is referred to as "culture wars."

Harvard history and economics professor Niall Ferguson (born 1964) identifies the growth and dominance of Western civilization in Europe and America with the influence of Christianity, particularly the Protestant work ethic. However, he notes that Christianity, along with industry and productivity, is now in decline within Western civilization; yet, in Sub-Saharan Africa and China, Christianity is on the rise.[7]

Christian apologist Os Guinness (born 1941) has repeatedly asserted that a free democracy requires religion. He speaks of the "golden triangle of freedom": "Freedom requires virtue; virtue requires faith; and faith requires freedom."[8] Yet, we live in a society where there "is the general disdain for religion that leads to a discounting of religious freedom, sharpened by a newly aggressive atheism and a heavy-handed separationism that both call for the exclusion of religion from public life."[9]

This has been noted by author and radio host Eric Metaxas (born 1963) as well, who sees America having "stepped backward to a cultural situation less like the earlier times in our own country than like the France of Tocqueville's day, in which religion and freedom were thought to be bitterest enemies."[10]

So, what are some of the consequences of living in a post-Christian Western society? Not only is there a decline in church attendance and membership, but Niall Ferguson says we are also left with "a vacuous consumer society and a culture of relativism." It's not that people believe in nothing; rather, "They believe in anything."[11] Stephen Carter states that the church then becomes a hobby, arbitrary and unimportant, a mystical irrationality held by only a few without political significance in the minds of many.[12] The practice of one's faith is then confined to the privacy of homes or within the walls of churches.[13]

---

6 Stephen Carter, *The Culture of Disbelief: How American Law and Politics Trivialize Religious Devotion* (New York: Basic Books, 1993), 51, 57–58. Also consider Bill Hecht, *Two Wars We Must Not Lose: What Christians Need to Know about Radical Islamists, Radical Secularists, and Why We Can't Leave the Battle Up to Our Divided Government* (Fort Wayne, IN: Concordia Theological Seminary Press, 2012), 393.

7 Niall Ferguson, *Civilization: The West and the Rest* (New York: Penguin Press, 2011).

8 Os Guinness, *A Free People's Suicide: Sustainable Freedom and the American Future* (Downers Grove, IL: InterVarsity Press, 2012), cited in Eric Metaxas, *If You Can Keep It: The Forgotten Promise of American Liberty* (New York: Viking Press, 2016), 54.

9 Os Guinness, *The Global Public Square: Religious Freedom and the Making of a World Safe for Diversity* (Downers Grove, IL: InterVarsity Press, 2013), 17.

10 Metaxas, *If You Can Keep It*, 67.

11 Ferguson, *Civilization*, 288.

12 Carter, *Culture of Disbelief*, 6–9.

13 Bill Wylie Kellermann, ed., *A Keeper of the Word: Selected Writings of William Stringfellow* (Grand Rapids: Eerdmans, 1994), 128.

As militant secularists fight to keep religion out of the political arena, the expression of one's faith or moral values based on faith is demonized. Believers are relegated to the margins of society or demoted to "second class citizens."[14] Ryan Anderson notes that both government and sexual values are changed. The progressive secular movement creates the administrative state, which assumes responsibility for more areas of its citizens' lives. The sexual revolution changed the American synthesis of faith and freedom, which sees religion at odds with "liberty" (actually understood now as license or emancipation from all authority outside the sovereign self).[15]

This is evidenced by the disregard or declining regard for the sanctity of life, marriage as a union between one man and one woman, and the family as foundational for society. With a state-directed secular education devoid of any subsequent religious influence, there is little to assist society in producing virtuous citizens. Meanwhile, the American federal courts have continued to lean against the public acknowledgment and accommodation of religion.[16] Richard John Neuhaus warned that without the value-bearing institutions of religion in culture, the state becomes totalitarian.[17]

Still, as bad as all that sounds, this shift is not completely negative. On the positive side, modern Christians in Western society are better situated to consider anew what is foundational to their faith, the true nature of the Church and her marks, the proper relation between the Christian and society, and their role as salt and light in the world. It is helpful to understand how this situation we now call post-Christian, post-Christendom, or post-Constantinian developed in order to assess both positive and negative aspects of these changes for the present and the future.

An Unfolding History

The first attack upon the Christian Church came soon after the ascension of our Lord Jesus Christ and the outpouring of the Holy Spirit at Pentecost. With the stoning of St. Stephen, a general persecution conducted by Jewish authorities

14 Nancy L. Rosenblum, ed., *Obligations of Citizenship and Demands of Faith: Religious Accommodation in Pluralist Democracies* (Princeton, NJ: Princeton University Press, 2000), 3, 9.

15 Ryan T. Anderson, *Truth Overruled: The Future of Marriage and Religious Freedom* (New York: Regency Publishing, 2015), 197.

16 Christopher Wolfe, ed., *The Naked Public Square Reconsidered: Religion and Politics in the Twenty-First Century* (Wilmington, DE: Intercollegiate Studies Institute, 2009), xvii, xxiii.

17 Neuhaus, *Naked Public Square*, 157.

broke out, extending throughout Palestine and into Syria (Acts 7–10). Persecution under the Roman government would follow:

> Christianity entered a world in which it was taken for granted that the state dominated religious activities. Prior to the advent of Christianity, the Romans made no distinction between the life of the state and the religious life of the people. The Romans felt that the gods had given them empire, peace, and prosperity as a result of their being pleased with the worship they received. . . . The maintenance of this covenant was the responsibility of the state.[18]

Certain Roman emperors and other government officials believed that Christians were putting the state's welfare at risk by worshiping their own God instead of the pagan gods and thereby violating the hallowed traditions of Rome. Persecutions were sporadic, and more often regional, occurring under specific emperors, including Nero (54–68), Domitian (81–96), Marcus Aurelius (161–80), Septimius Severus (193–211), Maximinus Thrax (235–38), Trajan Decius (249–51), and Valerian (253–60).[19] "The last universal and greatest persecution took place under Emperor Diocletian [303–11] . . . [who] ordered all Christian churches to be destroyed, Christian sacred books and vessels confiscated, and all Christian clergy imprisoned."[20]

Constantine (306–37) came to power over the western part of the Roman Empire after the death of his father, Constantius I. Before a battle with rival Maxentius at Milvian Bridge in 312, Constantine had a vision where he saw a cross and the words "By this sign conquer" inscribed on the midday sun. He then had his victorious legions fight with the *labarum* (the Greek letters Chi [X] and Rho [P], the first two letters for Christ) inscribed on their shields. Already in 311, the edict of persecution against Christians was withdrawn.

In 313, Constantine and co-regent Licinian issued the Edict of Milan, which made Christianity a legal religion in the Roman Empire and restored all property that had been confiscated under the previous persecution.[21] Constantine had been

---

18 Edward A. Engelbrecht, ed., *Church History: The Basics* (St. Louis: Concordia, 2016), 30–31.

19 Michael Grant, *Constantine the Great: The Man and His Times* (New York: Charles Scribner's Sons, 1993), 126–27; Justo L. González, *Church History: An Essential Guide* (Nashville, TN: Abingdon, 1996), 26.

20 Engelbrecht, *Church History*, 37. See also Justo L. González, *The Story of Christianity: The Early Church to the Dawn of the Reformation*, vol. 1 (San Francisco: Harper & Row, 1984), 104.

21 *Eusebius: The Church History*, trans. Paul L. Maier (Grand Rapids, MI: Kregel Publications, 2007), 322–24.

influenced by the Christian apologist Lactantius, who also tutored his children. Lactantius wrote *The Divine Institutes* (303–11), which called for not only the recognition of Christianity as a legal religion but also toleration for all religions by the state, as the Edict of Milan actually said.[22]

Although he wasn't baptized until just before his death (apparently believing that Baptism only covered original sin and all sins committed before Baptism, and not those after), it is reported that Constantine became Christian because he believed that Christianity would unify the empire and "give him a secure and successful reign."[23]

Like Roman emperors before him, Constantine saw his role as the sustainer of good order, which included all religion in the state. Although he maintained religious toleration throughout the empire, allowing pagan temples and ceremonies to continue unmolested, Constantine actively and openly supported Christianity. He sponsored the building of churches throughout the empire; declared Sunday to be a legal holiday; exempted Christian clergy from public service; exempted clergy and churches from taxes; used Christian bishops as local judges; and inserted himself in theological issues, including the Donatist controversy in North Africa and the Arian controversy, which motivated his calling and financing of the Council of Nicaea in 325. These were years of rapid growth for the Christian Church, and many who came into the church did so as part of a popular and politically expedient trend.

After Constantine's death, Christianity was torn by bitter theological controversies over the doctrine of the Trinity, the divinity of Christ, and the two natures of Christ, which brought imperial power into play in an attempt to maintain unity and peace. Then, just thirty years after Constantine's death, his nephew Julian (known as the Apostate) became emperor and launched an aggressive persecution in an attempt to undermine Christianity. He reigned for less than three years (December 361 to June 363) and was succeeded by Emperor Jovian, who reestablished Christianity's privileged position throughout the empire.[24] It was then under Emperor Theodosius I (reigned 379 to 395), that Christianity became the official religion of the Roman Empire. In 392, Theodosius passed

22 Robert Louis Wilken, "In Defense of Constantine," *First Things* (April 2001): 36–40, https://www.firstthings.com/article/2001/04/in-defense-of-constantine.

23 Wilken, "In Defense of Constantine."

24 Wilken, "In Defense of Constantine"; John Julius Norwich, *A Short History of Byzantium* (New York: Alfred A. Knopf, 1997), 20–28.

legislation prohibiting all pagan worship.[25] Negative consequences from this action were identified by Ken Wieting:

> All of society began to claim a nominal Christianity. There was increased indiscriminate admission to Baptism and confirmation. Careful concern for instruction in the faith under the threat of persecution gave way to political approval and popular applause of the church as an institution. It had become economically advantageous, socially stylish, and politically patriotic to join the Christian church. Receiving Christ in the humble means of Word and Sacrament is not a popular or patriotic act, however. It is the act of faith drawing its life from the promised presence of the Lord *for us.*
>
> . . . Amid all the outward excitement and expansion and enrichment, an inward decline in lay Communion began to set in. . . . A trend had started that was leading the church away from the steadfast devotion to Word and Sacrament in which the Holy Spirit had led the church after Pentecost.[26]

Theodosius was the last emperor to rule over a united Roman Empire. At the beginning of the fifth century, barbarians sacked Rome, and the West was divided from the Eastern or Byzantium Empire. Emperor Justinian (527–65) attempted to reunite the Roman Empire, but he was unsuccessful. He did, however, rewrite and codify Roman law and continued strict state regulation over the church, making the Nicaean-Constantinopolitan Creed the sole symbol of the Church and suppressing all heretics in the Eastern Empire.[27]

After Rome was sacked by the Goths (Germanic invaders) in 410, things changed abruptly in the western part of the Roman Empire. The reaction of many pagans was to blame Christianity, saying that if Rome had stayed with pagan deities, such a thing would not have happened.[28] The West's leading theologian, Augustine (354–430), the bishop of Hippo in North Africa, responded with his

25 Norwich, *A Short History of Byzantium*, 29–35. Although Theodosius placed the state over the church, he was called to account by Bishop Ambrose of Milan for massacring civilians in a conflict. Ambrose excommunicated Theodosius, calling him to repentance. Eventually, Theodosius did repent and was reinstated by Ambrose.

26 Kenneth W. Wieting, *The Blessings of Weekly Communion* (St. Louis: Concordia, 2006), 71.

27 Norwich, *A Short History of Byzantium*, 57–84.

28 Peter Heather, *The Fall of the Roman Empire: A New History of Rome and the Barbarians* (Oxford: Oxford University Press, 2006), 191.

magnum opus, *The City of God.* He took the concept of the heavenly Jerusalem with which Christians were familiar from the Book of Revelation (chs. 21–22) and applied it to the fall of Rome.

Christians were really citizens of a heavenly city. Rome, despite whatever benefits it offered Christianity after Constantine and other Christian emperors, was just like any other earthly city. In this world, citizens of the city of God may belong to different worldly cities or governments (cities of man). Even among the Goths who were sacking Rome, there might be heavenly citizens, while some fellow Romans might be enemies of Christ and His Church and therefore not members of the heavenly city. The heavenly city's citizens owe no more than a passing loyalty to any earthly government. Their true home is in heaven with Christ and the heavenly hosts.[29] Augustine "pointed out that the Church, the agent of the 'City of God,' must operate within every city of man and yet distinguish itself from it, functioning as its light."[30]

Rome's collapse was followed by another more destructive sacking by the Vandals in 455. In the West, the *pax romana* (Roman peace) gave way to feudalism with the lord or leader of one region warring against another. Bishops, including the bishop of Rome, became political leaders, often exerting secular authority within their territories, including the maintenance of armies with which to wage war. This paved the way for the assertion of papal supremacy.

The bishop of Rome claimed to be the vicar of Christ on earth based on an interpretation of Jesus' words to Peter in Matthew 16:13–19. This was given further emphasis by popes Innocent I (401–17), Leo I (440–61), and Gregory I (590–604). "The theory of papal primacy was not fully realized, however, until the pontificate of Innocent III (1198–1216)."[31]

Pope Gregory I did much to extend the power of the papacy from Italy all the way to Spain and Great Britain. But the ninth century witnessed a striking shift both politically and in the furtherance of the Western church:

> The crowning of Charlemagne's father by Boniface, the missionary bishop of Germany, and the crowning of Charlemagne himself by Pope Leo III on Christmas Day in AD 800 signaled a transition from

29 Heather, *The Fall of the Roman Empire*, 231.

30 Engelbrecht, *Church History*, 45.

31 Engelbrecht, *Church History*, 106.

> a Mediterranean, Eastern-oriented faith to an expressly European form of religion. . . .
>
> For the next nine hundred years, the politics, learning, social organization, art, music, economy, and legal system of Europe would be Christian in the sense of secular interest in and identification with churchly matters. That situation was not so much a result of the clear speaking of Law and Gospel in society but because the fate of the Western church, centered in Rome, had been so decisively linked with the new Roman emperor over the Alps. At the time of his death, Charlemagne's empire included areas of modern France, Belgium, Holland, Switzerland, northern Spain, and much of Germany and Italy.[32]

This began not only what became known as the Holy Roman Empire but also the concept we call Christendom. But who was the supreme authority within Christendom: the emperor or the pope? Charlemagne saw himself as the supreme protector of the church and the state, but the papacy and many leaders in the Western church disagreed. This was an issue that would continue back and forth into the seventeenth century. The forged Donation of Constantine supported papal claims of supremacy:

> It was fabricated in the Frankish empire sometime during the eighth century in order to support the claims of the Church against the state and in particular to strengthen the position of the pope. In it, Emperor Constantine purported to give to Pope Sylvester I the rulership over all of Italy and the West, in addition to Antioch, Constantinople, Alexandria, and Jerusalem. Lorenzo Valla (d. 1457) is credited with proving this document a forgery.[33]

In 962, King Otto I (936–73) invaded Italy from Northern Europe in order to defend Pope John XII against a military offensive, and in turn, the pope crowned Otto emperor, again furthering the concept of a Holy Roman Empire. But not long after, Otto deposed the pope and had one of his own choosing elected. Throughout the eleventh century, almost every bishop was appointed by the ruling monarch.

32 Wieting, *The Blessings of Weekly Communion*, 84–85.

33 Engelbrecht, *Church History*, 129–30.

The popes of that century continued to dispute the propriety and right of any lay ruler to exercise authority over clerical appointments. The issue came to a head when Gregory VII (also known as Hildebrand) was pope (1073–85):

> Gregory launched his attack against lay investiture in 1075. The penalty for ignoring his decree was automatic excommunication. In the same year, the pope wrote an aide-memoir for his private use. . . . The document, *Dictatus Papae*, made extravagant claims for papal primacy, including the first explicit claim that a pope could depose an emperor. King Henry IV in Germany (not yet crowned emperor) ignored the papal decree on lay investiture and appointed a bishop for Milan. . . . Gregory responded by deposing the king from office and excommunicating him. This act released all of Henry's subjects from their oath of allegiance to him. The turbulent princes of Germany, who were never happy under a strong king, used this occasion as a legitimate excuse for revolt, and Henry was forced to agree that a council be held in Augsburg during February of 1077 to determine his future role in Germany.
>
> In January 1077, the pope, en route to the Augsburg council, was resting at the castle of Canossa in northern Italy when the most dramatic episode of the controversy occurred. King Henry appeared outside the castle as a penitent, begging the pope's pardon.[34]

The pope absolved Henry, but left the deposition from office in force. The result was that the German lands were plunged into a civil war. Pope Gregory VII had declared for a rival king, Rudolph, who was eventually defeated and killed by Henry's forces. Henry IV then summoned a council of bishops and elected a counter-pope, Guibert (Clement III). Additionally, the German armies marched on Rome and besieged it for three years. Gregory VII died in captivity in 1085. Emperor Henry V (1111–25) continued the conflict with the papacy. However, the First Crusade diverted attention to what would prove to be other aspects of church and state confusion.

Since the eighth century, Muslim armies had pushed their way into Spain and the Mediterranean islands. By the middle of the eleventh century, they had

34 Engelbrecht, *Church History*, 134.

captured Bagdad in modern Iraq and were threatening the borders of the Byzantine Empire. In 1071, they conquered Syria and Armenia; Jerusalem followed in 1078, and Antioch in 1084. No longer did Christian pilgrims to the Holy Land have safe passage. Byzantine emperor Michael VII appealed to Pope Gregory VII for help, but the pope was too involved in the Investiture Controversy to offer assistance. By the end of the eleventh century, the Muslim armies had advanced to Nicaea, where they were threatening the gates of Constantinople, and again a plea for help went forth. Pope Urban II responded with the call for the First Crusade at the Council of Clermont in 1095, which appealed for Christians to rescue fellow Christians.[35]

> Economically and politically the Crusades were a vast outpouring of landless peasants and equally landless nobles, all hoping to carve a better future in the lands to be taken from the Muslims. Crusaders enjoyed a privileged status after assuming the cross. There was a moratorium on all their debts; they were promised the opportunity for new lands and property in the Holy Land; and they were granted a plenary indulgence that canceled the punishment for all previous sins.[36]

The practice of granting indulgences increased dramatically during the Crusades and helped augment the influence of the papacy.[37] From the end of the eleventh century to the end of the thirteenth century, nine crusades were mounted, and while Christians occupied Palestine for a brief period, ultimately the Holy Land remained in Muslim hands. In some ways, the Crusades set the papacy in place of the emperor as the head of Europe as well as the Roman Church, something that has been referred to as a papal monarchy.[38] This was solidified through the sale of plenary indulgences, which only the pope could grant.[39] It further connected the papacy and Christendom with militarism and feudal chivalry.[40]

---

35 Engelbrecht, *Church History, 85*; Margaret Deanesly, *A History of the Medieval Church 590–1500* (New York: Methuen, 1969), 106–7; George Holmes, ed., *The Oxford Illustrated History of Medieval Europe* (Oxford, U.K.: Oxford University Press, 1988), 135.

36 Wieting, *The Blessings of Weekly Communion*, 88.

37 Deanesly, *A History of the Medieval Church*, 112.

38 Geoffrey Barraclough, *The Medieval Papacy* (New York: W. W. Norton & Company, Inc., 1968), 91, 116.

39 R. W. Southern, *Western Society and the Middle Ages* (New York: Penguin Books, 1970), 136–37.

40 John H. Mundy, *The High Middle Ages, 1150–1309* (London: The Folio Society, 1998), 196–97.

Muslim armies continued their territorial conquest of Greece and Turkey, culminating in the fall of Constantinople on May 29, 1453. The Church of Hagia Sophia, constructed under Emperor Justinian in 537, the seat of the Patriarch of Constantinople, and actually the third church of that name to occupy that site (the first having been built under Emperor Constantine), was turned into a mosque.

The Investiture Controversy between Emperor Henry IV and Pope Gregory VII was eventually settled by the Concordat of Worms (1122), a compromise that left the secular ruler a voice in the election of bishops. Both sides continued to argue over which authority held the highest power. During the thirteenth century, the papacy reached the height of its power under the pontiffs Innocent III, Gregory IX, and Innocent IV. The papacy used military force, alliances, diplomatic pressures, and economic aid to influence or enforce its aims.

The majority of the leading theologians during the Middle Ages, the scholastics, supported papal primacy. Thomas Aquinas held that the pope is ultimately supreme and has the right to interfere in political affairs; but as long as the earthly ruler exercises power within his proper sphere, then there is no reason for ecclesiastical authority to interfere.[41] In his *Summa Theologiae*, Aquinas maintained that when ecclesiastical authority found someone to be guilty of heresy, then it was the responsibility of the state, for the good of society, to put the heretic to death.[42]

This contest over primacy moved to France in the early part of the fourteenth century when Philip the Fair, king of France (1285–1314), taxed the clergy to help finance a war. Pope Boniface VIII (1294–1303) issued a bull forbidding the clergy to pay the tax. When the nationalistic clergy paid the tax anyway, Boniface issued *Unam Sanctam*, which declared that subjection to the pope is necessary for salvation and that the state is under the authority of the church.

The controversy ended with what is called the Babylonian Captivity of the Papacy from 1309 to 1377, during which Avignon, France, became the papal seat and the papacy came under French influence. On September 13, 1376, Pope Gregory XI abandoned Avignon and moved his court back to Rome (arriving on January 17, 1377), officially ending the Avignon Papacy. The French cardinals were not pleased, though, and in 1378, they elected Clement VII as pope, beginning

---

41 Arthur Hyman and James J. Walsh, eds., *Philosophy in the Middle Ages* (Indianapolis: Hackett Publishing Company, 1973), 716–18.

42 David Bentley Hart, "No Enduring City: The Gospel Both Created and Destroyed Christendom," *First Things*, August 2013, https://www.firstthings.com/article/2013/08/no-enduring-city.

what is referred to as the Western Schism, which divided Christendom until 1417, with a pope in Rome and an antipope in Avignon.

Throughout Europe, people were calling for a general council to resolve the schism and assist in reforming the church. This ushered in what is known as the Conciliar Movement:

> In 1409, the College of Cardinals finally succeeded in calling a general council in Pisa, which deposed the popes at Rome and Avignon and elected Alexander V to succeed them. Neither of the deposed popes acknowledged the validity of the council, so there were now three popes claiming the allegiance of Christendom.[43]

The schism was finally healed at the Council of Constance (1414–18), which deposed all three popes and elected Martin V. The newly elected pontiff had to promise reforms for the church, which were not carried out. The council also condemned John Wycliffe, ordering that his body be exhumed from consecrated ground. It also condemned the Bohemian reformer John Hus. Even though he was promised safe passage to the council, Hus was declared a heretic and burned at the stake. "Although the schism had been healed, the council's treatment of Wycliffe and Hus, together with its failure to effect genuine reforms, made the Reformation of the sixteenth century inevitable."[44]

On October 31, 1517, an unknown Augustinian monk and University of Wittenberg professor, Martin Luther, nailed ninety-five theses to the town bulletin board, the doors of the Castle Church. Luther wanted to debate the sale of indulgences, which had been recently implemented in nearby Brandenburg.

Prince Albert of Brandenburg, a young man without theological training, was given dispensations to become the archbishop of Magdeburg, bishop of Halberstadt, and archbishop of Mainz by Pope Leo X. However, Albert had to pay Leo a considerable sum, which he borrowed from the Fugger banking house in Augsburg. To repay the loan, he was allowed to sell indulgences within German territories. A major portion of the money Albert raised went to building St. Peter's Basilica in Rome.

One of those selling indulgences was the Dominican friar John Tetzel, known for his interesting mercantile techniques. Among these was his slogan: "As soon

43 Engelbrecht, *Church History*, 155.

44 Engelbrecht, *Church History*, 155.

as a coin in the coffer rings / the soul from purgatory springs." Indulgences could be purchased for the forgiveness of one's own sins (past, present, or future) as well as those of loved ones who had already died and were supposedly languishing in purgatory.

Frederick III (also known as Frederick the Wise), elector of Saxony, who founded the University of Wittenberg, did not permit "the sale of [indulgences] in his lands because he was concerned about any competition [with his own] indulgence-granting collection of relics housed in the Castle Church at Wittenberg.[45] Frederick the Wise was one of seven "electors" in Germany who elected the emperor of the Holy Roman Empire. The emperor at this time was Maximilian I (March 22, 1459 to January 12, 1519), but Frederick was instrumental in electing Charles V as emperor in 1519.

Luther's Ninety-Five Theses were not intended to divide the Roman Church or Christendom; yet with those statements the Reformation began:

> The first two theses set the tone: "When our Lord and Master Jesus Christ said, 'Repent,' he willed the entire life of believers to be one of repentance. This word cannot be understood as referring to the sacrament of penance, that is, confession and satisfaction as administered by the clergy." The indulgence cannot take the place of the penance, the repentance required of the sinner. In other theses, he questioned the pope's power to remit all penalties and wondered why the pope did not use his own wealth to build St. Peter's instead of the money collected from the poor. If the pope could "empty purgatory" for money, why did he not do it out of charity? Luther did not reject papal indulgences at this time, but rather he warned of the dangerous misunderstandings and the extravagant claims for papal power current among the purchasers and preachers of indulgences.[46]

Because of the invention of the printing press by Johannes Gutenberg around 1440, Luther's theses were copied, translated, and published throughout Europe. A pamphlet war began, the sale of indulgences dropped significantly, and Luther was called to appear before Cardinal Cajetan, the papal legate, in October 1518.

---

45 Engelbrecht, *Church History*, 164; E. G. Schwiebert, *Luther and His Times: The Reformation from a New Perspective* (St. Louis: Concordia, 1950), 306–14.

46 Engelbrecht, *Church History*, 165.

Cajetan was ordered to call the upstart monk a heretic if he did not recant. Yet, Luther refused to recant his views, which were developing further and being expressed in various published writings.

At the Leipzig Debate in July 1519, Luther contended with theology professor Johann Eck. Luther questioned the primacy of the Roman papacy, holding that both popes and councils have erred, even contradicted one another, and were not infallible. He also asserted that John Hus, a condemned heretic, held views that were "plainly Christian and evangelical."

In 1520, Luther's *To the Christian Nobility* appealed to the German princes to cast off the chains that bound them to the Roman papacy. Here Luther asserted the priesthood of all believers, to which all Christians belong through Holy Baptism. Through this priesthood, all believers are responsible for the spiritual welfare of their neighbors and have the essential right to read and interpret Holy Scripture. Christian laity, especially the princes, should exercise their Christian duty by calling a council to reform the Church. Luther called for the elimination of canon law, the ending of required clerical celibacy, and the establishment of a German national church.

In June 1520, Pope Leo X issued a bull of excommunication against Luther and ordered that he report to Rome in sixty days. However, Frederick the Wise, elector of Saxony, protected his subject Martin Luther. In response to the bull of excommunication, Luther published *The Babylonian Captivity of the Church* in October 1520. Here Luther took issue with the entire sacramental system of Rome. He asserted that only Baptism, the Lord's Supper, and possibly penance (confession of sins and pronouncing absolution) have the promises of Christ attached to them, offering forgiveness of sin. Martin Luther would publicly burn the papal bull of excommunication on December 10, 1520.

In order to deal with the excommunicated "heretic," the newly elected Holy Roman Emperor, Charles V, called a diet to meet in the German city of Worms in 1521. Luther was granted safe passage, and on April 17, he appeared before the emperor, the assembled princes, clergy, and representatives of the free cities. The diet did not allow Luther to discuss his views. Instead, he was presented with his books, asked if they were his, and ordered to recant. Luther asked for time to consider and was allotted twenty-four hours. When again asked to recant,

> Luther pointed out that no simple answer was possible, as he had written on a variety of things, some of which were truly Christian and in

> defense of the Word of God. He asked to be corrected on the basis of Scriptures. Then, after being asked for a clear and simple answer, Luther made his historic response: "Unless I am convinced of error by the testimony of Scripture or by clear reason . . . I cannot and will not recant anything, for it is neither safe nor honest to act against one's conscience. God help me. Amen."[47]

After leaving Worms on April 26, while traveling through the Thuringian forest, Luther was "kidnapped" by some of Elector Frederick's knights and whisked off to the Wartburg castle near Eisenach. There Luther would remain until March 1522, translating the New Testament into German and writing *On Monastic Vows* (1521), which attacked the medieval monastic system as well as the vows taken by monks, nuns, and regular clergy. Here Luther also asserted that not only church professions, but also all worthwhile occupations were vocations or callings from God, and even the common laborer could give witness to the Gospel in his or her work.

Luther returned to Wittenberg to stem the radicalism of Andreas Karlstadt and others who were destroying statues and stained glass windows, discarding clerical vestments, and disregarding other Christian traditions. In a series of sermons, Luther showed that there were many traditions that Christians were free to use or discard; images, ceremonies, symbols, vestments, festivals, fasting, and other outward customs could be useful in devotion as long as they were not worshiped or used to bind people's conscience.

In 1523, Luther published *Temporal Authority: To What Extent It Should Be Obeyed*, which shared similarities with what was put forth by Augustine in *The City of God*. Here he articulated his doctrine of the two kingdoms. God rules the world in a twofold way: the kingdom of the right, or the spiritual kingdom, and the kingdom of the left, or through secular government. The spiritual government is the "kingdom of grace," which brings the kingdom of God into being. Here Christ exercises His government through the preaching of His Word and the administration of His Sacraments. There is no force used in this kingdom. Everything takes place through the compelling power of the Holy Spirit who works through God's Word and Sacraments.

The secular government, or the kingdom of the left, is instituted by God to maintain order in a fallen, sinful world. Here God works through human

47 Engelbrecht, *Church History*, 167–68.

authority, the Law, and even the use of force. For Luther, this includes much more than political authorities and governments, rather everything that contributes to the preservation of earthly life, especially marriage and the family, along with property, business, and all the stations and vocations that God instituted for people to serve their neighbors. In the spiritual kingdom, Christ rules personally as the Holy Spirit works through the Gospel. In the secular kingdom, reason rules through natural law.

In this world, both kingdoms need each other, and yet the two kingdoms cannot be mixed. The spiritual kingdom needs the secular government to maintain a peaceful society and encourage and protect marriage and families. The secular government needs citizens who understand and respect the authority of the civil government and the various stations of society as God's work and will.

Luther asserted that the Roman papacy was especially guilty of mixing the two kingdoms. Through its canon law, the papacy sought to gain control of secular law and make itself master over secular authorities. Yet, the Enthusiasts like Karlstadt also confused matters by attempting to derive laws for secular government from the Gospel. On the other hand, Luther condemned political authorities who sought to take control over the church.

The evangelical teaching of Martin Luther spread to many other areas in Germany and was supported by a number of princes. Meanwhile, Charles V was occupied by a war with France, and the Muslim armies were advancing toward Vienna. A diet was called at Speyer in 1526. Charles V was not present but was represented by his brother Ferdinand, who ordered all the princes to enforce Roman Catholicism in their lands. The evangelical princes issued a statement holding that the Word of God was above all temporal authorities and offered a list of grievances to the emperor, stating that they would protest if these were not acted upon. Thereafter, they were dubbed "Protestants" by those who sided with the Roman Catholic Church. The Diet of Speyer resolved that "each German ruler should so 'live, govern and carry himself as he hopes and trusts to answer to God and his imperial majesty.'"[48]

Charles V ignored the list of grievances and called a diet to meet at Augsburg in 1530. On June 25, those princes holding to the Christian evangelical doctrine of Martin Luther put forth a document drafted by Luther's colleague, Philip Melanchthon. (Because Luther was considered an outlaw after the Diet of

48 Engelbrecht, *Church History*, 174.

Worms, he remained at Koberg Castle in protected evangelical territory during the Diet of Augsburg.)

The Augsburg Confession articulates the apostolic Christian faith as set forth in the Ecumenical Creeds (Apostles', Nicene, and Athanasian). This includes faith in the triune God (Article I), the total corruption of mankind through sin (Article II), the divine and human natures of Jesus Christ (Article III), and that justification before God was earned solely by the perfect life, death, and resurrection of Jesus Christ, and not by any merits or worthiness in sinful human beings. This justification or the forgiveness of sins becomes ours solely by God's grace through faith in Jesus Christ (Article IV), which is worked by the Holy Spirit through Baptism and God's Word. So that people may obtain such faith, God instituted the preaching office, proclaiming the Gospel and administering the Sacraments (Article V), and this office comes only through a proper call (Article XIV). Where the Gospel is preached and the Sacraments are administered, there the Church is to be found (Article VII). Strictly speaking, the Church is the gathering of all true believers, which is one holy, Christian Church. However, in this sinful world, there are hypocrites mingled in with true believers in the visible Church. Yet, even if evil men preach the Word and administer the Sacraments, God's Means of Grace are valid and effective because of Christ's institution and command (Article VIII).

The Augsburg Confession also articulated the two-kingdom teaching of Martin Luther. Almighty God works through two distinct kingdoms in this world, each having its own goals, sphere, and means. Regarding the two kingdoms, Article XXVIII asserts,

> There has been great controversy about the power of the bishops, in which some have terribly confused the power of the Church with the power of the State. This confusion has produced great war and riot. All the while the popes, claiming the Power of the Keys, have instituted new services and burdened consciences with Church discipline and excommunication. But they have also tried to transfer the kingdoms of this world to the Church by taking the Empire away from the emperor. Learned and godly people have condemned these errors in the Church for a long time. Therefore, our teachers, in order to comfort people's consciences, were constrained to show the difference between the authority of the Church and the authority of the State.

> They taught that both of them are to be held in reverence and honor, as God's chief blessings on earth, because they have God's command.
>
> Our teachers' position is this: the authority of the Keys [Matthew 16:19], or the authority of the bishops—according to the Gospel—is a power or commandment of God, to preach the Gospel, to forgive and retain sins, and to administer the Sacraments. . . .
>
> Therefore, the Church has the authority to grant eternal things and exercises this authority only by the ministry of the Word. So it does not interfere with civil government anymore than the art of singing interferes with civil government. For civil government deals with other things than the Gospel does. Civil rulers do not defend minds, but bodies and bodily things against obvious injuries. They restrain people with the sword and physical punishment in order to preserve civil justice and peace [Romans 13:1–7]. (AC XXVIII 1–5, 10–11)

Furthermore, concerning life in the kingdom of the left, Article XVI states:

> Our churches teach that lawful civil regulations are good works of God. They teach that it is right for Christians to hold political office, to serve as judges, to judge matters by imperial laws and other existing laws, to impose just punishments, to engage in just wars, to serve as soldiers, to make legal contracts, to hold property, to take oaths when required by the magistrates, for a man to marry a wife, or a woman to be given in marriage [Romans 13; 1 Corinthians 7:2]. (AC XVI 1–2)

Although both Luther and the Augsburg Confession taught that the two kingdoms, church and state, should be distinct, it was the evangelical princes, all of whom believed it was their responsibility to uphold the Christian faith in their lands and to maintain or uphold Christendom, who presented the Confession before the Holy Roman Emperor. This understanding of the state being responsible for the church would continue in Europe, even to the present.

It was not until after the death of Martin Luther, February 18, 1546, that Holy Roman Emperor Charles V was able to devote his attention to the "Protestant problem," having established peace with France, at least for the time being, and having held the Muslim armies in the Balkans at bay. Within a few months of Luther's death, he declared war against the Lutheran princes' Smalcald League. Due largely to the betrayal of Duke Maurice of Saxony (who gained the position of elector of Saxony from John Frederick I by switching sides), the Lutheran princes lost the Smalcald War (1546–47), and Charles V imposed the Augsburg Interim on the Lutheran territories, forcing certain aspects of Roman Catholic teaching and practice upon the Lutherans.

The edict resulted in a rebellion in 1552 by the Protestant princes, only this time it was led by Elector Maurice of Saxony (who switched sides again!) and now also supported by King Henry II of France. The conflict was finally settled at the Peace of Augsburg on September 25, 1555. The Peace established the principle *cuius regio, eius religio* (He who rules determines the religion). This allowed the princes of the Holy Roman Empire to choose either Lutheranism or Roman Catholicism within the domains they governed, which upheld their rule over their lands, including rule over the church. Those subjects who did not wish to hold to the prince's religion were given a period in which they were allowed to emigrate to a principality that held to their desired religion.

Elsewhere in Europe, other forms of state-endorsed religion were taking shape. King Henry VIII of England (1509–47) was not happy when the pope would not authorize his divorce. He went through six marriages in an effort to gain a male heir, and by way of a series of decrees between 1532 and 1537, established the Church of England, with himself as the Supreme Head. Conflicts between Protestants and Roman Catholics in the British Isles would continue well into the twentieth century.

In Switzerland, a more radical Reformation took place, first under Ulrich Zwingli, who died October 11, 1531, in the Battle of Kappel. The Swiss cantons had been divided between Protestant and Roman Catholic sides and Zwingli took up arms in the battle. John Calvin, a Protestant reformer from France, settled in Geneva, Switzerland, and continued the Reformation there. Geneva would be governed by a theocratic consistory that maintained a close relationship between citizenship and church membership. Calvin's doctrine and polity would spread to the Netherlands, the Palatinate, England, and Scotland.

Although things seemed to settle down briefly, military conflict became a way of attempting to resolve religious differences again in the seventeenth century, specifically with the Thirty Years' War on the European continent (1618–48) and the civil war and commonwealth period in England (1642–60, also called the English Revolution). In both cases, political motivation and intrigue were involved and were sometimes the driving force in the conflict.

The Thirty Years' War decimated the population and landscape of Germany (some estimates hold that upwards of two-thirds of the population was lost due to war and plague during this time), involved most of the nations of the European continent in the conflict, and resulted in the status quo being reinstated: *cuius regio, eius religio* (He who rules determines the religion).

The English Revolution ended with Charles II being reinstated as both the King of England and sovereign over the Church of England (1660–85). However, he was followed by James II (1685–89), who tried to restore Roman Catholicism. He was forced to flee to France and was succeeded by William of Orange and Mary in 1689. That year, the British Parliament passed the Toleration Act and the Bill of Rights, which guaranteed civil rights and religious freedom. However, the British sovereign was still the head of the Church of England, and only Anglicans could serve in the government and the military.

Among other things, the religious wars of the seventeenth century paved the way for the rise of the Enlightenment in the eighteenth century. The Enlightenment invoked a number of ideals, including liberty, progress, tolerance, fraternity, constitutional government, and separation of church and state, although those ideals were not always practiced by its adherents (i.e., the French Revolution). It placed human reason as the main authority in determining what is true.[49] Although it did not result in the dissolution of state churches, it did decimate church attendance and religious influence throughout Europe. Niall Ferguson notes,

> The case of Britain is especially interesting in view of the determination with which Britons sought to spread their own religious faith in the nineteenth century. Today, according to the World Values Survey, 17 percent of Britons claim they attend a religious service at least once a week—higher than in continental Europe, but still less than half of the American figure. . . . When Christian Research conducted a census of 18,720 churches on Sunday 8 May 2005, the real rate of attendance was just 6.3 per cent of the population, down 15 per cent since 1998. On closer inspection, Britain seems to exemplify the collapse both of observance and of faith in Western Europe.[50]

49 Dorinda Outram, *Panorama of the Enlightenment* (Los Angeles, CA: Getty Publications, 2006), 29.

50 Ferguson, *Civilization*, 267–68.

The concept of freedom of religion that we have in the United States developed out of a unique mix of Christian and Enlightenment thought.[51] The British colonies in North America began with state churches. At the outbreak of the Revolutionary War, "Nine of the thirteen colonies had conferred special benefits upon one church to the exclusion of others."[52] When the Bill of Rights was adopted in 1791, the First Amendment to the Constitution had two purposes. First, there would be no established national church for the united thirteen states. Second, government should not impede or interfere with the free practice of religion.[53] Nevertheless, a number of the states continued to have state churches, which was not considered to be in conflict with the First Amendment:

> In all but one of the thirteen states, the states taxed the people to support the preaching of the gospel and to build churches. It was not until 1798 that the Virginia legislature repealed all its laws supporting churches. In Massachusetts, the Massachusetts Constitution was not amended until 1853 to eliminate the tax-supported church provisions.[54]

Bill Hecht holds that these and other state regulations (some requiring mandatory church attendance and tax support for clergy, anti-blasphemy laws, and Sabbath regulations) "argue strongly that most Americans believed America to be a Christian nation, at least in a broad sense of the term."[55] Christopher Wolfe asserts,

> While there have always been certain tensions in America regarding the relationship between religion and politics, until relatively recently in our history these tensions have concerned what role religion should play in our national life and what sort of religion it ought to be that was playing this role. Only in the second half of the twentieth century

51 Colson, *Kingdoms in Conflict*, 119–20.

52 Schaeffer, *How Should We Then Live?* 433, citing Herbert W. Titus, "Education, Caesar's or God's: A Constitutional Question of Jurisdiction," *Journal of Christian Jurisprudence* (1982): 101–80.

53 Legal expert Stephen Carter asserts that "the metaphorical separation of church and state originated in an effort to protect religion from the state, not the state from religion. The religion clauses of the First Amendment were crafted to permit maximum freedom to the religious" (*Culture of Disbelief*, 105–6).

54 Schaeffer, *How Should We Then Live?* 433, citing Titus, "Education, Caesar's or God's."

55 Hecht, *Two Wars We Must Not Lose*, 422.

did the question become whether religion as such had any role to play in American politics.[56]

Although it would be technically inaccurate to say that the United States of America is a Christian nation or a Christian republic, it may be fair to say that the United States began and continued at least into the twentieth century with a Christian culture. It was a Christian culture in the sense that the predominant choice of religious people was a form of Christianity, and in the sense that most members of the culture were familiar with the basic truth claims and ethical principles associated with Christianity.[57] Niall Ferguson holds that the nationalization of the church or specific religious confessions in Europe led to the downfall of both religion and, to an extent, the state ("In religion as in business, state monopolies are inefficient"), while in the United States, the lack of a state-established religion led to open competition between multiple denominations: "And this may be the best explanation for the strange death of religion in Europe and its enduring vigour in the United States."[58]

It was to this pluralistic religious culture, with no specific established national church and the freedom of religion guaranteed under the First Amendment, that a group of almost seven hundred Saxon Lutheran emigrants came in 1838, settling in St. Louis and Perry County, Missouri. They fled Germany because they believed they could not continue to be orthodox, confessional Lutherans under the state church of Saxony, which had been influenced by the rationalism of the Enlightenment.

In Germany, the prince of a kingdom[59] oversaw the state church in his territory, usually through an appointed consistory, which placed and assigned pastors and was responsible for the maintenance of church buildings and the salaries of church workers through taxes paid by citizens of the kingdom.

Since the Saxon Lutherans were leaving this state church system and coming to a country with no established state church, they based their status as a church upon the allegiance they pledged to their leader, Martin Stephan, proclaiming

56 Wolfe, *Naked Public Square Reconsidered*, xiii.

57 T. David Gordon, "The Decline of Christianity in the West? A Contrarian View," *Ordained Servant Online*, May 2007, http://www.opc.org/os.html?article_id=44. Eric Metaxas discusses how this spread through early colonial America and paved the way for the unique mix that resulted in the First Amendment through the preaching of George Whitefield in what has been referred to as the First Great Awakening (*If You Can Keep It*, 79–114).

58 Ferguson, *Civilization*, 275.

59 Before 1871, Germany was a collection of independent kingdoms.

him bishop, and giving him complete control over all ecclesiastical and fiscal matters in their emigration company.

However, only months after their arrival, they removed their bishop from office for immorality and sent him away from the colony. This resulted in two years of turmoil and threatened dissolution, including near starvation for some, outbreaks of disease, several deaths, animosity and accusations toward the clergy, calls for repentance, and calls to return to Germany. The Saxons questioned whether they were indeed members of the Christian Church, whether their pastors had valid calls, whether the Word preached and the Sacraments administered in their midst were even valid.

In April 1841, one of the pastors, Carl Ferdinand Wilhelm Walther, debated one of the leading laymen, Franz Marbach, concerning their situation. Marbach held that they had sinned by following Martin Stephan, and the only solution was to repent and return to Germany. Walther argued his position on the teaching of Holy Scripture, the Lutheran Confessions, Luther, and other prominent Lutheran theologians. He showed that even though they had sinned and could possibly be considered a heterodox company, they still were part of the Holy Christian Church (*una sancta ecclesia*), the invisible Church of all true believers. He asserted that the priesthood of all believers held all churchly authority and powers, and that this royal priesthood in their midst could therefore call ministers to preach the Word and administer the Sacraments, and that those Means of Grace were valid and marked the Church in their midst.[60]

After the formation of what has become The Lutheran Church—Missouri Synod in 1847, synodical president C. F. W. Walther would further articulate the church body's position on church and ministry in a series of theses that were adopted in 1851 and published as *Church and Ministry: The Voice of Our Church on the Question of Church and Office*. Here Walther and the Missouri Synod asserted that the true Church, the Holy Christian Church of all true believers, is invisible, known fully only by God. To this true Church of believers, Christ has given the keys of the kingdom of heaven.

> Thesis V: Although the true Church in the proper sense of the word is in its essence invisible, nevertheless its existence can be (definitely)

60 Walter O. Forster, *Zion on the Mississippi* (St. Louis: Concordia, 1953). Also consider William J. Schmelder, "Walther at Altenburg," *Concordia Historical Institute Quarterly* 34:3 (1961), 65–81; Jack D. Ferguson, "Mid Tumult of Her War: The Doctrine of the Church and the Office of the Holy Ministry Following the 1841 Altenburg Debate," *Concordia Historical Institute Quarterly* 89:1 (2016), 7–34.

> recognizable, namely, by the marks of the pure preaching of God's Word and the administration of the Sacraments according to Christ's institution.
>
> Thesis VI: In an improper sense, Scripture also calls the visible entirety of all the called—that is, of all who confess and adhere to the proclaimed Word and use the holy Sacraments—which consists of good and evil [persons], "Church" (the universal [catholic] Church); so also it calls its several divisions, that is, the congregations that are found here and there in which the Word of God is preached and the holy Sacraments are administered, "churches" (particular or individual churches). This it does especially because in this visible assembly is hidden the invisible, true, and properly so-called Church of believers, saints, and children of God; outside this assembly of the called no elect are to be sought.[61]

So, in a very real sense, The Lutheran Church—Missouri Synod has been coping with the loss of the Constantinian accommodation since its founding. The understanding and basis of being part of the Christian Church did not depend on recognition or support by the state, but instead on the marks of the Church in their midst: the pure preaching of God's Word and the administration of the Sacraments according to Christ's institution.

Consequences of "Constantinian" Christianity

In studying the historic concepts of both Constantinianism and Christendom, one sees that Emperor Constantine did not establish the idea of Christendom, nor did he establish Christianity as the state church of the Roman Empire. Both came later. Constantine legalized Christianity but tolerated other religions. Still, like emperors before him, he believed it was his responsibility to oversee religion in the state, he saw religion as a unifying force in the empire, and as the first Roman emperor to identify as a Christian, he favored the Christian Church.

The placing of the state over the church would continue even after the fall of the Roman Empire in the West through what eventually became the Holy Roman Empire. With the concept of Christendom, the state continued in its place over

61 C. F. W. Walther, *The Church & The Office of The Ministry* (St. Louis: Concordia, 2012), 3.

the church even after the Reformation through the state-established religion of the Peace of Augsburg and the Treaty of Westphalia. However, it did not continue in the United States of America, at least not nationally (although some states did provide state support for churches into the middle of the nineteenth century). The development of civil and religious rights and liberties in the United States came through a mixing of both Enlightenment thinking and a culture that was decidedly Christian. The Lutheran Church—Missouri Synod was founded not by identifying with state support and sanction but as the triune God worked through the marks of the Church.

What became known as the Constantinian accommodation has had both positive and negative consequences. On the plus side, the persecution of Christians was terminated, the church was united by calling councils of bishops to deal with heretical teaching, Christians were allowed to freely spread the truth of God's Word in their day-to-day vocations, and the church was permitted to openly proclaim God's Word and administer the Sacraments in lawful public Divine Services.[62] By legalizing Christianity and through various forms of legislation, Constantine and other Christian emperors allowed Christianity to change a hedonistic, corrupt society to one that valued the sanctity of human life (ending infanticide and the gladiatorial games); esteemed the sanctity of marriage between one man and one woman; respected overall sexual morality; respected the dignity and freedom of women; fostered charity and compassion toward the less fortunate, which resulted in the establishment of orphanages and hospitals; and, over time, advanced education throughout society.[63]

In the category of mixed blessings, the church experienced a significant upgrade in social status as Christians went from being a persecuted minority to a legal and even protected religious majority. Although this resulted in more people becoming members of Christian churches, many were joining for the wrong reasons, and there was a growing number of nominal Christians.[64] Additionally, "A certain amount of triumphalism crept into the church which began to view itself more and more as a spiritual/political force destined to 'rule' the world."[65]

---

62 John C. Nugent, "A Yoderian Rejoinder to Peter J. Leithart's *Defending Constantine*," in John D. Roth, ed., *Constantine Revisited* (Eugene, OR: Pickwick Publications, 2013), 3–4.

63 Consider Alvin J. Schmidt, *How Christianity Changed the World* (Grand Rapids: Zondervan, 2001); Matthew Rueger, *Sexual Morality in a Christless World* (St. Louis: Concordia, 2016).

64 Ken Wieting notes, "The active participation of the laity in weekly Communion began to decline during the rule of Constantine. For various reasons—including political and social turmoil, unsteady church leadership, and doctrinal confusion—this period of history did not foster a recovery of the understanding of the true nature of the Lord's Supper" (*The Blessings of Weekly Communion*, 81).

65 Mark William Worthing, "Twenty-Five Theses concerning Cultural Christianity and Its Adherents," *Lutheran Forum* 28:2

This "certain amount of triumphalism" points to the decidedly negative consequences that developed out of the so-called Constantinian accommodation. From 312 until the present, the accommodation resulted in an inappropriate mixing of church and state. With emperors, kings, and princes managing the affairs of the church, many vested with secular authority used the spiritual authority of the church to serve their own ends. On the other side, leaders in the church assumed secular power and authority, using it to serve their worldly ends as well. There is the long, sad history of competition and rivalry between the leaders in the two kingdoms, wrangling over who was supreme.

Perhaps even more devastating to the spiritual welfare of so many is that this mixing of the two kingdoms resulted in the "secularization of the church in the West and the inception of Christendom as the worldly embellishment of Christianity." This sadly resulted in a marked corruption of the proclamation of the church so that the biblical integrity of the Gospel was obscured and the church became indistinguishable from worldly principalities.[66] Furthermore, by attempting to assert itself through power, the church actually gave up its ability to influence the state in a more Christlike way. Stephen Carter put it this way:

> The church, by becoming the state, surrendered the possibility of acting as an intermediary. It yielded its essential role as the protector of the people of God; it ceased to be able to preach resistance. One might even say that in its grasping for power, the institutional church gave up the right to die for its beliefs in exchange for the right to kill for its beliefs.[67]

Put another way, through the mixing of church and state, along with its confusion of the distinct nature, means, and goals of the two kingdoms, the church became a purveyor of a theology of glory instead of the saving theology of the cross.

Christ Builds His Church

Jesus asked His disciples, "Who do you say that I am?" Simon Peter replied, "You are the Christ, the Son of the living God." To which Jesus responded:

(1994): 45, cited by Mark E. Braun, "Only in the Eye of the Beholder?" *Logia* 26:1 (2017): 35.

66 Kellermann, *A Keeper of the Word*, 259–60.

67 Carter, *Culture of Disbelief*, 82.

"Blessed are you, Simon Bar-Jonah! For flesh and blood has not revealed this to you, but My Father who is in heaven. And I tell you, you are Peter, and on this rock I will build My church, and the gates of hell shall not prevail against it" (Matthew 16:15–18). The whole concept of papal supremacy and papal succession that developed subsequent to the time of Emperor Constantine, that contributed greatly to a mixing of church and state together with the espousing of a theology of glory throughout the Middle Ages and even to the present, is connected to an erroneous interpretation of this significant Scripture verse. The "rock" (*petra*—feminine) on which the Church is built is not the person of Peter (*petros*—masculine) nor, consequently, his successors in the humanly established office of the Bishop of Rome. Rather, it is the "ministry of the confession Peter made, in which he proclaims that Jesus is the Christ, the Son of God [Matthew 16:16]" (Tr 25).

Jesus builds His Church! He does so on the ministry of the confession that Peter made, proclaiming that Jesus is the Christ, the Son of God. Before ascending into heaven, Jesus would tell His disciples, "Go therefore and make disciples of all nations, baptizing them in the name of the Father and of the Son and of the Holy Spirit, teaching them to observe all that I have commanded you" (Matthew 28:19–20). The Word and Sacraments are the means by which Christ builds His Church. The Augsburg Confession puts it this way:

> So that we may obtain this faith, the ministry of teaching the Gospel and administering the Sacraments was instituted. Through the Word and Sacraments, as through instruments, the Holy Spirit is given [John 20:22]. He works faith, when and where it pleases God [John 3:8], in those who hear the good news that God justifies those who believe that they are received into grace for Christ's sake. This happens not through our own merits, but for Christ's sake. (AC V 1–3)

The instruments or means by which Christ builds his Church, the Word and Sacraments, are also called the marks of the Church. Where the Word is proclaimed and the Sacraments are administered, there is the Church:

> Our churches teach that one holy Church is to remain forever. The Church is the congregation of saints [Psalm 149:1] in which the Gospel is purely taught and the Sacraments are correctly administered. For

> the true unity of the Church it is enough to agree about the doctrine of the Gospel and the administration of the Sacraments. (AC VII 1–3)

So, the Church is not identified with the predominant worldview in society (pre-Christian, Christian, or post-Christian); it is not identified with the influence that Christian churches have on a society or government (pre-Christendom, Christendom, or post-Christendom); and it is not identified with the promotion of Christianity by the state (pre-Constantinian, Constantinian accommodation, or post-Constantinian).

Jesus Christ, who builds His Church so that the gates of hell will not prevail against it, establishes, upholds, and protects His Church through weakness. Jesus tells Pontius Pilate, "My kingdom is not of this world" (John 18:36). To His disciples, Jesus says, "Truly, I say to you, whoever does not receive the kingdom of God like a child shall not enter it" (Mark 10:15). This "weakness" is combined with what is called the "hiddenness of God." Isaiah writes: "Truly, You are a God who hides Himself" (Isaiah 45:15). Gene Veith articulates it this way:

> God conceals Himself, often in things that we would least expect—a crucified criminal, a book, water, bread, wine, a gouty pastor, trials and suffering, human beings working and raising their families.
>
> The hiddenness of God is one of the most profound themes in Lutheran spirituality. It is part of what is termed "the theology of the cross."[68]

At the beginning of the Reformation, Martin Luther was asked to defend his teaching before his fellow Augustinian monks at the Heidelberg Disputation of 1518. Here, he asserted,

> That person does not deserve to be called a theologian who claims to see into the invisible things of God by seeing through earthly things (events, works). But [that person deserves to be called a theologian] who comprehends what is visible of God . . . through suffering and

68 Gene Edward Veith Jr., *The Spirituality of the Cross: The Way of the First Evangelicals*, rev. ed. (St. Louis: Concordia, 2010), 70.

the cross. The theologian of glory calls evil good and good evil. The theologian of the cross says what a thing is.[69]

A theology of glory looks to outward, worldly success as a sign of God's blessings and thus gets it all wrong. The theology of the cross recognizes our lost, sinful condition and then clings to the cross of Jesus, trusting our Savior to do for us what we cannot—rescuing us from sin, death, and the devil; giving forgiveness of sins and eternal life through His perfect life, suffering, death, and resurrection. The theology of the cross recognizes that Jesus says, "If anyone would come after Me, let him deny himself and take up his cross daily and follow Me" (Luke 9:23). This cross is not of our own choosing or making, but is instead the trials and difficulties that come upon us in life because we are followers of Jesus. This cross can involve living in a society that does not share our Christian worldview, a society that ostracizes, ridicules, and even persecutes us for our Christian faith. It can involve having to cope with life under a government that no longer provides religious accommodation for those who profess Christ.

A theology of the cross also recognizes that being a Christian is not identified with our citizenship in an earthly kingdom, even when the culture of that kingdom has been predominately Christian for some time. Jesus tells Nicodemus, "The wind blows where it wishes, and you hear its sound, but you do not know where it comes from or where it goes. So it is with everyone who is born of the Spirit" (John 3:8). Martin Luther warned the Germans: "God's Word and grace is like a passing shower which does not return where it once has been."[70] President Friedrich Pfotenhauer used this to caution and encourage The Lutheran Church—Missouri Synod at its 1930 synodical convention to make use of and hold fast to the grace and Word of God while it is here.

That warning holds just as true for us today, if not more so. Church attendance and membership in all historic American Christian denominations is on the decline, and Christian worship attendance has dropped most significantly in historically Christian Europe, which was once the center of Christendom. Reasons for the decline within the Missouri Synod are well documented in a recent issue of *Journal of Lutheran Mission*.[71] Meanwhile, the number of Christians

69 Gerhard O. Forde, *On Being a Theologian of the Cross: Reflections on Luther's Heidelberg Disputation, 1518* (Grand Rapids: Eerdmans, 1997), 71.

70 Quoted by Friedrich Pfotenhauer in a 1930 synodical convention sermon, "God's Word and Grace Are a Passing Rain Shower," in Matthew Harrison, *At Home in the House of My Fathers: Presidential Sermons, Essays, Letters, and Addresses from the Missouri Synod's Great Era of Unity and Growth* (St. Louis: Concordia, 2011), 777n1.

71 *Journal of Lutheran Mission* 3:3 (2016), https://blogs.lcms.org/2016/journal-of-lutheran-mission-december-2016.

in Africa, South America, and Asia is on the rise.[72] Some scholars are saying that the center of Christianity has shifted from Europe to the global South.[73] All Christians do well to hold firmly in faith, clinging to God's grace through Jesus Christ by making regular use of His Means of Grace, the marks of the Church, God's Word and Sacraments. Stuart Murray noted, "Post-Christendom could be more Christian than Christendom, not less."[74]

Coming to grips with a post-Christian, post-Christendom, post-Constantinian culture means also embracing evermore firmly God's mission for Christ's Church. Klaus Detlev Schulz notes four classical categories that define the Church's role in God's mission: the Church is missional, evangelical, vocational, and confessional:

> First, the Church is *missional*. As God's redeemed community, she continues to receive life from God but then also unselfishly passes on the gift of life in Christ to the world (John 3:16). The Church administers the precious lifelines of Word and Sacrament, not only in the context of worship but also in a kerygmatic-sacramental activity to the unbelieving world. . . .
>
> Second, the Church is *evangelical* in that she possesses the salutary Gospel. This Gospel is the only remedy to sin, death, and the devil. . . . The evangelical character of the Church expresses the Gospel in a number of visible forms. The Church is evangelical through witnessing, preaching, and administering the Gospel. . . .
>
> Third, the Church is also *vocational* in her service to and in the world. In addition to the ordained ministry of the Church, mission includes the sanctified life of all Christians by structuring itself around the manifold vocations of Christians. Through their witness and conduct, all

---

72 Setrige Crawford, "Christianity Declines in Europe, Increases in Africa and Asia, Says Survey," *The Christian Post*, December 23, 2011, http://www.christianpost.com/news/christianity-declines-in-europe-increases-in-africa-and-asia-says-survey-65619. This was also noted by Gene Edward Veith, "Postmodernism under the Cross," in *The Theology of the Cross for the 21st Century*, ed. Alberto L. García and A. R. Victor Raj (St. Louis: Concordia, 2003), 172–74; Ferguson, *Civilization*, 277–78; and Klaus Detlev Schulz, *Mission from the Cross* (St. Louis: Concordia, 2009), 3.

73 Trevor Grundy, "Shift of center of Christian gravity to Global South 'most dramatic in history,'" *Ecumenical News*, November 4, 2013, http://www.ecumenicalnews.com/article/shift-of-center-of-christian-gravity-to-global-south-most-dramatic-in-history/22528.htm.

74 Stuart Murray, "Post-Christendom, Post-Constantinian, Post-Christian . . . does the label matter?" The Anabaptist Network, May 10, 2008, http://www.anabaptistnetwork.com/node/506. While I do not agree with Murray's radical reformation Anabaptist views, his statement about post-Christendom rings true.

> Christians serve the mission of the Church by extending the Word into all realms of society. . . .
>
> Fourth, the Church's mission is *confessional* in that all proclamation and every Christian's vocational witness must be articulated clearly and with fidelity to Scripture.[75]

Conclusion

How do we cope with the death of the Constantinian accommodation or life in a post-Christian, post-Christendom culture? We cope in the same way that Christians have throughout the history of the Church: solely by God's grace through the power of the Holy Spirit, clinging in faith to Jesus Christ as our Lord and Savior as we make regular use of God's Means of Grace, His Word and Sacraments. Nourished and encouraged by these means, we go forth into a fallen world to give witness to the new life that is ours solely through Jesus Christ, and then the Holy Spirit will use that witness as Christ continues to build His Church by the Word (Romans 10:17). Additionally, we exercise our vocation as Christian citizens in a democratic nation to vote for candidates and regularly express our views to our elected officials regarding the sanctity of human life, unborn to aged, the sanctity of marriage between one man and one woman, and the maintaining of religious freedom throughout society.

We also recognize that throughout her history, God has been at work in the life of His Church through His Means of Grace, the marks of the Church—despite the fallen, but forgiven, nature of its members. There has always been one Holy Christian Church whose members are known only to God, and there has always been a visible Christian Church that has included true believers as well as hypocrites. Synodical President Matthew Harrison helps us find comfort in this fact:

> The Church is a paradox. She is the bride of Christ, "spotless," "holy," "washed," (Ephesians 5:25–27), the "pillar and foundation of truth" (1 Timothy 3:15), the body of Christ (1 Corinthians 12:1ff.). And yet she only appears in this world hidden under the guise of poor sinners,

75 Schulz, *Mission from the Cross*, 299–300.

> flawed leaders, tensions, divisions, and even false teaching. This is at once both disturbing and comforting.[76]

Whether we live in a Christian culture or post-Christian culture, whether we have the accommodation of the civil government for our churches and their members, Jesus Christ will build His Church, and the gates of hell will not prevail against it.

Soli Deo Gloria

76 Matthew C. Harrison, *A Little Book on Joy: The Secret of Living a Good News Life in a Bad News World* (St. Louis: Concordia, 2011), 163.

Study Questions

1. What is meant by post-Christian, post-Christendom, and post-Constantinian? Are they the same? Do any of these terms apply to our situation as Lutheran Christians living in the United States of America? Why?

2. Did Emperor Constantine establish Christianity as the state religion of the Roman Empire? If not, when did that occur? And what impact did this have on the Christian Church with respect to church attendance, catechesis, and use of the Means of Grace?

3. How did the conflict between church and state, together with the use of indulgences by the papacy, lead to the Reformation?

4. What were some of the teachings of Martin Luther that differentiated him from the theologians of the medieval Roman Catholic Church? What was his teaching on the two kingdoms or church and state?

5. Was the United States of America Constantinian in its founding? Was it a Christian "nation" or a Christian "culture"?

6. Did the resolution reached by the early Saxon Lutheran immigrants in Perry County, Missouri, depend on a Constantinian accommodation? Why? How did they identify themselves as "church"? What are the identifying marks of the Church?

7. How does living under the theology of the cross help one cope in a post-Christian, post-Christendom, post-Constantinian world? What opportunities are ours in a post-Christian, post-Christendom, post-Constantinian age?

8. Why should we not despair despite the rapidly changing relationship between the church and our surrounding culture?

9. **Are there any signs in that relationship for which we should thank God and express optimism?**

11

The Gates of Hell: Defying the Devil in International Mission Work

Rev. Dr. Daniel O. S. Preus

If the gates of hell are not able to prevail against Christ's Church that is built on the rock (Matthew 16:18), it is absolutely essential that the Church understand what the rock is. What is not built on the rock is not the Church. And what is not the Church is incapable of carrying out the Church's mission. Jesus makes it clear in His conversation with Peter in Matthew 16 what the rock is on which the Church is built. His declaration that He would build His Church on the rock immediately followed Peter's confession about Him, namely, that He is "the Christ, the Son of the living God." This confession about Jesus is the rock.

To destroy the Church, the devil has only one real objective—to move her off the rock. That which is built on the rock is safe; that which is not belongs to the devil. Thus, only a few moments after Jesus had identified Peter's confession as the Church's rock, the devil, through Peter, was already trying to push the Church to a sandy foundation upon which she could find no hope or life. With Peter's suggestion that Jesus not go to Jerusalem to die, Satan would entirely deprive the Church of the very content of her confession. For without the sacrificial death of Jesus on the cross for the sins of the world, there would be no atonement for sin, no promise of resurrection, no hope of everlasting life, no confession, and no rock. Jesus rightly identifies Satan as the source of this suggestion.

If the confession is the rock on which the Church is built and if, in her mission, the Church is to follow the example of her Savior in defying Satan, then the Church must be absolutely clear and confident regarding her confession. Therefore, at the very beginning, it might be helpful to state what the mission of the Church, in the context of foreign missions, is *not*. The mission of the Church of Christ is not to impose our ideas upon others. The Church does not send pastors and missionaries to foreign lands because our ideas are better than those of foreigners. The mission of the Church is not an attempt to force or persuade others to conform to our preferred beliefs, as though we have evaluated their religious ideas and want them to accept ours because they are superior to theirs.

Nor is the mission of the Church in foreign countries an imperialistic or paternalistic attempt to make others accept a religion that is more culturally advanced than theirs. As though our missionaries would say, "Your religion is more primitive than ours. Ours is more enlightened and suitable for living in this modern age." This view might see religious thought as having evolved, with the Church's task to provide the primitives of the world with the latest fad along the perceived religious, evolutionary chain.

Neither is it the mission of the Church in foreign lands to accommodate its message to the cultural mores and traditions of those to whom she goes. For example, in our own country, one trend among many Protestant and Lutheran churches is to adapt the Divine Service to the culture in the form of contemporary services, which supposedly relate better to those of our time and place, although it is questionable as to how frequently they relate to those upon whom they are imposed.

Another trend popular among some missionaries is to encourage people of other cultures to retain as much of their culture as possible in their worship services, and this without significant thought given to whether such cultural practices are compatible with the teachings of Christianity. But harmony between cultural preferences and worship style has nothing to do with the mission of the Church and, in fact, the Church frequently needs to act counter to the culture in order to confess the Gospel in its purity.

In the late 1980s, I attended a convention of the Northern Illinois District of the LCMS where they had a guest speaker from Ghana named Paul Kofi Fynn. Today, Dr. Fynn is the president of the Evangelical Lutheran Church in Ghana. At any rate, Dr. Fynn talked about how some of the missionaries encouraged their pastors in Ghana to retain as much of their culture in their worship services as possible. His response was, "Why do you ask us to keep our culture? It is part of our culture to sprinkle the blood of a chicken in front of the place where we worship to keep out the evil spirits. Why do you ask us to keep our culture? When we became Christians, Christ became our culture."

I have never forgotten that testimony from Paul Fynn. It demonstrated profound understanding of an extremely simple concept on the part of a pastor of a very young church body, a pastor who understood that for the Church to be engaged in mission, she must be built on the rock in doctrine and in practice. Apart from her confession, she is not the Church. Thus, the mission of the Church is intimately connected with Jesus, whom the Church confesses, and with the proclamation of the Gospel that is the good news about Him and what He has done for sinners.

The mission of the Church in foreign lands is no different from the mission of the Church in this country. There is only one mission, and it is a very simple mission—proclaim the Gospel about Jesus, the Christ, the Son of the living God. This is the same Gospel that you, the reader, should hear proclaimed from the pulpit of your congregation each Sunday. In our congregations, we bring to other weak and suffering sinners the same message of forgiveness, comfort, hope, peace, life, and joy that we have as Christians. It is a message about a Savior who came to wash away sin and give eternal life to all who believe in Him. And since this is the only message that builds the Church upon the rock, this is the message that is at the center of the Church's mission proclamation.

It is common in some churches today to call all sorts of things mission work—building hospitals, rebuilding homes destroyed by wars or storms, providing for orphans, teaching English as a second language to help people become more employable, or leadership training. These are all wonderful things to do, and we applaud those who do them. They truly help people for the needs of this life. But the mission of the Church is not to do these things. The people of God should do these things in response to God's love and out of love for the neighbor. But these are not her mission.

The mission of the Church, given to her by Jesus Christ, is to show people the way to eternal life. It is to show them Jesus. It is to give them the confession upon which the Church is built. That confession, originally made by Peter, contains two basic elements: (1) a description of who Jesus is, namely, the Son of the living God, and (2) why He has come, namely, to be the Christ, the Savior of the world. The Gospel is the confession on which the Church is built and must therefore be the content of the Church's mission. Otherwise, the Church is not one, built together on the same foundation and rock.

Since we are talking about the Church's mission, it would be good to ask the question, "What is the Church?" Of course, every good Lutheran knows what the Church is. This knowledge is fairly basic and not particularly difficult to understand. In fact, our Lutheran Confessions say in Article XII of the Smalcald Articles, "Thank God, ‹today› a seven-year-old child knows what the Church is, namely, the holy believers and lambs who hear the voice of their Shepherd [John 10:11–16]" (SA III XII 2–3). And how are believers made? How is the Church created? The Smalcald Articles answer, "In issues relating to the spoken, outward Word, we must firmly hold that God grants His Spirit or grace to no one except through or with the preceding outward Word [Galatians 3:2, 5]" (SA III VIII 3). The Word of God, the Gospel and the Sacraments, the Means of Grace are alone that which causes the Church to be born, to be nourished, and to grow.

How does the Church grow? This question has to be addressed in an age where every gimmick under the sun is applied with the objective of growing the Church. How many books, how many pastoral conferences, how many discussions, how many journal articles have been devoted to this topic of church growth? One would think it was a difficult and complicated science to establish how the Church grows. But every Lutheran who has been confirmed in an orthodox Lutheran congregation already knows the answer to this question. How does the Church grow? The Word of God gives birth to the Church; the Word of God nourishes the Church; the Word of God strengthens the Church; the Word of God preserves the Church; the Word of God sustains the Church to the end. All growth of the Church and in the Church is caused by the Word and by the Word alone.

How to grow the Church? That is really not a question for us at all. That's a question for God. And God has already answered the question. "As the rain and the snow come down from heaven and do not return there but water the earth, making it bring forth and sprout, giving seed to the sower and bread to the eater, so shall My word be that goes out from My mouth" (Isaiah 55:10–11). The Spirit grows the Church through the Word.

Unfortunately, when people lose their love for the Word of God and the Gospel, they begin to think that the Church can grow in other ways as well, and that perhaps these other ways will be even more effective. This type of thinking necessarily perverts the mission and plays into the hands of Satan himself. Thus, Dr. Anssi Simojoki points out in an article entitled "Mission and the Lutheran Confessions" that many who conduct mission work have forgotten what the mission is. He talks about the danger to the health of the Church when theologians and church leaders become content to mirror their society rather than to lead people in the truth of God's Word even when it conflicts with the views of society.

He states that this is exactly what happened in Scandinavia, and then he says, "When the society changed, the church mirroring the society changed, too."[1] When the Church takes its cue from the culture, eventually the two become virtually indistinguishable. At that point, the slogans of the world become the slogans of the Church. Simojoki refers to the missiology of the liberal churches as "a junkyard of slogans, . . . changing fashion throughout the 1920s, 1930s, 1940s and so on."[2] "Discarded over the decades in this junkyard have been slogans such as: Kingdom of God, shalom principle, liberation, justice, peace, kenosis, kerygma, 'Church Growth,' theology of diaconia, theology of liberation, incarnational mission, and so forth. . . . Many Lutherans . . . ," according to Simojoki, "have responded to this phenomenon by attempting to incorporate as many Lutheran principles as possible into the ecumenical missiological sausage."[3]

In other words, everything goes into it. But in all that sausage, is the one thing needful discernible? Only the Word of God, the Gospel, grows the Church.

> One thing's needful; Lord, this treasure
> Teach me highly to regard.
> All else, though it first give pleasure,
> Is a yoke that presses hard!
> Beneath it the heart is still fretting and striving,
> No true, lasting happiness ever deriving.
> This one thing is needful; all others are vain—
> I count all but loss that I Christ may obtain!
> (*LSB* 536:1)

If we are not bringing people the Word, if we are not bringing them the Gospel, the things we bring will prove only to be burdens that never bring true happiness.

1 Anssi Simojoki, "Mission and the Lutheran Confessions," paper delivered in Pretoria, South Africa, August 19, 2008, 1.

2 Simojoki, "Mission and the Lutheran Confessions," 2.

3 Simojoki, "Mission and the Lutheran Confessions," 4.

Only the Gospel can give joy above measure and fill all their needs. This is true whether for the local church or for the foreign mission. Christ's mission to the foreign mission field is the same as it is to the local congregation. The Spirit of God works through the Word and only through the Word, whether here or there.

This simple truth needs to be emphasized in our age when Satan is challenging the church in our country with a number of severe challenges.

- Secularism encourages people to believe that fulfillment can be found in the things of this life and this world. Its partner, materialism, focuses attention on the importance of self-gratification and pleasure. Symptoms accompanying secularism and materialism are arrogance, selfishness, and narcissism. If a church, in its desire to mirror the culture, embraces secularist views, it will also ultimately proclaim a kingdom that has little to do with the kingdom of repentance and faith Jesus proclaimed and will simply validate the base desires of sinful humans. Of great harm in this regard has been the message of the so-called prosperity preachers whose proclamation would have people believe that the kingdom of God is comprised not of those who in faith look to Jesus for mercy, but of those whose faith is so powerful that it has provided them with the very kingdom Jesus said He had no part of. "My kingdom is not of this world" (John 18:36).

- Pluralism encourages people to believe that no one ideology, philosophy, or religion should be promoted above others. Pluralism is quite popular in the United States and can be known by such insipid statements as, "Well, there are many ways to God," or "We're all trying to get to the same place." Symptoms accompanying a pluralistic mind-set are doctrinal indifference, religious apathy, intolerance toward claims of absolute truth, and a temptation to secularism. When a church embraces pluralism, it is inevitable that it will eventually lose the Gospel itself, for it will not even know the difference between the true God and false gods, much less will it know the only way of salvation in Christ.

- Relativism is a close cousin of pluralism and proclaims that absolute truth is not attainable by humans. The concept of truth as a revelation of God that never changes and that applies to all people on earth is rejected. "You have your truth; I have mine; and don't tell me that yours is superior." The implications for the mission of the Church are obvious. A church that embraces relativism will not be able to retain a meaningful creed and the members of such a church will be left to wander in the swamp of their own speculation as they consult not Scripture, but the teachings of the most recent religious fads and their own sinful minds in a futile search for truth.

- The Church Growth Movement aims to grow churches with its entertainment worship style and claims of church growth resulting from the application of tested methods, shown to be successful in the marketing and entertainment industries. Symptoms common among those enamored with the Church Growth Movement are

    - a tendency toward an emotionalism that mistakes feelings for faith;
    - a kind of worship that downplays the Means of Grace;
    - a theology that focuses primarily on the First Article of the Creed, placing little emphasis on the doctrine of justification by grace through faith in Christ;
    - a type of church service that separates people from the historic worship of the church and therefore from its doctrine; and
    - an attempt to relate in its worship to the culture of the day.

These challenges not only create difficulties for those who wish to be faithful Lutherans, but they are also influential in establishing the basis for much of what happens in mission work. Unless a church body is very careful in resisting the popular ideas of our time, that church body may find itself mirroring the society instead of carrying out its true mission of proclaiming the Word of God in its truth and purity.

In 2005, the Luther Academy and the Association of Confessional Lutherans, at their annual Congress on the Lutheran Confessions, held a conference titled *Mission Accomplished*? The conference was meant to address the challenges and opportunities facing Lutherans in the twenty-first century in connection with the mission Christ has given His Church. The papers delivered at the conference were later published together in a book by the same title. This volume can act to some degree as a corrective against the many mission fads that seem to be afflicting churches today. It is truly refreshing in its authentic Lutheran presentation. To demonstrate the value for an understanding of true mission work, I quote from it at some length.

The first article is written by a well-known Lutheran theologian, historian, missionary, and Confessions scholar, Dr. Klaus Detlev Schulz. Very helpful is his encouraging observation that Martin Luther did not speak only occasionally about the importance of mission to the heathen. Rather, his concern for mission actually permeated his entire theology.[4] Of course, this mission took place when the Word of God was proclaimed. Thus, the focus on the importance of bringing the Gospel to the nations is basic to the roots of Lutheranism.

The articles that follow repeatedly demonstrate this same truth. There is a wonderful unanimity among the authors of this book, as they understand that only the Word of God can create, nourish, grow, and preserve the Church. To speak of mission in any sense apart from the proclamation of the Word and the administration of the Sacraments is unbiblical. Thus, Roland Ziegler describes the mission perspective of Wilhelm Loehe, a man as responsible as any other for the early missionary work that took place in America among Germans around the middle and end of the nineteenth century. "Loehe was convinced," says Ziegler, "that only the proclamation of the gospel as the message of justification, rooted in the *extra nos* (outside us) as it is taught in the Lutheran Church, can be the basis of any missionary work."[5] In addition, Loehe saw that "For true mission it is imperative to retain the purity of proclamation. Since Loehe was convinced that the Lutheran Church was the church of the pure Gospel and Sacraments, he opposed any tendencies against confessional Lutheranism."[6]

Since some of Loehe's insights have clear application to our situation today, I think a bit more attention to his views will be helpful. According to Loehe, the

4 *Mission Accomplished?: Challenges to and Opportunities for Lutheran Missions in the 21st Century* (St. Louis: Luther Academy, 2008), 3.

5 *Mission Accomplished?*, 39.

6 *Mission Accomplished?*, 39.

mission of the Church is carried out only through Word and Sacrament. As a result, Loehe was opposed to the so-called "New Measures" of the Methodists that had greatly influenced the Lutherans in the East around the time of the formation of the Missouri Synod. These New Measures bear a remarkable resemblance to the methods of the Church Growth Movement today. Characteristic of both is the view that the application of certain "tried and true methods" will cause the Church to grow. According to Loehe,

> Every form of Methodism, wherever it might be, is a human unordered use, indeed abuse of available means. Everybody turns to the natural powers of man, instead of bringing heavenly powers of renewal. . . . Every form of Methodism is from a Pelagian root, comes out of a wrong understanding of the powers of man (nature and grace), and brings false doctrine. This is also the case of the Lutheran Church in America. It would not be so indifferent to the doctrine and eternal truth if it were not so external, if it would not regard so highly Methodist driving of emotions and works.[7]

Loehe says, "Mission is therefore nothing but the task to call, gather, enlighten, and keep the church of Jesus to life eternal."[8] And, of course, this calling, gathering, enlightening, and keeping of the Church is done by the Holy Spirit through the Gospel.

In the same article, Ziegler describes the work of Louis Harms, most well-known for his establishment of the Hermannsburg Mission Society, responsible for sending many pastors to the New World and to other places around the globe. Harms emphasized the importance not only of the Means of Grace but also of well-trained missionaries. "Preachers must be sent out," he said, "with the means of grace, but regularly called, instructed, and ordained preachers, not such as have been a little bit prepared in three or four weeks and then are sent out. The disciples, too, learned for three years with Jesus."[9]

Louis's brother Theodor, who succeeded Louis as director of the Hermannsburg Mission Society and who was suspended from office for his opposition to theological liberalism, likewise placed great emphasis on the Means of Grace and

7 *Mission Accomplished?*, 41.

8 *Mission Accomplished?*, 41.

9 *Mission Accomplished?*, 46.

the importance of Lutheran worship. In 1851, he said about the missionaries sent out from Hermannsburg, "Three things that they have experienced and learned here, they shall carry out into the heathen world; the glory of our divine service, the pure gospel and the pure sacrament of our church, and the power of our singing, and these immense treasures of our church they shall give our heathen brethren in full."[10]

In another of the articles in this book, we hear from Mark Braun that the early Wisconsin Synod *Reiseprediger* (traveling preacher) shared the same view of the Gospel's proclamation as that which defined the Church's mission. He writes about the early traveling preachers in the United States and says,

> [They] were sent out without having received any sort of "philosophy of missions." There was no "chair of missiology" at the fledgling seminaries where they were trained. They went instead, as one of them later confessed, "with the faith that the gospel alone is the power that saves, and that when and where this gospel is preached it will not return without accomplishing that which God pleases."[11]

Orthodox Lutherans have always agreed that the mission of the Church is to bring to people the Means of Grace, the Gospel and the Sacraments. Where these are absent, there is no Christian mission. As Timothy Quill puts it in his article on global missions, today, when we separate the Holy Spirit "from the means of grace, the means of grace themselves are replaced by human experience, enthusiasm, and moralism."[12]

This separation of the Holy Spirit from the Means of Grace seems to have become commonplace today as neo-Pentecostalism, unanchored in the Word, has become a threat to authentic Christianity all over the world. But when the mission is no longer the proclamation of the Word and this alone, assemblies that arise as the result of the mission will not bear the true marks of the Church. And Lutheran churches have not been immune from the temptation to enlarge the Church's mission as one that goes beyond the proclamation of the Gospel. The Mission Affirmations of the Missouri Synod, a series of resolutions adopted

10 *Mission Accomplished?*, 49.

11 *Mission Accomplished?*, 71.

12 *Mission Accomplished?*, 134.

beginning in 1965 at synodical conventions, are a case in point. One of them reads as follows:

> Resolved, That we affirm that the church is God's mission to the whole man. Wherever a Christian as God's witness encounters the man to whom God sends him, he meets someone whose body, soul and mind are related in one totality. Therefore Christians, individually and corporately, prayerfully seek to serve the needs of the total man. Christians bring the Good News of the living Christ to dying men. They bring men instruction in all useful knowledge. They help and befriend their neighbor to improve and protect his property and business by bringing him economic help and enabling him to earn his daily bread in dignity and self-respect. Christians minister to the needs of the whole man, not because they have forgotten the witness of the Gospel but because they remember it. They know that the demonstration of their faith in Christ adds power to its proclamation.[13]

Now almost everything stated in this resolution is true. The only problem is that it confuses mission with vocation and makes almost all Christian activity over against others mission work. As Klemet Preus says in his article entitled "Pietism in Missouri's Mission,"

> The problem is that these statements purport to be mission affirmations, not guidelines on Christian living. Is it really the mission of the church to help our neighbor in his body or help him protect his business? If that is the case, then it seems as though anything a Christian does in faith is the mission of the church. Everything becomes mission work. This is what happens when the love of the Christian is viewed as a mark of the church.[14]

Now it may seem that I am belaboring this whole point of the definition of what mission work is, but I think it is necessary when there seems to be so much confusion today regarding exactly what the mission of the Church is. As an example, I point to an issue of the *Fan into Flame* magazine connected with the

---

13 *Mission Accomplished?*, 101–2.

14 *Mission Accomplished?*, 102.

Ablaze! movement of the Missouri Synod, which described as mission projects a number of "outreach ministries" performed by a congregation. They include

- open gym for neighborhood teens to play basketball, dodgeball, and kickball, with fifteen to twenty-five teens participating weekly;
- a low-impact aerobics session, which generated a group that exercises on a weekly basis;
- a needy family ministry that has been able to provide emergency funds and food for thirty-nine individuals and families; and
- "Marriage Is like Dancing," with six couples participating in dance classes and Bible study.[15]

As I said, there seems to be quite a bit of confusion today, or at least a lack of definition, regarding the meaning of words such as *outreach*, *evangelism*, and *mission*. Just as the meaning of the word *minister* has undergone a radical redefinition to include almost any work done by a Christian in the church, resulting in great confusion as to what the office of pastor is, so these other words also seem to be changing in their meaning as far as the public is concerned. As a result, many no longer seem to know what the mission is.

Perhaps part of the reason for this confusion is that the mission paradigm has changed. The mission itself has not changed, but all around the world, the way in which the mission is being carried out has changed. The church's former model of sending a theologically well-trained pastor to another country together with his wife and children to serve the indigenous people has gone almost entirely by the wayside, not because there was anything wrong with the model, but because most people today want their own ethnic pastors. As a result, the practice of sending Western missionaries to be pastors in other countries is becoming more and more uncommon.[16]

With this shift in mind, away from the former model toward the practice of more indigenous pastors serving congregations, how does the church respond? In 2004, the three officers of the Luther Academy asked themselves precisely that question. At that time, I was the president, Kurt Marquart was the vice president,

15 *Fan into Flame* magazine, not dated, but appeared in September 2009, p. 5.

16 Though in the last several years, the LCMS has been sending more missionaries overseas.

and Martin Noland was the secretary and treasurer. We had recently received a couple of generous bequests and were asking ourselves how the work of the Luther Academy could best be expanded in a way that carried out the Church's mission. Up until that time, Luther Academy had been primarily a publisher of Lutheran books and journals.

We made a conscious decision that we wanted to be more active in foreign mission. We asked ourselves how we could do that in light of the change in the mission paradigm and came to the conclusion that the most effective way was to teach. What becomes apparent as one travels overseas and visits various churches, Lutheran and non-Lutheran, is that the change in the mission paradigm has both positive and negative aspects. One of the positive aspects is that most people now have their own indigenous pastors. These pastors do not need to learn a new language to begin their service to the people. They will not in any way be put off by the culture of the people. But perhaps the most negative aspect about this new paradigm is that in many parts of the world, these pastors have received only minimal theological training.

To demonstrate, I refer to an experience I had in 2007. I was serving as a professor for one semester at Lutheran Theological Seminary in Pretoria, South Africa. One day, as I was teaching, I began to sense that there were some rather severe gaps in the understanding of my students in respect to Christology. Now, these were first year students, so one would expect their doctrinal understanding to be somewhat incomplete. At the same time, all but one or two of the seventeen students in my class that day had been evangelists in their churches before they came to the seminary. They came from Liberia, Uganda, Sudan, Kenya, Botswana, and South Africa. They had been teaching and preaching in the congregations of their church bodies, some for just a year or two, some for quite a bit longer. So one would expect them to have a good understanding of the person of Jesus—who is He? what has He done? But I sensed that they didn't, so I asked them a question to test my theory. I asked them, "Is Jesus a man still today?" No hands went up. "Come on guys," I said. "It's not that hard a question. Is Jesus, our Savior, the one who died on the cross for us and rose again, still a man today?" I saw only blank faces. Some looked at other students and then back at me, but no one had enough confidence to answer the question. It's a pretty important question. Did the eternal God the Son, the Second Person of the Holy Trinity, take on my flesh to be my brother for all eternity? Or was the incarnation simply a temporary intrusion on the part of God into the affairs of man? I have never had a confirmand—child or adult—who could not answer that question.

The point is that in many third-world countries, the men who are studying to be pastors or the men who are already ordained are in serious need of further theological education. And it is in this area, I believe, that a church like ours, The Lutheran Church—Missouri Synod, can do its best mission work.

The Luther Academy concluded that the most effective way to use our resources was to teach. So that's what we began to do. We sent teachers overseas to teach pastors—not to make pastors, but to teach those who have already been ordained. And we are engaged in that teaching still today. We don't teach leadership training, we don't teach English as a second language; we teach the Word of God and we teach the Lutheran Confessions. Now that is our only mission overseas. Currently we hold over fifteen annual conferences in several world areas.

In each place we teach, we work with a local church leader to determine who to invite to our conferences and what topic we should address. We choose topics that are of importance to the pastors and churches of the areas in which we teach. For example, in Africa, where syncretism is so prevalent, our first conference dealt with pluralism and the challenges it presents to the African Lutheran churches. The second year, we taught a class on the proper distinction between Law and Gospel and when Law and Gospel need to be applied. At our first conference in South America, we dealt with the person and work of the Holy Spirit to help the Lutheran pastors there deal with the dangers of the unscriptural Pentecostalism that is rampant all over South America. In India, our first conference dealt with prayer in a land that prays to and worships thousands of gods. In Indonesia, we taught a class on the priesthood of all believers and the Office of the Holy Ministry, of great interest to those whose churches have ordained women.

Generally, we teach for one week from eight in the morning to five in the afternoon. And everywhere we teach, the response is the same—enthusiastic, grateful, happy. When we first taught in West Africa, in Ghana, it took the men from Sierra Leone over a week to reach the conference site. But they were eager to come. They wanted the teaching. The first time I taught in Panama, I taught about fifteen men on the topic of justification. Toward the end of the course, I asked these men, "What is the most important way we can help you?" Now, these men were all poor, and they served poor congregations. None of the pastors or the evangelists in the class owned a car. They traveled by bus or bicycle to visit their congregations. They lived in very modest or even poor homes. By our standards as Americans, they were profoundly poor. But how did they answer my question? They all said the same thing: "Send us more teaching. Give us more teaching." In our country, we take the opportunity to receive education for granted. It is not so in most third-world countries. These men in Panama considered precious the opportunity to learn. There is no better way to do mission work today than to send teachers and teaching to those who need and treasure it.

Clearly, the Luther Academy is not the only organization that does this kind of work. The Missouri Synod's Office of International Mission and both of our synodical seminaries also send men overseas to teach pastors. As for the Luther Academy, this is the only work we do overseas. We teach the Word of God to pastors who very much want to learn. They want to be faithful. We teach the Word according to the Lutheran Confessions, which means that we teach it in its purity. We believe strongly that it is the most effective way to do mission work overseas today. Only the Word of God creates the Church. Only the Word of God sustains and grows the Church. And our only task overseas is this teaching of the Word of God. As always, the growth of the Church is not discernible with human eyes. But we have God's promise that His Word will create faith and strengthen faith; we have God's promise that where the Word goes, the Spirit goes; and where the Spirit goes with His Means of Grace, the Gospel and the Sacraments, the Church is born and lives and thrives under God's grace.

The truth of the Gospel never changes; thus, the mission to proclaim that Gospel never changes. Paradigms change, cultures change, nations come and go, theories arise and die, alliances may change, styles may change, the climate may change. But one thing never changes. The message of the Gospel remains the same throughout the ages. And so we sing:

> God's Word is our great heritage
> And shall be ours forever;
> To spread its light from age to age
> Shall be our chief endeavor.
> Through life it guides our way,
> In death it is our stay.
> Lord, grant while worlds endure,
> We keep its teaching pure
> Throughout all generations. (*LSB* 582)

This commitment of the Church to keep the teaching of God's Word pure is not just to preserve a Word from God that never changes. That alone would be a precious thing in a world of constant change. But this changeless message actually saves forever those who believe it. It is an absolutely indispensable message, for without it, there is no hope for anyone of reconciliation with a righteous God or of life after death. Without this message of the Gospel, we who are sinners can only despair. Without this message of the Gospel, the gates of hell prevail and the Church dies.

But God, in His love, will not permit Satan to have His way. From eternity, He has determined to save sinners and to lift them out of despair, and He does this not just by telling us about a possible hope or a potential solution. He acts out His love through His Son and effects our eternal salvation. The Son of God takes on human flesh, becomes one of us, to live for us, to obey God's Law for us, to suffer God's wrath and punishment in our place, for our sin, to die for us and then to rise for us to redeem us from sin and death and hell. This is the changeless Gospel that the Church treasures and proclaims to the end of the age. This is the rock upon which we are built and it is not only a message that never changes; it is also a message that never ceases to create, nourish, and comfort the Church.

This message about Jesus, this beautiful, comforting message, is the one that is proclaimed when the Church carries out the mission God has given her. The mission work of the Church is very simply the proclamation of the Gospel, the same Gospel we hear proclaimed from our LCMS pulpits each Sunday. We take what God gave us and give it to others. We bring to other sinners, to other weak and suffering and vulnerable people, the same message of forgiveness, comfort, hope, peace, life, and joy that come from knowing the beautiful message about the Savior, who will never break a bruised reed and never snuff out a smoldering wick (Isaiah 42:3), who has come not to condemn or destroy, but to give life eternal.

As noted earlier, it is common in some churches today to call all sorts of things mission work, activities that help needy people with basic human needs. The building of wells would be an example or bringing dental work to those who otherwise would never have it. There are many wonderful things that churches, mission societies, and congregations do for fellow Christians in need and also for those who have not yet embraced the Gospel. And we applaud those who do them. They truly help people in the needs of this life. In fact, as Detlev Schulz points out, "The missionary tasks of human care and service . . . have been part of Christian mission since its inception."[17] Christians are not heartless and selfish people who care nothing about the health and physical welfare of others. Because of God's love in Christ and the mercy that our gracious Father in heaven has shown to us in many ways, we truly want to help others in their physical needs. And, as Detlev Schulz correctly observes, the Church has always exercised mercy to accompany its proclamation of the Gospel.

But the true mission of the church, accompanied though it may and indeed must be by meaningful acts of mercy, is always the proclamation of the Gospel—it is to show people the way to eternal life. It is to show them Jesus. For as long as the Missouri Synod has existed, our pastors and missionaries have shown the people Jesus. This is our mission, a mission to our congregations and communities and a mission that extends beyond the borders of our nation or continent or hemisphere to all the corners of the earth. It is a mission to show all people the one who came to save the lost, the sinful, the miserable—to save them from sin and from eternal death.

There are many threats to the Church's mission. These threats are not new. Neither are they, for that reason, any less dangerous or satanic. Certainly, one of the most serious threats is that which attacks the unique role of Jesus as Savior. This threat is particularly pervasive and enticing in our culture, which has become increasingly pluralistic. Even churches that have been historically Christian have succumbed to this temptation to concede Jesus' role as the only mediator between God and men. Surely one of the most powerful expressions of this threat to the unique role of Jesus as sole hope for sinners is the so-called interfaith service. When Christians, Muslims, Jews, Buddhists, and representatives of other religious bodies or cults participate together in a common or single service, a number of messages are broadcast, whether intentionally or not:

- Those who are participating may expect help from the deity to which they pray.
- All the religions represented provide hope to their followers.
- No religion can claim it alone offers hope to the needy.
- All faiths represented are equally legitimate.

17 Klaus Detlev Schulz, *Mission from the Cross: The Lutheran Theology of Mission* (St. Louis: Concordia, 2009), 82.

Those Christians who participate in such services may proclaim loudly and sincerely that it is absolutely not their intention to promote such messages, but whether they like it or not, these are the messages the world will hear. The average observer will certainly not distill the pure Christian Gospel from such a mishmash of religious expression. On the contrary, such views as those expressed above, if they prevail, will spell the death of true Christian mission work. If there is hope for Muslims that God will answer their prayers apart from faith in Jesus, what shall be the incentive of the Church to conduct mission work among Muslims? If Jews, who reject Jesus as their Messiah, nevertheless have access to the heavenly Father and may hope for salvation from Him, why should we bring the Gospel to them? If Buddhists can achieve peace, true peace, without the aid of the Prince of Peace, why should the Church evangelize Buddhists? In short, if Jesus is to take an equal place on the stage with the gods of the various world religions, the purpose of Christian mission work must either evaporate or, at best, be reduced to mercy work—but it will be mercy work without the mercy of Him who gave His own Son as the fullest expression of divine mercy the world has ever experienced, in fact the only expression of mercy that offers hope to lost sinners.

It appears that interfaith services will become more common in our land, as well-meaning but misled people attempt to respond to various attacks or tragedies that befall us. These events force upon us an unavoidable question: Is Jesus' claim to be the only way to the Father (John 14:6) true? It appears today that many "Christians" are reluctant to answer this question in the affirmative.

I recently had an interesting discussion with a man I met casually at a social event. He was describing how he and his wife, who were from different religious backgrounds, decided to resolve their differences. "We decided to join the Methodist Church. They don't stand for anything." I have become accustomed to hearing people tell me that they joined churches because of what they teach or did not teach. Needless to say, this man offered a different perspective. I thought about him as I considered the direction of many mainline churches today. In an attempt to appeal to those who don't really wish to stand for anything, are the churches, little by little, sacrificing their distinctive teachings? And are the person and work of Jesus becoming less and less necessary for mission work? Or are the mainline churches today simply becoming embarrassed to continue teaching a body of doctrine that the "enlightened" world considers primitive and outdated for thinking people? Have the churches become simply a mirror of the culture?

May it never be so among us! There is only one Lamb who took upon Himself the sin of the entire world (John 1:29). There is only one scapegoat upon which was placed the guilt of all people and was then sacrificed for their atonement (Leviticus 16:8–10). There is only One who raised Himself from the dead and who therefore has the power to raise from death to life all who trust in Him. There is only One through whom the Father pours out His grace in Word and Sacrament in order that the faithful might live and grow. There is no other source for Christians or for anyone apart from the One who gave Himself into death in order that all who trust in Him might live. The Church is therefore bound in her mission to the proclamation of Jesus as Savior, and as the only Savior. To neglect this proclamation is to remove the rock on which we are built.

There is another threat, also not new, that threatens the Church's mission. This threat would limit the atonement of Jesus to only some. Not long after the Reformation began, a theologian named John Calvin began to teach such a limited atonement. He taught that God did not send His Son for everyone, He did not intend to save everyone, Jesus did not die for everyone. He died only for the elect. Calvin's teaching was horrible. It was a denial of the Gospel, which teaches that, "God so loved the world, that He gave His only Son, that whoever believes in Him should not perish but have eternal life" (John 3:16). Calvin's heresy was particularly insidious because it is already natural for sinful human beings to doubt that God could love them. The teaching of a limited atonement was therefore a terrible barrier to faith among those to whom Calvinists attempted to preach.

Calvin's view of a limited atonement, though still taught by a few, is not a particularly pervasive view today. But the idea that Jesus is not a Savior for everyone is! This fact is truly ironic because there is no more-inclusive religion than Christianity. It is true that Christianity, at first glance, may appear to be exclusive. After all, Christianity does teach that only through Christ can a person be saved. However, nobody is forbidden to be a Christian. Nobody is excluded from Christianity by virtue of color, language, sex, race, intelligence, virtue, or any other characteristic. Everyone on earth is invited to be baptized, to receive the forgiveness of sins in Jesus, and to be saved by Him. Every other religion in the world has rules or laws or standards by which people will be excluded. Christianity does not. Rather, Christianity includes all under sin in order that all might be justified by God through His Son and be included under His grace (Romans 3:23–24). Because Christ has died and risen, all are invited to live through Him. "Come to Me," Jesus says, "all who labor and are heavy laden, and I will give you rest" (Matthew 11:28). The apostle Paul assures us, "If you confess with your mouth that Jesus is Lord and believe in your heart that God raised Him from the dead, you will be saved" (Romans 10:9).

It is as though God is saying to all of us who doubt that He could be merciful to people like us, "I do not exclude you. My Son did not die simply for mild sinners; He died for all. Nor did He die just for some of your sins; He died for all of them—from the time you were born until the time you die, His blood washes you clean from every sin. I do not exclude you. There is only one way in which you can be excluded and that is if you do not believe Me when I tell you that I love you, that I sent My Son to die for you, that for His sake I forgive you and that I give the kingdom of heaven to all who look to Him for salvation. You see, My grace is universal. It's meant for everybody. It's meant for you.

"Look at the Christmas story. My angels came and proclaimed the birth of My Son to shepherds. Doesn't that show you that My grace extends to all people regardless of station in life? Look at the story of the Wise Men. They were Gentiles. Doesn't that tell you that My grace extends to all people regardless of race or color? Look at My Son talking to the Samaritan woman at the well. Look at the sinful woman washing His feet. Look at Him visiting Mary and Martha. Look at the women coming to His grave on Easter morning. Doesn't that tell you that My grace goes out equally to men and women? Look at the Great Commission of My Son. He says, 'Go and make disciples of all people.' Πάντα τα έθνη the Greek says—all the peoples. Doesn't that tell you that My grace is offered to everybody in the world? Look who My Son chose as apostles! Matthew, a thieving tax collector; Peter, a denier; Thomas, a doubter; Paul, a murderer of Christians. Doesn't that tell you that My grace extends to you—even if you are the worst of all sinners?"

God's universal grace is a theme that must not be stifled—it is too precious to keep silent; it must never be a secret but must constantly be proclaimed. There is always an urgency about the preaching of the Christian message of God's grace in Christ because "there is no other name under heaven given among men by which we must be saved" (Acts 4:12). To deny that God's grace is universal is truly satanic!

The universal grace of God through Jesus is the source of our beauty as God's people. This grace brings into the church men, women, and children of every language, nation, and race. Thus, Zion lives in no single place and speaks no single language. Zion is God's people living all over the world, wherever the Gospel of Jesus Christ is preached and confessed. The universality of God's grace was demonstrated to me in a wonderful way in the great ethnic diversity I experienced in the parish. In my two most recent congregations, members whom I served as pastor have been of Swedish, Philippine, Hispanic, African American, Vietnamese, Italian, French, Danish, Russian, Greek, Norwegian, Finnish, Estonian, Czech, Indian, Native American, Slovakian, and German backgrounds—to mention only a few. This same ethnic panorama is true in many of our congregations and in our entire church body, and this panorama is beautiful.

And this focus on all nations and the desire to have those of all nations walk with us in faith is not new. Already in 1915, those who were members of the Synodical Conference together with The Lutheran Church—Missouri Synod were rejoicing in the evidence of God's love for all nations. One observer described a meeting of the Synodical Conference: "Here you may see a German, an Englishman, a Slovak, a Norwegian, a Negro, and an Indian—so different in background—yet one in doctrine, one soul, one heart, one theological language, one purpose, one spirit. To see such a gathering fills one with spiritual joy."[18]

As Christians, we know our Christ is for everyone. We have a desire, therefore, to see the precious Gospel of Jesus Christ, which alone can save, go out to all nations and peoples and tongues. Without Jesus, you and I should forget whatever Christian service or ministry we are involved in; find a position in which we can make some good money; and eat, drink, and be merry until the day we die. But we can't do that, because without Jesus, we are still in our sins. Without Jesus, we have no hope. Without Jesus, we are without our rock, adrift without anchor in an endless tempest.

One final threat to the mission should be mentioned. It is a threat implied in the title of this essay. The Church must not lose sight of the fact that Satan himself is plotting the demise of the Church and of individual Christians. He is certainly intent upon confusing the Church's understanding of mission and of thwarting the Church's mission altogether if he can. In our "enlightened age," many are embarrassed to speak about Satan as a real person or demons as real entities. If God's Word is to be our guide, however, we cannot ignore the presence and activity of the demonic without great risk. As the hymn teaches,

18 Carl S. Meyer, *Moving Frontiers* (St. Louis: Concordia, 1964), 261.

I walk in danger all the way.
    The thought shall never leave me
That Satan, who has marked his prey,
    Is plotting to deceive me.
    This foe with hidden snares
    May seize me unawares
If I should fail to watch and pray.
I walk in danger all the way. (*LSB* 716:1)

The Church is enjoined to be vigilant in its defiance of Satan not only by the hymnwriter, but also by the apostle Peter himself. The one whom Satan used to tempt Jesus to abandon His salvific mission knew better than most the reality of Satan's mission to destroy the Church by removing it from the rock on which it is built. He warns us in his first epistle, "Be sober-minded; be watchful. Your adversary the devil prowls around like a roaring lion, seeking someone to devour. Resist him, firm in your faith" (1 Peter 5:8–9).

In two recent books, Dr. Robert Bennett makes clear that the activity of Satan and his angels is vicious and ongoing both in our nation and abroad. In one of his books, he focuses on demon possession in Madagascar and how the Christians there deal with it.[19] In the other book, he talks about the activity of the demonic in the United States and demonstrates that, contrary to the view of many, more Americans today than ever are becoming involved in occult behavior or being afflicted with demonic oppression.[20] Dr. Bennett's books are somewhat unnerving, to say the least. But they are biblical and a necessary corrective in a rationalistic age that is inclined to reject out of hand anything that smacks of the supernatural. Bennett also provides a word of comfort to the Church in the face of a truly frightening enemy. In a chapter entitled "Christ Bound Satan So That We May Be Free," Bennett points out that when exorcisms are performed, the one doing the exorcism is Jesus Himself.[21] Just as Jesus Himself baptizes using the hands and the voice of the pastor, so also Jesus uses the voice of His Christian disciple to exorcize, but He Himself is the exorcist. Bennett goes on to explain that an exorcism in Jesus' name is effective not because the name itself

---

19 Robert H. Bennett, *I Am Not Afraid: Demon Possession and Spiritual Warfare* (St. Louis: Concordia, 2013).

20 Robert H. Bennett, *Afraid: Demon Possession and Spiritual Warfare in America* (St. Louis: Concordia, 2016).

21 Bennett, *I Am Not Afraid*, 118.

has some magical power, but "The command to 'depart' must be spoken in the faith that Jesus will be the active force in the exorcism."[22]

Later he says about Jesus' name, "The name had power, not as an incantation, but as a connection to Jesus' very person."[23] By requiring the exorcism to be connected to Jesus' person and to be performed with faith in Jesus, Bennett is saying, in essence, that the effectiveness of exorcisms is intimately joined with the Christian confession. When Satan is dashed against the rock, he cannot prevail. Those who stand upon the confession belong to Jesus, and Satan may not have them. Far from being possessed by a demon, Jesus promises those who confess Him that He and the Father will make their home with them. "If anyone loves Me, he will *keep My word*, and My Father will love him, and We will come to him and make Our home with him" (John 14:23, emphasis added).

In both Luther's morning and evening prayers, we pray, "Let Your holy angel be with me, that the evil foe may have no power over me." We pray these prayers with confidence that our petition will be granted because we have prayed to our heavenly Father, "through Jesus Christ, Your dear Son." Calling to Him in Jesus' name, we know that He will hear us and answer our prayer that the evil foe indeed may have no power over us. Prayer is not answered because Jesus' name is some magical incantation but because the one who prays does so with faith in Jesus, in other words, embracing Peter's confession that Jesus is the Christ, the Son of the living God.

So also, when the Church carries out the Lord's mission to the world, it proclaims Peter's confession, it preaches the Gospel, not as a magical formula that defeats Satan by virtue of its special or unique wording, but because it is a confession about the Lamb of God who takes away the sin of the world. The Church's mission is powerful because the absolving word of the Gospel is powerful, which is to say the Church's confession is powerful. And so Paul confesses, "I am not ashamed of the gospel, for it is the power of God for salvation to everyone who believes, to the Jew first and also to the Greek" (Romans 1:16).

The Gospel has power not only to forgive sins, but also to save forever. Satan cannot withstand this power, for it is the power to call people out of his kingdom of darkness into God's marvelous light in Jesus (1 Peter 2:9). It is the Church's mission to preach this Gospel with the assurance, in fact, the promise, that God will not permit His Word to return to Him empty (Isaiah 55:11). In fact,

22 Bennett, *I Am Not Afraid*, 119.

23 Bennett, *I Am Not Afraid*, 122.

the gates of hell cannot prevail against the Church's confession about Jesus, the Christ, the Son of the living God. And so it is that around the entire world, each Christian may pray,

In Thine arms I rest me;
Foes who would molest me
    Cannot reach me here.
Though the earth be shaking,
Ev'ry heart be quaking,
    Jesus calms my fear.
    Lightnings flash
    And thunders crash;
Yet, though sin and hell assail me,
Jesus will not fail me. (*LSB* 743:2)

Soli Deo Gloria

Study Questions

1. To build on the rock is to build on

    A. Peter

    B. The Church

    C. The Old Testament

    D. Peter's confession

Explain why the correct answer is the correct answer and why the wrong answers are wrong.

2. Can it be said that to build on Peter's confession is to build on Christ? Explain your answer.

3. How is the Church created? Does God use a different "means" to sustain the Church than He does to create it?

4. What is the danger in putting Lutheran principles into the "ecumenical missiological sausage"?

5. Why will churches lose the Gospel when they embrace pluralism?

6. Which central Christian teaching should be at the heart of all mission work? Why?

7. How has the mission paradigm changed in the last fifty years?

8. How is the Gospel attacked by John Calvin's view of a limited atonement?

9. Defend the following statement: "Christianity is the most inclusive religion in the world."

10. Why can we say that the Church's confession is powerful?

12

The Gates of Hell and the Table of the Lord

Rev. Christopher S. Esget

Food and the Fall

God made our first father, Adam, from the earth. We are material creatures—souls and bodies joined in a beautiful union. As embodied souls, we are dependent on our Creator who sustains our life. God sustains our life through food to nourish the body and His Word to nourish the soul. Both are gifts of His grace.

God created the world for man's benefit. He presented the world as a gift to our first parents. "Behold, I have *given* you every plant yielding seed that is on the face of all the earth, and every tree with seed in its fruit. You shall have them for food" (Genesis 1:29, emphasis added). This food was life to the man. Yet one source of food was death.

The tree of the knowledge of good and evil was appealing to almost every aspect of human longing: "The woman saw that the tree was good for food, and that it was a delight to the eyes, and that the tree was to be desired to make one wise" (Genesis 3:6). Little children have a habit of sampling everything, often to the horror of their parents. Twigs, rocks, fabric, coins—everything goes in the mouth. Some things positively delight us upon sight. For our first mother, Eve, such was the fruit of this tree. Food, sex, a cool breeze, a warm bath, soft clothing, all manner of creaturely activities and experiences bring pleasure to the human body. Received as gifts of God in accordance with His Word, they are good. But experience teaches us that not everything is good for food. Grasped outside of His Word, they are expressions of lust. That which is grasped in passion brings death.

As the food was seized in the passion of *bodily* lust, so was it also taken as independent *aesthetic* ideal: "A delight to the eyes." She gazed enraptured by beauty separated from the Artist and His intention. The "lust of the eyes" (1 John 2:16 NKJV) is an increasing plague upon her children. The allure of the television has transformed modern dining habits. Where once there was conversation and storytelling, now all eyes gaze at the screen, silent and obedient. The advent of pocket devices with their own screens leads to ubiquitous slavery. On sidewalk and roadway, in bathroom and in bed, the lust of the eyes holds worshipers enthralled.

These first two, bodily lust and aesthetic ideal, have been cunningly joined by the enemy in pornography. Pornography was once the province of seedy parts of town, delivered in the shame of brown paper obscuring the contents, traded by pubescent boys in secret. But cable television began to change all that. By the 1980s, middle-class homes were hardwired to MTV. With the late-night offerings on Cinemax or HBO, a thing once reserved for marriage was opened up to the immature and innocent.

With cable television, access to pornography increased, but restrictions remained in place. Attentive parents could still maintain a godly home. Within a few decades, that task became nearly impossible. The internet offered free and instant access to pornography to everyone. A new sexual revolution dawned, attacking the foundation of human civilization: the family. It objectified women and glorified abusive behaviors; it harmed careers and threatened marriages.

The marriage of a man and a woman is a divine institution, centered around the procreation of children. The legalization of homosexual "marriage" detaches this institution from its essential biological components, a potential father and mother. In the 1990s, homosexual "marriage" was a fringe movement; now it has grown to complete acceptance. Major global corporations celebrate "pride," and any objection from religion or natural law is labeled "hate." As sex is further detached from biology in the transgender movement, the serpent's third appeal is fully in view: "The tree was to be desired to make one wise."

The wisdom offered in this food is a diabolical wisdom, fully contradicting the Word of the Creator. Such thinking—especially moral and ethical thinking—divorced from the mind of God is a descent into madness and nihilism. We observed above that this food offered *almost* everything that humans long for: the lust of the flesh, the lust of the eyes, and the pride of the mind. But it lacks one thing: the love and good will of God, apart from which there is no life. Grasping for food to satiate their lusts, our first parents poisoned both body and soul.

Why was this tree of the knowledge of good and evil there? Augustine of Hippo suggests it was a test and a pedagogical tool: "In order that [God] might show man, to whom submission to such a Master would be very useful, how much good belonged simply to obedience."[1] God had blessed man with both food and His Word. In the battle against desire, it was not the hunger of the body that prevailed. Our first parents had been given all the food they needed. The tree of the knowledge of good and evil offered a life outside of God's gifts, a life on man's own terms. Yet grasping the food of empty promise gave them not life but death.

Refraining from what God has not given, and rejoicing in what He has given, is the exercise of piety. The Ninth and Tenth Commandments prohibit coveting. When expressed positively, these commandments teach us to be content with what God has given, certain that He has given us precisely what we need. This contentment is the path to joy. Not eating this tree was their act of worship. Martin Luther writes in his commentary on Genesis:

> After everything had been entrusted to him to make use of it according to his will, whether he wished to do so for necessity or for pleasure, God finally demands from Adam that at this tree of the knowledge of good and evil he demonstrate his reverence and obedience toward God and that he maintain this practice, as it were, of worshiping God by not eating anything from it. (AE 1:94)

Learning contentment and maturing through obedience, they would receive His highest gift: food joined with His Word and promise. For in the center of the garden that God cultivated and set in order was His greatest gift: the tree of life. Its mention in Genesis 3:22 suggests they were meant to eat from the tree of life, and that it confirms the eater in a deathless state.

1 Augustine, *A Treatise on the Merits and Forgiveness of Sins, and on the Baptism of Infants* II.35, in *Nicene and Post-Nicene Fathers: First Series*, vol. 5, ed. Philip Schaff (Peabody, MA: Hendrickson, 1995).

> Then the LORD God said, "Behold, the man has become like one of Us in knowing good and evil. Now, lest he reach out his hand and take also of the tree of life and eat, and live forever—" therefore the LORD God sent him out from the garden of Eden to work the ground from which he was taken. He drove out the man, and at the east of the garden of Eden He placed the cherubim and a flaming sword that turned every way to guard the way to the tree of life. (Genesis 3:22–24)

The food of concupiscence brought our race into destruction. Their desires had become disordered. As their children, we have the same proclivities creeping in us: the lust of the flesh, the lust of the eyes, and the pride of life (1 John 2:16). What we eat, what we desire, is killing us.

Food now is produced by sweat, hard labor unto death. Creation is hostile to us, bringing forth thorns, choking life, and leaving us bleeding until our body breathes its last and is divided from the soul in a terrible sundering. Whether one dwells in a deserted wilderness or among towering skyscrapers, all mankind is east of Eden, lost in the wasteland, laboring for food but finding none that can give real life. The way to the tree of life, once known by Adam but guarded by cherubim, is now hidden to his offspring. With the portal to the tree of life closed, the gates of hell revealed themselves to man in his hungry wandering.

God Remembers His People

Joseph's brothers had sold him into slavery, unaware they were preparing the way for their own. Warned of an impending famine through Pharaoh's dreams, Joseph rose to prominence with a plan to store and ration Egypt's harvests (Genesis 41). That famine brought the sons of Israel to Egypt for bread. After Joseph's death, they were reduced to slavery. The Egyptians "made their lives bitter with hard service. . . . In all their work they ruthlessly made them work as slaves" (Exodus 1:14).

This historical event also typifies the entire human experience. The pursuit of bread makes life bitter. Uncertainty about tomorrow leads to anxiety. We are held in bondage throughout our life by the fear of death (Hebrews 2:15). This fear of death is not an obsession with various medical maladies, or fears surrounding catastrophic events. The fear of death that grips humanity is recognition that everything we have and experience is transitory. Bones break. Hearing fades. Automobiles lose their new-car smell—and then get dented, scratched, and rust away. Try as we may to retain our earthly treasures, we experience what Jesus says of them: "Moth and rust destroy and . . . thieves break in and steal" (Matthew 6:19). That is the fear of death: slavery to things that perish, making our "lives bitter with hard service."

It is tempting to cry out with the Preacher, "Vanity of vanities! All is vanity. What does man gain by all the toil at which he toils under the sun?" (Ecclesiastes 1:2–3). Comfort comes in the memory of God.

> During those many days the king of Egypt died, and the people of Israel groaned because of their slavery and cried out for help. Their cry for rescue from slavery came up to God. And God heard their groaning, and God remembered His covenant with Abraham, with Isaac, and with Jacob. God saw the people of Israel—and God knew. (Exodus 2:23–25)

Mark well the actions of God when Israel cried out for help. God heard, God remembered, God saw, and God knew. When God remembers, it is not the sudden recollection of something long forgotten. I make long lists of tasks I must do, tasks I know I should do, ideas I have, and names and events I want to remember. Without the lists, I may forget. But God does not forget as you and I do.

In our fear that God has forgotten, we imagine we are all alone, that because nothing has happened, God has abandoned us, He does not care, or He is angry with us. But when the Bible speaks of God's memory, the Holy Spirit is comforting us. God's remembering is His promise to us that He will act in just the right way at just the right time. In the time of famine, in the bitterness of hard service, and in the fear of death, this word for Israel is also for us. God hears. God remembers. God sees. And God knows.

After the Exodus

Led to the house of bondage through famine, the Lord's rescue from that place came through a meal. Israel's children ate the meat of the Passover lamb as its blood dripped from their doors. This was no ordinary meal; it had God's promise attached to it. "On all the gods of Egypt I will execute judgments: I am the Lord. The blood shall be a sign for you, on the houses where you are. And when I see the blood, I will pass over you, and no plague will befall you to destroy you, when I strike the land of Egypt" (Exodus 12:12–13).

Passing from pain to freedom through the Red Sea waters, the rescued went on but found no water to drink. After three days in the parched wilderness, they finally came upon water, only to find it undrinkable. They named it *Marah*, Hebrew for "bitter." The people grumbled, Moses cried out to God, and the Lord showed him wood. Wood thrown into the bitter waters made them sweet. Here we may find an analogy to the blessed Virgin Mary, whose name comes from the same Hebrew word meaning bitterness and rebellion.[2] In the bitter waters of the woman's womb, cursed with pain and sorrow in childbearing (Genesis 3:16), mankind is given Jesus. From Him, rivers of living water flow (John 7:37–39), and all who believe are invited to drink the sweetness of His Gospel, found in the wood of the cross on which was hung all the world's bitterness.

For Israel, the sweetness of those waters did not foster trust in God or in Moses. The bitterness of their hearts kept them in a greater slavery than they knew in Egypt: the slavery of the fear of death. "You have brought us out into this wilderness to kill this whole assembly with hunger" (Exodus 16:3). Despite their grumbling and rebellion, the Lord cared for His people as He once cared for our first parents, providing them food without labor. Unencumbered by sweat or thorns, each evening the Lord gave them quail to eat, and in the morning *manna*—bread from heaven (Exodus 16:12). In this bread from heaven, the Lord was again teaching His people the blessing of contentment. Whether one gathered little or much, it was enough.

The Lord did give one command concerning the manna: "Let no one leave any of it over till the morning" (Exodus 16:19). Consuming each day's bread demonstrated their faith that God would faithfully provide manna the next day. His Word promising to provide bread day by day foreshadowed the prayer Jesus gave us: "Give us this day our daily bread" (Matthew 6:11). The substance of that petition is trust that God will care for us day by day, as the version of the Lord's Prayer in St. Luke's Gospel emphasizes: "Give us each day our daily bread" (Luke 11:3).

Even in the wilderness, God promises to care for us. His heavy sentence in Eden of hard labor followed by death is lightened along the way for His saints, giving them a foretaste of the feast to come. Therefore, Jesus asks us, "Why do you worry?" The Father knows what we need and is teaching us contentment in the wilderness. He will provide what we need for today. And the next day. And the

2 Paul J. Achtemeier, ed., "Marah," *Harper's Bible Dictionary* (San Francisco: Harper & Row, 1985), 610.

next. Day by day. "Therefore do not be anxious about tomorrow, for tomorrow will be anxious for itself. Sufficient for the day is its own trouble" (Matthew 6:34).

This is a hard lesson. It certainly was for Israel with their daily bread. "They did not listen to Moses. Some left part of it till the morning, and it bred worms and stank" (Exodus 16:20). Like a corpse, their food was full of creatures of the soil, and foul. This is the destiny of the fallen human body. Without the hope of the resurrection, there would be nothing else. Dr. Luther often spoke of his own body as a "maggot sack" to remind himself of the grave that all men must inhabit. In one instance, he touches on a theme we will explore later, how the Lord's food will transform our bodies:

> Since this poor maggot sack, our body, also has the hope of the resurrection of the dead and of the life everlasting, it must also become spiritual, and digest and consume everything that is fleshly in it. And that is what this spiritual food does: when the body eats it physically, this food digests the body's flesh and transforms it so that it too becomes spiritual, i.e., alive and blessed forever as Paul says in I Corinthians 15[:44], "The body will rise spiritually." (AE 37:100–101)

Eating and Drinking in God's Presence

Continuing on their journey, the Israelites arrived at Mount Sinai. There God gave the *Torah*. Often translated "Law," that term carries overtones of demand, accusation, and condemnation. As a theological category, the Law does have such a function. One of our Lutheran Confessions, the Formula of Concord, explains the uses of the Law like this:

> God's Law is useful (1) because external discipline and decency are maintained by it against wild, disobedient people; (2) likewise, through the Law people are brought to a knowledge of their sins; and also, (3) when people have been born anew by God's Spirit, converted to the Lord, and Moses's veil has been lifted from them [2 Corinthians 3:13–16], they live and walk in the Law [Psalm 119:1]. (FC SD VI 1)

However, the Hebrew term *Torah*[3] expresses a broader idea encompassing all that God has to say to us, both Law and Gospel. It is "instruction on the Will of God."[4] That will of God is revealed in the first of the Ten Words (nearly always called the Ten Commandments): "I am the LORD your God, who brought you out of the land of Egypt, out of the house of slavery" (Exodus 20:2). It is as though God were saying, "Do you see what I have done for you? I have taken care of you all along the way. I rescued you from bondage, I turned your bitter waters into sweet, I fed you with bread from heaven, and I have continued to do so day by day. You can trust Me. I will be your God, and you will be My people. Do not be anxious! I will take care of you." That first word is a word of promise from the One who gives bread in the wilderness. The First Commandment, "You shall have no other gods before Me," is grounded in the relationship between God and Israel, which God established by His own action and initiative. Every other commandment likewise flows from the relationship God has established with His people. Every transgression against one of the Commandments is a breaking of this relationship, a worship of something or someone else as god.

The Lord's Torah established a gracious relationship between God and Israel, a covenant (or testament) God ratified in blood. After God expressed His Torah, Israel pledged fidelity: "All that the LORD has spoken we will do, and we will be obedient" (Exodus 24:7). Their obedience comes not as the legal requirement of the covenant, but as their joyful response to it. "And Moses took the blood and threw it on the people and said, 'Behold the blood of the covenant that the LORD has made with you in accordance with all these words'" (Exodus 24:8). Another way to translate this is, "This is the blood of the covenant," words that the Lord Jesus will echo when He establishes the new covenant.

Then the representatives of Israel are invited into the Lord's presence and they eat at His table:

> Then Moses and Aaron, Nadab, and Abihu, and seventy of the elders of Israel went up, and they saw the God of Israel. There was under His feet as it were a pavement of sapphire stone, like the very heaven for clearness. And He did not lay His hand on the chief men of the people of Israel; they beheld God, and ate and drank. (Exodus 24:9–11)

3 "The more precise meaning of the noun would be 'teaching' or 'doctrine' rather than 'law'" (B. Grossfeld, "Torah," *Dictionary of New Testament Background*, ed. Craig A. Evans and Stanley E. Porter [Downers Grove: InterVarsity Press, 2000], 1242).

4 F. L. Cross and E. A. Livingstone, eds., *The Oxford Dictionary of the Christian Church*, 3rd rev. ed. (Oxford: Oxford University Press, 2005), 1643.

No one can see God and live (cf. Exodus 33:20), and yet they see God and do not die. This unique experience in Israel's history looks back to Eden, where our first parents ate the food God provided and knew His presence as He walked among them (Genesis 3:8). It also anticipates another day when the Son of God would eat and drink with His people, when "in the fullness of time He would assume human nature personally."[5]

Man is an embodied soul. Whether in Eden, on Mount Sinai, or all the other places man has dwelt, we experience life in the body. This is how God deals with us. Through food, and water, we experience with physical senses like seeing and hearing the gifts He desires to bestow on us. "They beheld God, and ate and drank." This peculiar theophany would not be repeated—but God would continue to be known among His people through eating and drinking. He would set His table among them, and they would rejoice.

Joy in His Peace

The sacrifices the Lord established to be offered at His altar were not designed to be constant reminders of a vengeful God, full of wrath. The atmosphere of His house, though never irreverent, was characterized by gladness.

> Splendor and majesty are before Him; strength and joy are in His place. (1 Chronicles 16:27)

> Glad songs of salvation are in the tents of the righteous. (Psalm 118:15)

> [The Lord said:] "On the day of your gladness also, and at your appointed feasts and at the beginnings of your months, you shall blow the trumpets over your burnt offerings and over the sacrifices of your peace offerings. They shall be a reminder of you before your God: I am the Lord your God." (Numbers 10:10)

The sacrificial life in God's presence was meant to bring Israel back to the first word of the Torah: "I am the Lord your God." There in tabernacle and temple, the Lord's people were invited into His splendor, bidden to rejoice with glad songs in the memory of God.

5 Johann Gerhard, *On the Nature of God and on the Most Holy Mystery of the Trinity*, Theological Commonplaces, ed. Benjamin T. G. Mayes, trans. Richard J. Dinda (St. Louis: Concordia, 2007), 392.

As with the rescue from the house of bondage, God's memory brings His past words and promises into the present. Man remembers God, while God also remembers man, and delivers His benefits now. A beautiful example of this is found in the Lord's gift of the peace offering. Perhaps you've received a gift from someone after having an argument or being involved in a conflict. Often the offending person brings a gift to symbolize an apology and an intention to live in harmony going forward. The peace offerings of the tabernacle and temple were *not* like that.

Peace offerings did not *make* peace, but rejoiced in the One who had *already given* peace to His people. The Lord established the peace offering so Israel could come and rejoice in His presence. The peace offering was a type of communion with God.[6] The Lord received the food brought to His altar, but unlike the whole burnt offering, He did not consume it all. The kidneys and certain fatty portions were consumed in the fire and so "eaten" by the Lord (Leviticus 3:3–16). He gave a portion to His priests (Exodus 29:27–28), and the rest was eaten by the person bringing the offering, along with his family and guests. John Kleinig observes, "The peace offering may have been the most popular sacrifice because it provided meat for a festive meal. Since animals were, by and large, too valuable to be eaten by ordinary people as part of their regular diet, they were usually eaten only on high holy days and other special occasions."[7]

It is easy to think of offerings as giving away something that belongs to you and thus interpret the Old Testament sacrifices in the same way—that the Israelites are giving away something that belongs to them. This, however, is to forget the first word: "I am the LORD your God, who brought you out of the land of Egypt, out of the house of slavery" (Exodus 20:2). Since He brings them into His land, everything they have is a gift from Him. Kings of old demanded rent from their tenants, just as landlords today require regular payments from those living on their properties. With God as the land's Lord, He invites His people to bring their rent into His presence. In His royal house, He invites His people to dine with Him. The rent they have brought is partially returned to them, as God, priests, and people eat together with joy.

6 John W. Kleinig, *Leviticus*, Concordia Commentary (St. Louis: Concordia, 2003), 37, figure 3. See also Allen C. Myers, *The Eerdmans Bible Dictionary* (Grand Rapids: Eerdmans, 1987), 807.

7 Kleinig, *Leviticus*, 91.

> The holy meal in which the holy meat from the peace offering was eaten united the Israelites as a holy people with their holy God; it confirmed their right to live on his land; it empowered them with his blessing to serve him as his royal priestly servants in their daily work on his land. The God of Israel, the land of Israel, and the people of Israel were all integrated harmoniously and productively by means of this pivotal sacrifice.[8]

The Book of Numbers adds a fascinating detail to the festive meal of the peace offering:

> And when you offer a bull as a burnt offering or sacrifice, to fulfill a vow or for peace offerings to the LORD, then one shall offer with the bull a grain offering of three tenths of an ephah of fine flour, mixed with half a hin of oil. And you shall offer for the drink offering half a hin of wine, as a food offering, a pleasing aroma to the LORD. (Numbers 15:8–10)

Added to the bull is flour mixed with oil, and wine. Flour for bread, along with wine, looks ahead to the central elements of the meal the Lord would later establish, the greater peace offering where Jesus Himself dines with His people and joins Himself to them. For He is the God who gives "wine to gladden the heart of man, oil to make his face shine and bread to strengthen man's heart" (Psalm 104:15).

The Lord who "ate" the fatty portions in the peace offerings promises a coming feast where the people will share even in the Lord's portion. Isaiah 25 anticipates a feast on a different mountain than in Exodus 24. Sinai is changed to Zion, and the reproach of Sinai—the disobedience of the people—is taken away. Here on this mountain, the feast of Exodus 24 is recapitulated, that is, repeated, but also enhanced and made perfect. Now, not only Moses, Aaron and his sons, and the seventy elders of Israel will eat, but this will also be a feast "for all peoples." This feast celebrates that death is trampled down. In this end-times peace offering that the Lord Himself hosts, He will share His portion and give fat things full of marrow[9] to His guests, as well as the finest of wines. Foretold

8 Kleinig, *Leviticus*, 94.

9 Kleinig, *Leviticus*, 95.

here is a resurrection meal where embodied souls freed from death eat and drink with God. All tears are wiped dry, and mourning is replaced with the new song of joy: "Behold, this is our God; we have waited for Him, that He might save us. This is the LORD; we have waited for Him; let us be glad and rejoice in His salvation" (Isaiah 25:9).

The New Passover

The Lord's Supper arises within the context of how God dealt with His people throughout history. It is the culmination of all that the children of Adam, and Abraham, and Israel were given and promised by God. The journey from Adam's feasting in the garden and the lost promise of the tree of life to the bread of sweat and death set man's memory and hope on God, who creates food and once was present with them in their place of feasting. When they cried out in slavery, the Lord remembered His people. Even in the wilderness, He turned their bitter waters sweet and gave them day by day bread from heaven. When He gave them His Torah, He invited their leaders into His presence, where they saw Him and ate and drank. Through the long centuries of success, sin, and trouble, He was with His people in the peace offerings, and He promised a day when death would be destroyed and He would give them His own portion of the meal that celebrates peace.

All this sacred history prepared Israel for the moment when God, standing as a man on the earth, walked among His people healing His creation, then sat at Table with them and said, "Take, eat; this is My body, given for you. Take, drink, this is My blood of the new testament, shed for you for the remission of sins."

Jesus institutes His Supper at the Passover meal. By Jewish reckoning (where the day begins at sundown and continues until the next evening), Jesus establishes His Supper on the same day He is crucified. He is "the Lamb of God, who takes away the sin of the world" (John 1:29). Luther's great Easter hymn puts it like this:

> Here is the true Paschal Lamb
> Which God himself attested.
> That was on the tree of shame
> In flaming passion roasted
> His blood on our doorpost lies;
> Faith holds that before Death's eyes;
> The smiting angel can do nought. Alleluia! (AE 53:257)

The blood of lambs dripping from the doors of enslaved Israelites now touches the door of the body, the mouth. The Table of the Lord is our new Passover.

This Passover, or *Pascha*, becomes the meal by which we remember something greater than the first Passover. Above we observed how God remembered His people in the house of bondage (Exodus 2:24). The Passover meal was also established as an annual meal for remembering: "This day shall be for you a memorial day, and you shall keep it as a feast to the Lord; throughout your generations, as a statute forever, you shall keep it as a feast" (Exodus 12:14; cf. Exodus 12:24–27; 13:3, 8–10, 14).

When Jesus celebrates the Passover meal with His disciples on the night of His betrayal, He evokes the theme of memory: "This is My body, which is given for you. Do this in remembrance of Me" (Luke 22:19). The strong command "Do this" means that Jesus wishes for the Lord's Supper to be repeated. We see from the Acts of the Apostles that the earliest Christians did this regularly, devoting themselves "to the apostles' teaching, and to the communion in the breaking of the bread, and to the prayers" (Acts 2:42, author's translation). From our earliest Christian documents outside the New Testament to the Lutheran Confessions, we see that the Lord's Supper was celebrated every Sunday according to this word from Jesus. However, what is more important than simply performing the action is the eating and drinking in faith. This is the chief meaning of "remembrance" in Jesus' words. Jesus wishes for us to meditate in faith on who He is and what He has done for us.

Remembering Jesus is like the Jewish recollection of the Passover: when God instituted that meal, He wanted His people to recall how He had saved them from death and delivered them from slavery. When we bring to our memory Jesus at the Supper, we are remembering all that He has done for us. This is more than simply pious feelings; it is a meditation on the Word. How can you remember Jesus when you go to the Supper? You can start by considering your sins and how every one of them has been dealt with by Jesus who takes away the world's sin. Then you can consider the specific words and deeds that you heard in the Gospel that day, and the pastor's exposition of it in his sermon. Finally, you can think about His great promises to you, how He has prayed for you (John 17), sent the Holy Spirit to be your Counselor (John 14–16), and promised to be with His Church always, even to the end of the age (Matthew 28:20).

You can also remember that Jesus remembers you. We saw above that God remembered Israel in Egypt. The Psalms teach us to ask God to remember us:

"Remember Your mercy, O Lord, and Your steadfast love, for they have been from of old. Remember not the sins of my youth or my transgressions; according to Your steadfast love remember me, for the sake of Your goodness, O Lord!" (Psalm 25:6–7). Three times in two verses, the psalmist puts "remember" on our lips. We ask God to remember His mercy, and to remember us; and sandwiched between these divine remembrances is a divine forgetfulness: God will no longer remember our sins! Consider all the other ways the Bible speaks about how God deals with our sins: blotting them out, covering them up, casting them into the depths of the sea, and putting them away from Him as far as the east is from the west. Behold, here is a great mystery: God, who knows all things, chooses to forget our sins!

Perhaps most significant in the theme of memory is the promise of Jesus on the cross. When one of the rebels who was crucified with Jesus had come to faith in Him, he implored Christ, "Jesus, remember me when You come into Your kingdom" (Luke 23:42). And Jesus promised him that he would be with Jesus in paradise that very day! Sometimes people use biblical examples such as the thief on the cross to try to tear down the Bible's teaching on Baptism or the Lord's Supper. The argument goes like this: "Since the thief on the cross wasn't baptized and didn't eat the Lord's Supper, we don't need those things either."

But this puts things topsy-turvy. It makes the Sacraments not less important, but more important! We do not have the honor of being crucified next to Jesus. We do not have a time machine where we can travel back and have Jesus lay His hand on us, hear Him speak to us, receive the Supper from His hand. But He has given us something in which, by a great mystery, He is present in His body and blood and speaks His own words to us. When we go to the Supper, hear the Word, and receive the Lord's body and blood, we are getting what the thief on the cross got: a personal word of promise.

The thief on the cross is not an exception to the Bible's teaching; his experience shows us that what he got directly from Jesus, we get through the means He established for all the disciples throughout time to hear His Word: "This is My body, given *for you*; this is My blood, shed *for you*." All this we remember when we go to the Supper, our new and greater memorial meal.

The New Manna

The institution of the Lord's Supper is repeated in each of the Synoptic Gospels (Matthew, Mark, and Luke), and also by Paul in 1 Corinthians. John's Gospel is unique in that it contains no institution of the Lord's Supper (or Baptism), although there are many passages in this Gospel where Christians through the centuries have seen themes of Baptism and Communion.

One of these places is in John 6, where Jesus feeds the five thousand. The people are in the wilderness and have run out of food. They are in a similar situation as the Israelites were after the crossing of the Red Sea. Following the Lord has put them in a place where there is no earthly hope. Only God can provide. When Jesus tests His disciples, their only solution is money—money that they do not have. "Two hundred denarii worth of bread would not be enough for each of them to get a little" (John 6:7).

Nevertheless, Jesus has the people sit down and get ready for a meal. Taking the little bit of bread and fish that a young boy has offered, Jesus speaks words that sound similar to the words He would later use on the night He was betrayed: "Jesus then took the loaves, and when He had given thanks, He distributed them to those who were seated" (John 6:11). Some Greek manuscripts add, "To the disciples," strengthening the resemblance to the Words of Institution. The recipients of the meal in the wilderness immediately recognize the significance. "This is indeed the Prophet who is to come into the world!" (John 6:14). They are well aware of the prophecy to Moses: "I will raise up for them a prophet like you from among their brothers. And I will put My words in His mouth, and He shall speak to them all that I command Him" (Deuteronomy 18:18).

After this sign, Jesus teaches in the synagogue in Capernaum on the topic of bread, manna, life, and death. "Do not work for the food that perishes, but for the food that endures to eternal life, which the Son of Man will give to you" (John 6:27). Since being exiled from Eden, every man has labored among the thorns for the food that perishes, eventually perishing himself. He has been cut off from the tree of life, and so cannot live as God intended. Now Jesus suggests the possibility that they might receive this food. "Sir, give us this bread always" (John 6:34), they cry, and we along with them.

What Jesus says next was an absolute shock to His hearers, and still causes scandal today. "I am the bread of life; whoever comes to Me shall not hunger, and whoever believes in Me shall never thirst" (John 6:35). Jesus Himself is the food by which people can live. Now comes into view what God intended by the gift of Eden and His presence among our first parents. God created man to bestow on him His benefits, but what is more, God intended to join man within the creation, and ultimately to bring man into communion with Himself. The incarnate God will gather humanity into a perfect unity, and Himself be joined to them. Immediately before His arrest in another garden, the Son prays to the Father for the unity of all disciples, "That they may be one even as We are one, I in them and You in Me, that they may become perfectly one, so that the world may know that You sent Me and loved them even as You loved Me" (John 17:22–23). Beyond all human understanding, St. Peter speaks of this communion as sharing in God's nature: "He has granted to us His precious and very great promises, so that through them you may become partakers of the divine nature, having escaped from the corruption that is in the world because of sinful desire" (2 Peter 1:4).

All the gifts of the Lord's Table throughout sacred history have had this in view, escaping the world's corruption. This corruption is moral and spiritual, as seen in the myriad ways men worship the idols of covetousness and self-seeking. This corruption is also bodily, leading to death. When St. Paul says that the wages of sin is death (Romans 6:23), he speaks a truth that goes back to the one original commandment and threat: "The day that you eat of it you shall surely die" (Genesis 2:17).

The meal of faith that Jesus offers is the promise that undoes that threat. The fruit of His flesh is the tree of life. Jesus anticipates the Supper He will establish, and the benefits of the cross to believers, joining them to the Old Testament themes of Eden and the end-times meal that swallows up death (Isaiah 25).

> Truly, truly, I say to you, unless you eat the flesh of the Son of Man and drink His blood, you have no life in you. Whoever feeds on My flesh and drinks My blood has eternal life, and I will raise him up on the last day. For My flesh is true food, and My blood is true drink. Whoever feeds on My flesh and drinks My blood abides in Me, and I in him. As the living Father sent Me, and I live because of the Father, so whoever feeds on Me, he also will live because of Me. This is the bread that came down from heaven, not like the bread the fathers ate, and died. Whoever feeds on this bread will live forever. (John 6:53–58)

The manna kept our spiritual fathers alive in the wilderness. The food Jesus gives bestows everlasting life. The Table of the Lord is the new manna.

The New Covenant

At Sinai, the people were splashed with the blood of the covenant as they promised obedience to God's Word. Then Moses, Aaron, Nadab, Abihu, and the seventy elders of Israel were invited to a covenant ratification meal where they ate and drank with God. Israel's pledge of obedience was broken repeatedly, leading to their exile and captivity. "Behold the blood of the covenant" (Exodus 24:8) became for many an antiquated reminder of an irrelevant relationship. Israel largely forsook obedience to God's Word and embraced covetousness and idolatry.

While Jesus institutes the Sacrament of the Altar at the Passover meal, and that meal joins us to His death and resurrection, the words Jesus uses at the Supper recall that key moment in Israel's life. With the blood of the sacrifice marking them, Israel promised obedience. Now, hours before His arrest, Jesus speaks nearly identical words that reckon with Israel's disobedience: "Drink of it, all of you, for this is My blood of the covenant, which is poured out for many for the forgiveness of sins" (Matthew 26:27–28). The words of Moses, "This is the blood of the covenant," now become on Jesus' lips, "This is *My* blood of the covenant [or *testament*]."

"Covenant" often carries the connotation of a contract, an agreement by two parties. The biblical use of "covenant" does not express that kind of contract, but rather a promise on the part of God to His people. The term *testament* better expresses the idea that a gift is being imparted, showing the will of the testator upon his death. In this solemn moment, as Jesus is preparing for His crucifixion, the Lord gives His last will and testament, reiterating God's ancient promise to His people.

Other New Testament writers report the word *new* as part of the institution: "This cup that is poured out for you is the *new* [testament] in My blood" (Luke 22:20, emphasis added; cf. 1 Corinthians 11:25). In the blood of Jesus, a new testament is made that speaks better things than the blood of the first. The blood of Sinai was sprinkled and Israel promised obedience. This new testament reaffirms God's gracious relationship with His people, promising them forgiveness. The Table of the Lord is this new testament.

The blood of the old covenant sprinkled the outsides of the body. The blood of the new testament sprinkles the inside. The old testament strictly forbade the drinking of blood:

> If any one of the house of Israel or of the strangers who sojourn among them eats any blood, I will set My face against that person who eats blood and will cut him off from among his people. For the life of the flesh is in the blood, and I have given it for you on the altar to make atonement for your souls, for it is the blood that makes atonement by the life. Therefore I have said to the people of Israel, No person among you shall eat blood, neither shall any stranger who sojourns among you eat blood. (Leviticus 17:10–12)

Israel's surrounding neighbors used blood for idolatrous rituals. By drinking the blood or eating it with its flesh, pagans believed they would gain the power of its life. They also used blood as offerings of food to the spirits of the dead, to appease gods of the underworld, for fertility rituals (both agricultural and human), and to ward off bad luck. God's direction for His people reminded them that He alone is the Lord and giver of life, and He alone had the right to blood. Blood would not be "eaten" to gain life, but would only be used for atonement, at His specific direction.[10]

Imagine, then, the absolute shock and horror at the seemingly blasphemous words of Jesus, "Take and drink, this is My blood of the new testament"! On its face, this seems to go against the heart of God's Law. Yet, precisely here we see the culmination of all the Old Testament teaching on blood and its life. By giving His disciples *His* blood, He is giving them His own life, the benefits of His atonement. Where the blood of Sinai sprinkled them on the outside, this new testament in the blood of Jesus would sprinkle them on the inside, making them clean and holy. Life does not come from any animal, but from God Himself, the God who took on human flesh and blood to bring man into communion with Himself.

This blood then gives us a clean conscience! How easy it is to think of a clean conscience as the result of our own works. If we have lied, stolen, committed adultery, or betrayed a friend, our conscience ought to accuse us. Our conscience is not clean. Yet, when God's Word speaks of a clean conscience, it is not the result of our works, but God's own work of forgiveness.

> For if the blood of goats and bulls, and the sprinkling of defiled persons with the ashes of a heifer, sanctify for the purification of the flesh, how much more will the blood of Christ, who through the eternal

10 Kleinig, *Leviticus*, 365–66.

> Spirit offered Himself without blemish to God, purify our conscience from dead works to serve the living God.
>
> Therefore He is the mediator of a new covenant, so that those who are called may receive the promised eternal inheritance, since a death has occurred that redeems them from the transgressions committed under the first covenant. (Hebrews 9:13–15)

The clean conscience does not come from us, but from Jesus. The sprinkling of His blood inside us as we drink marks us as clean and holy. Our conscience need not accuse us, because Jesus' blood delivers forgiveness to us and summons us to a new kind of life in communion with Him.

When we go to Holy Communion, wherever our church may be located, we travel to Mount Zion, and there God speaks to us a new word as we are sprinkled with a blood that speaks forgiveness and gives life.

> You have come to Mount Zion and to the city of the living God, the heavenly Jerusalem, and to innumerable angels in festal gathering, and to the assembly of the firstborn who are enrolled in heaven, and to God, the judge of all, and to the spirits of the righteous made perfect, and to Jesus, the mediator of a new covenant, and to the sprinkled blood that speaks a better word than the blood of Abel. (Hebrews 12:22–24)

Jesus Eats with His Disciples

After His resurrection and before His ascension, the Lord Jesus continued meeting with His disciples in significant ways that taught the Church and established a pattern. Luke's Gospel is unique in presenting to us the Easter account of two disciples on the road to Emmaus (ch. 24). They have heard news of the resurrection, but they remain in doubt. Jesus comes and walks along with them, but His identity is hidden from them. Jesus shows them that the entire Hebrew Scriptures taught that the Christ was to suffer, be crucified, die, and rise again on the third day.

When they arrive at their lodging, they invite Jesus to remain. Instead of acting as a guest at dinner, as would be expected, Jesus assumes the role of host.

In language reminiscent of the Lord's Supper, Jesus "took the bread and blessed and broke it and gave it to them. And their eyes were opened, and they recognized Him. And He vanished from their sight" (Luke 24:30–31). Here we see a pattern of teaching from Scripture and eating, with Jesus as host and delivering both rebuke and good news to His disciples.

These disciples immediately return the seven miles to Jerusalem and report to the others that Jesus had made Himself known to them "in the breaking of the bread" (Luke 24:35). Jesus' vanishing from their sight does not indicate His absence, but rather that He is present in a new and different way: "In the breaking of the bread." In St. Luke's second volume, the Acts of the Apostles, he uses this term in a technical way for the Lord's Supper, referring to it as "communion" in the Greek (*koinōnia*, Acts 2:42; cf. 1 Corinthians 10:16).

Immediately after this event, Jesus appears again among these same disciples and others gathered in Jerusalem. He reveals to them that He has bodily risen from death by inviting them to touch Him and then by eating a meal of fish before their eyes. Then in a critical passage, Jesus "opened their minds to understand the Scriptures" (Luke 24:45), showing them that the right understanding of the Bible is to see Christ as *the* message, throughout "the Law of Moses and the Prophets and the Psalms" (Luke 24:44). He then gives them a commission to preach repentance and the remission of sins in His name. This becomes the basic pattern of all true Christian worship: Word and Meal, with preaching of repentance and the forgiveness of sins. They go together, Word and Sacrament. Still today, this is how Jesus is known to us, how He is present with His Church: Christ-centered Bible teaching, and the Meal He instituted to remember Him, receiving life in His body and a clean conscience in His blood.

The Lord's Table before the Gates of Hell

How can we apply the Bible's teaching about the Lord's Table to our own present situation? The Lord Jesus builds His Church on the confession given to St. Peter: "You are the Christ, the Son of the living God" (Matthew 16:16). Against this Church, "The gates of hell shall not prevail" (Matthew 16:18). Our experience in a hostile world can often make us doubt this. Radical Islam terrorizes the West. In America, people are abandoning Christianity in droves, and a new generation is arising that doesn't even know the basic Christian message. Churches are closing, others are without pastors. The culture has rapidly embraced homosexual marriage, discarding millennia of tradition and rejecting natural law.

The concrete, scientific reality of the human body as male or female is discarded for a new age that rejects what every previous age understood, inventing the idea that gender can change—and even be fluid—based upon feelings. It seems as though the gates of hell are indeed prevailing.

When we are prone to despair, whether about our own lives or the state of the culture or the church, it is imperative to remember Jesus' promise: "On this rock I will build My church, and the gates of hell shall not prevail against it" (Matthew 16:18). What Jesus promises to Peter in Matthew 16, He reaffirms to the twelve disciples in John 20, where the whole Church is given the keys first announced to Peter upon the good confession of Jesus as the Christ. So we need not fear. Jesus is still with His Church, wherever two or three gather in His name. Strength is not found in numbers or worldly success, but our strength is entirely in the weakness of Jesus crucified. For when we are weak, then the strength and power of Jesus is made manifest.

Among the most comforting passages of Scripture in every generation is the Twenty-Third Psalm. And there we have a verse that captures our theme, "The Gates of Hell and the Table of the Lord": "You prepare a table before me in the presence of my enemies" (Psalm 23:5). What kind of strange way is this to deal with enemies? Will the Lord set up a picnic before us as the gates of hell open up, pouring forth demons, armies, and beasts to devour us? Dr. Luther says of this verse, "I should think He would prepare before him a mighty wall, a strong rampart, a deep moat, an armor, and other arms and weapons that have to do with battle, through which he might be safe from his enemies or put them to flight" (AE 12:172).

Instead, the Lord gives us a table. The Table He has now given in Jesus is fully set. There is a rich meal of life-giving, conscience-cleansing food: the body and blood of Jesus. And preached through that meal is the Word, the remembrance of God's creation of our first parents and how He provided for them. How He rescued our spiritual fathers from bondage, bloodying their doors to protect them from death as they ate safely inside. How He gave them safe passage through the waters, turned their bitter waters sweet, and fed them with bread from heaven. How He established His Divine Service whereby they could know peace and joy in His presence. And how He promised them a meal of everlasting life when death was swallowed up forever.

The Lord Jesus now brings us to this beautiful table. To the world, it appears to be nothing, and sadly, to some Christians, too, who do not believe that Jesus can or does mean what He says, "This is My body; this is My blood." Yet, surrounded by enemies—arguments in the church, hatred from the world, cancer and disease creeping in our bodies, experiences of sadness breaking our hearts—the Lord sets a table where our cup runs over with goodness. Jesus is saying to us, "I Myself am with you. I will not leave you nor forsake you. I know you feel guilty, but I have taken your guilt upon Myself. Your conscience is clean. I know you feel weak. But My body is true food. By it, you will live. I will raise up your body. Inside you is anger and sadness, betrayal and pride, frustration and feelings of worthlessness. Come to Me, come to My Table; here you will find rest. Here you will find that I have done everything for you already."

This is far better protection than any wall, moat, nuclear missile, or Navy Seal team could provide. The Lord God who commands angelic armies, who creates and brings to nothing by His Word, has invited us to His Table. What other comfort do we need? Truly the gates of hell shall not prevail where the Lord sets His Table.

Into our mad world and frenzied hearts comes Jesus. He sets Himself as host at the Table in each of our congregations and repeats His Easter word: "Peace!"

> Jesus Himself stood among them, and said to them, "Peace to you!" But they were startled and frightened and thought they saw a spirit. And He said to them, "Why are you troubled, and why do doubts arise in your hearts?" (Luke 24:36–38)

> On the evening of that day, the first day of the week, the doors being locked where the disciples were for fear of the Jews, Jesus came and stood among them and said to them, "Peace be with you." When He had said this, He showed them His hands and His side. Then the disciples were glad when they saw the Lord. Jesus said to them again, "Peace be with you. As the Father has sent Me, even so I am sending you." And when He had said this, He breathed on them and said to them, "Receive the Holy Spirit. If you forgive the sins of any, they are forgiven them; if you withhold forgiveness from any, it is withheld." (John 20:19–23)

The central word of the resurrection appearances of Jesus is peace. In the Easter appearance to the disciples in John's Gospel, Jesus repeats it, framing the display of His wounds. The wounds of Jesus make for our peace. Jesus is our peace offering, and the Supper of Jesus is the joyous meal where, like the ancient Israelites, we enjoy a festive time with our family celebrating the Lord's peace and goodness to us. Our true family is the Church, for there we are joined together not through the bloodlines of our parents and grandparents, but through the blood of Jesus. This means that a new family is created, through a new birth whereby we are born, with Jesus, "not of blood nor of the will of the flesh nor of the will of man, but of God" (John 1:13).

In the Divine Service liturgies, after the pastor has spoken the Word of Jesus over the bread and wine, celebrating His gift of body and blood to us, the pastor faces the people, holds up the cup and bread, and announces the words of Jesus, that this is His peace offering: "The peace of the Lord be with you always." The joyful response of His people is "Amen!" We are by this Amen saying, "True, dear Lord. Your body and blood is my peace, for You have made peace between man and God, even breaking down the wall of separation. You have opened the way back to paradise. Your Word is truth. Thank You." This is what the Amen means, and it is fitting for God's people to say it with vigor and rejoicing!

After the Meal, the liturgies offer to us the option of singing the words of holy Simeon, who held the infant Jesus in his arms on the day Mary and Joseph brought Him to the temple in Jerusalem for His presentation and Mary's purification. Simeon had been given a great promise that before he died, he would see the Messiah. By the Holy Spirit, Simeon knew immediately that this child was that Messiah. Cradling Jesus in his arms, Simeon uttered the words that are now so often sung by Christians as they depart from the Lord's Table:

> Lord, now You are letting Your servant depart in peace, according to Your word; for my eyes have seen Your salvation that You have prepared in the presence of all peoples, a light for revelation to the Gentiles, and for glory to Your people Israel. (Luke 2:29–32)

We are singing with Simeon that Jesus is our true peace offering, and we are now ready to die. God has fulfilled His promises in Jesus. He is salvation for Gentiles and Israelites. When the gates of hell pour forth death, we who have been comforted at the Table of the Lord see it for what Jesus has made it by the power of His resurrection: a portal to paradise, where we await our own resurrection in the body in the life of the world to come.

Worthy and Unworthy Eating

So how can I be certain that this is for me? As a pastor, on several occasions, I have been told by Christians troubled by their sins that they did not or will not receive the Lord's Supper because they are not worthy. How can we know if we are worthy to receive the gifts from the Lord's Table? We will first look at Scripture, then see how that Scripture is applied in the Small Catechism.

After teaching that participating in Holy Communion is a fellowship (Greek *koinōnia*, communion, sharing) in the body and blood of Jesus (1 Corinthians 10:16–17), St. Paul goes on to say that this participation excludes participation in the fellowship rites of other religions: "What pagans sacrifice they offer to demons and not to God. I do not want you to be participants with demons. You cannot drink the cup of the Lord and the cup of demons. You cannot partake of the table of the Lord and the table of demons" (1 Corinthians 10:20–21). This strong language means that for Christians, the Table is open only to those who have absolute loyalty to Christ, and do not have any ritual associations with non-Christian religions.

This does not mean that a person cannot have everyday contact or friendships with non-Christians. St. Paul discussed that earlier when he spoke about the importance of discipline within the Church (1 Corinthians 5:9–13). There he called the Church to remove from fellowship those whose life goes against the Ten Commandments. A common argument against excluding manifest sinners from Communion is that we are all sinners. This is true! The key distinction to make is repentance—turning away from sin and petitioning the Lord's forgiveness. This is why St. Paul, still instructing on the Lord's Supper, calls upon us to examine ourselves (1 Corinthians 11:28) and judge ourselves (1 Corinthians 11:31). All of the people coming to Communion are sinners. The Bible calls us to examine and judge ourselves as sinners in need of a Savior. The person who is excluded from Communion is not excluded because of his sins, but because he refuses to turn away from the sin and ask for forgiveness. Repentance is the issue.

So far, we've seen how the Word of God instructs the Church to close the Communion Table to those who participate in other religions and those who are practicing an unrepentant, immoral life. There are several additional words from Scripture that we need to consider. Those who come to Communion must "discern the body" (see 1 Corinthians 11:29). Communicants know what Jesus teaches about His Supper, and they discern that the bread is the body of Jesus and the wine is the blood. To our great sadness, this excludes us communing with those who deny the Lord's Word and teach that the Lord's Supper is just a symbolic meal. Many of the churches around us teach this way.

When people participate in Communion, they "proclaim the Lord's death until He comes" (1 Corinthians 11:26). Communicants are proclaimers! They preach about the Lord's death—the cross and what Jesus accomplished there—by participating in the meal. Going to an altar for Communion means that you are proclaiming the same thing the other communicants there are proclaiming. Inviting people to our altars means we say the same thing—we hold to the same creeds, the same confession of faith.

Besides the stern warning in God's Word about Communion fellowship, we should also recognize that when we ignore God's Word on these points, we are saying that His Word is not important and communicants can believe whatever they want. While it is natural to want to avoid conflict—closed Communion seems terribly unfriendly!—we are not being truly kind by practicing open Communion. What we are teaching by an open Communion practice is that you can ignore parts of God's Word and we won't take that seriously.

Every Sunday, my congregation has visitors—people whom I don't know. Many of them want to come to Communion. How can I be faithful to God's Word and also loving to these visitors at the same time? The pastor has to take his responsibilities seriously, which requires knowing who the people are who are presenting themselves for Communion. This requires a conversation. Closed Communion doesn't mean that only Missouri Synod Lutherans are going to heaven, or that we are superior to everyone else. What it does mean is that if a visitor comes to me and says, "I am a member of a Missouri Synod congregation," then my Communion fellowship with all other LCMS congregations means I can now assume that another pastor has done the work of baptizing and teaching this person. That's a short and easy conversation.

When someone comes to me who is a member of a different church body, or no church at all, then I need to have a longer and more intentional conversation with that person. In the sixty to ninety seconds you might get right before Divine Service, it's impossible to find out about the person's faith and life. Pastors do have the right to make exceptions; the important thing is that the pastor talks with a person and comes to know her Christian faith; sees to it that she is baptized, knows the Ten Commandments, has been taught to examine herself and repent, and knows what the Supper is; and gets to know her manner of life. These are not always easy conversations to have; sometimes people get very angry. I try always to remember a conversation I had that turned out differently.

One Easter Sunday, a visitor came to the altar. I hadn't talked with him beforehand, so I discretely asked him about his faith and what church he was a part of. After realizing I couldn't commune him yet ("yet" is always the key word!), I gave him a blessing and sought him out after the service. Concerned that he would be upset, I found instead a person who wanted to learn more. "This is the only church I've been to that takes the Lord's Supper seriously! I want to learn more." A few months later, he was confirmed, and he is still a member after more than a decade. Closed Communion is not saying, "Never," but, "Not yet." Closed Communion treats every human being as important, requiring that the pastor talk with the people God sends his way and take seriously Jesus' instruction to make disciples by baptizing and teaching. Communing people without that pastoral conversation ignores the Great Commission and the spiritual needs of people, turning the Lord's Supper into the churchly equivalent of an automated checkout machine at the supermarket.

Luther's Small Catechism is very helpful for framing these conversations, and also for giving pastoral care to the troubled soul afraid of God's judgment:

> *Who receives this sacrament worthily?*
>
> Fasting and bodily preparation are certainly fine outward training. But that person is truly worthy and well prepared who has faith in these words: "Given and shed for you for the forgiveness of sins."
>
> But anyone who does not believe these words or doubts them is unworthy and unprepared, for the words "for you" require all hearts to believe. (SC Sacrament of the Altar)

The key to proper preparation is faith! The person who knows and feels his sins is not unworthy to come to the Supper, just as sickness doesn't make you unworthy to go to the physician. Yet this is not just any sort of faith; it is faith in a specific object—Jesus—with specific meaning: "Given and shed for you for the forgiveness of sins." Let's examine this point by point:

Given and shed—The bread is the body of Jesus given into death, and the wine is the blood of Jesus shed on the cross. This means that the communicant will have at least a basic understanding of the cross and the atoning work of Jesus. The communicant will also know that the bread *is* the body of Jesus, and the wine *is* the blood of Jesus, according to His clear words.

For you—The Christian's faith is not simply a knowledge of history, but a certainty that what happened in history—the death of Jesus and the institution of His Supper—happened for me.

For the forgiveness—The communicant comes seeking forgiveness, knowing that Jesus invites sinners to Himself, and calls them to "go, and from now on sin no more" (John 8:11).

Of sins—The communicant will know the Ten Commandments by heart so he can examine himself.

With a member of the church who is troubled by sin and worried about eating and drinking judgment to himself (1 Corinthians 11:29), I have the following type of conversation: "Do you believe that you are a sinner?" "Yes, I do." "Do you want to be forgiven and freed from your sins?" "Yes, more than anything!" "Dear friend, this is why Jesus gave us this Sacrament! He invites you to come and be forgiven. Things won't get better by you staying away. St. Ambrose said about the Supper, 'Because I always sin, I always need the medicine.' If you were sick, you would go to the doctor. You are a sinner, so you should go to the Supper. Do you think you are not worthy? It's true, you're not! None of us are. But when the Bible talks about worthy eating and drinking, the worthy person is the one who confesses sin and looks to Jesus for forgiveness. So by all means, come!"

Worthiness consists in recognizing your unworthiness.

The Bodily Benefit

We live in an age that is both obsessed with body image and denies the body has any lasting significance beyond death. One day the body is honed and toned through exercise and plastic surgery, and the next it is cremated and scattered to the winds.

The Christian view of the body recognizes its value now and calls us to holiness in our bodily actions. "Do you not know that your body is a temple of the Holy Spirit within you, whom you have from God? You are not your own, for you were bought with a price. So glorify God in your body" (1 Corinthians 6:19–20; cf. Romans 12:1). At the same time, we recognize the great value of the body after death, knowing that God will raise us up again from the dead. The Lutheran rite of burial includes a passage that reminds the mourners that God is not finished with this body we now lovingly lay in the ground. "Our citizenship is in heaven, and from it we await a Savior, the Lord Jesus Christ, who will transform our lowly body to be like His glorious body, by the power that enables Him even to subject all things to Himself" (Philippians 3:20–21).

At the Supper, the Christian is fed both body and soul. Some have inferred a bodily benefit to the Lord's Supper through the admonition St. Paul gives about unworthy eating. "Anyone who eats and drinks without discerning the body eats and drinks judgment on Himself. That is why many of you are weak and ill, and some have died" (1 Corinthians 11:29–30). This bodily benefit that comes from the forgiveness of sins is not one that we should look to for giving us athletic prowess or to free us from every infirmity. It is a much greater benefit: the power of the resurrection. That is one majestic result of being in communion with the resurrected Jesus. We shall also rise from the dead on the strength of His victorious body and blood. In one of Luther's two great works about the Lord's Supper, he connects the Lord's Supper with our coming resurrection.

> This is a bodily benefit . . . an extraordinarily great one, and it follows from the spiritual benefit. . . . If we eat him spiritually through the Word, he abides in us spiritually in our soul; if one eats him physically, he abides in us physically and we in him. As we eat him, he abides in us and we in him. For he is not digested or transformed but ceaselessly he transforms us, our soul into righteousness, our body into immortality. (AE 37:132)

This bodily benefit leads us back to the beginning, where man was created by God to live and not die, to partake of the tree of life. In the parables of Jesus, the kingdom of God is often likened to a great banquet, such as a feast for the marriage of the king's son (e.g., Matthew 22:1–14). The Book of Revelation takes up this same theme: "Blessed are those who are invited to the marriage supper of the Lamb" (19:9). This marriage takes place in a new city, new Jerusalem, where God dwells with man (Revelation 21:2–3), where the feast-prophecy of Isaiah 25 is fulfilled: "He will wipe away every tear from their eyes, and death shall be no more, neither shall there be mourning, nor crying, nor pain anymore" (Revelation 21:4). There in that city, new Jerusalem, is the tree of life, perpetually in bloom, a tree that heals the world (Revelation 22:2).

In the Supper, we receive Jesus in His body and blood. This moment, as the church gathers together around Jesus and His Word, is the one moment that makes sense out of all the other troubles and arguments and sins and death. There at His Supper, Jesus is putting everything to rights for us. The Holy Communion is the Gospel, and while it is everything, it is also provisional. In His Supper, Jesus is preparing us for a yet greater feast, when we shall walk in the new city, free from sadness, free from shame, and be truly alive. Nothing shall harm us, for we will have free access to the tree of life, whose leaves are for the healing of the nations.

This is our great hope. This Table of the Lord is our great protection against the gates of hell. When the Table is set for us, there is nothing left to say but the Bible's closing prayer: "Amen. Come, Lord Jesus!" (Revelation 22:20).

Study Questions

1. What is the "fear of death" (Hebrews 2:15), and how does it affect you?

2. What is a "peace offering," and how does it differ from the way we commonly use the term today?

3. How can we remember Jesus when we go to Holy Communion?

4. What are the similarities and differences between the old covenant and new testament?

5. How can we know if we are receiving the Sacrament worthily?

6. What did Luther identify as the bodily benefit to the Lord's Supper?

13

The Gates of Hell and the Urgency of Preaching

The Purpose, Power, Perils, and Privilege of Preaching!

Rev. Nabil S. Nour

Introduction

In the April 24, 2015, edition of *The New York Times*, David Brooks unwittingly wrote a plea for preachers to proclaim justification by grace through faith in Jesus apart from the works of the Law; for this teaching alone delivers and frees one to see the depth and height, width and length of the nature of unconditional love.

The title of Brooks's opinion piece was "Love and Merit." He opined that well-meaning parents have fallen into a trap. In their efforts to push their children to be all that they can be, they are proclaiming a message of conditional love. If you get straight As, if you get into a prestigious college, if you rank on the top of the academic or athletic heap, we will lavish you with praise, affirmations, and rewards.

The result? Students feel that unless they measure up to the standard of the law imposed on them by parents and those in authority, they are not loved. Anxiety, depression, and fear arise when these students fall short of the steep standards placed on them by the law.

"The wolf of conditional love is lurking in these homes," wrote Brooks. The dominant note of the parent-child relationship is not unconditional love. Instead, the message is "I love you when you stay on my balance beam," not simply, "I love you."[1]

The religions of self-justification take many lethal forms. For example, a pastor recently told me of a mother who was twisting the arm of her teenage son to steal copper in order to pay for her drug habit. "Son, this is what you must do to put yourself in a right relationship with me."

Schools today have become fanatical about sports. Beneath it all is the drumbeat of self-justification—what you must do to put yourself in a right relationship with the social engineers. This emphasis on athletics is weakening families and emptying churches. Young people must give their all to sports. Sports have contributed substantially to major dips in church attendance and to family dysfunction. But sports are just one of the competing claims that seek to silence the Gospel by drawing people away from church. The reason our nation is drifting more and more toward social chaos is because apostolic, evangelical preaching is a dim, distant voice in the lives of many people. "Where there is no prophetic vision the people cast off restraint" (Proverbs 29:18).

If our nation is to maintain liberty, it must have a revival in preaching. To be sure, this is a penultimate concern. Nations come and go. Ultimately, there is a much larger issue. Biblical preaching in sync with the God of all grace is necessary for the gathering of the elect and the saving of people from the damnation self-justification brings. To this end, we look at the purpose, power, perils, and privilege of preaching in our age where we may well be living in the last days.

The Purpose of Preaching

David Buttrick, in his book *Homiletical Moves and Structures*, provides a commendable summary of the purpose of preaching.

> The purpose of preaching is God reconciling the world through Christ. In Jesus Christ, we see the mysterious Love of God reaching out with spectacular modesty to the human world. . . . Thus God's purpose—however, whenever, wherever—must be conceived as communion

1 David Brooks, "Love and Merit," *The New York Times*, April 24, 2015, https://www.nytimes.com/2015/04/24/opinion/david-brooks-love-and-merit.html?mcubz=0.

> with a reconciled world. The purpose of preaching, broadly considered, is nothing less than the saving purpose of God.[2]

The fingerprints of God's grace and purpose of salvation are clearly revealed in Scripture. St. John declares, "For God so loved the world, that He gave His only Son, that whoever believes in Him should not perish but have eternal life. For God did not send His Son into the world to condemn the world, but in order that the world might be saved through Him" (John 3:16–17). Throughout Scripture, we see the God of all grace demonstrating His unconditional love to His created beings. This is the purpose of preaching. Paul, the apostle, speaks of that blessed grace with these words: "God shows His love for us in that while we were still sinners, Christ died for us" (Romans 5:8).

Through Gospel-centered preachers, this saving message brings people comfort, hope, joy, peace, and a sense that they are loved unconditionally. Luther explained this Gospel aspect of the message of our preaching in a magnificent manner in his 1518 *Heidelberg Disputation*, in which he contrasted God's love with man's love: "The love of God does not find, but creates, that which is pleasing to it. The love of man comes into being through that which is pleasing to it" (AE 31:41).

The "purpose" of God was addressed specifically by St. Paul as he proclaimed it in his letter to congregations at Ephesus. In the context of his trinitarian tribute to God the Father as the author of salvation, Jesus as the agent of salvation, and the Holy Spirit as the administrator of it, Paul sets forth God's great goal of which preaching is a key instrument. He writes,

> In Him we have redemption through His blood, the forgiveness of our trespasses, according to the riches of His grace, which He lavished upon us, in all wisdom and insight making known to us the mystery of His will, according to His purpose, which He set forth in Christ as a plan for the fullness of time, to unite all things in Him, things in heaven and things on earth. (Ephesians 1:7–10)

In preaching, there is a cosmic purpose, not a mere cosmetic purpose. Through the powerful message of the riches of God's grace in Christ, God is putting together this broken planet, this Humpty Dumpty, post-fall world. Therefore, the purpose of preaching will have an eternal ripple effect of the most sublime proportions.

2 David Buttrick, *Homiletic Moves and Structures* (Philadelphia: Fortress Press, 1988), 452.

Martin Luther gives us biblical insight into the work of the Holy Spirit through preaching. Preachers serve as the mouthpiece of the Holy Spirit where and when they proclaim the fabulous facets of the grace of God—like a beautiful brilliant diamond showing its glorious features. The fabulous facets of the grace of God are proclaimed through the message of the preacher. "Preach, not because you want to say something, but because you have something to say."[3] Yes, the preacher has a great deal to say. It is the message of the greatest story in all of human history—the salvific story of Jesus, coming to earth, living the perfect life, dying for the sins of the world, and rising again to give believers life and salvation.

Such passionate proclamation about the life, death, resurrection, and ascension of Jesus brings about a host of wonderful results. At the same time Luther explains the work of the Holy Spirit, he also describes what occurs through the Gospel harmoniously proclaimed in scriptural preaching. His explanation to the Third Article of the Apostles' Creed reveals the rich realities at work in the powerful purpose of preaching:

> I believe that I cannot by my own reason or strength believe in Jesus Christ, my Lord, or come to Him; but the Holy Spirit has called me by the Gospel, enlightened me with His gifts, sanctified and kept me in the true faith.
>
> In the same way He calls, gathers, enlightens, and sanctifies the whole Christian church on earth, and keeps it with Jesus Christ in the one true faith. (SC Creed, Third Article)

The purpose of evangelical preaching is also specified in Article V of the Augsburg Confession. Philip Melanchthon declares that the office of preaching, like salvation, is a gift of God. It is not something we do on our own authority, but God calls us to do it.

> So that we may obtain this faith, the ministry of teaching the Gospel and administering the Sacraments was instituted. Through the Word and Sacraments, as through instruments, the Holy Spirit is given

3 Richard E. Lauersdorf, *Together with Jesus: Daily Devotions for the Year* (Milwaukee: Northwestern, 2003), devotion for March 17.

> [John 20:22]. He works faith, when and where it pleases God [John 3:8], in those who hear the good news that God justifies those who believe that they are received into grace for Christ's sake. This happens not through our own merits, but for Christ's sake. (AC V 1–3)

Isaiah, the fifth evangelist, records these words from the God of all grace, "Comfort, comfort My people" (Isaiah 40:1). Here we have a double imperative where God graciously gives what He commands. What follows is a divine announcement of pardon. The details of that pardon center on the story of the coming Savior. This story culminates with the revelation of Good Friday and the day of resurrection (Isaiah 40–53). Essentially, fourteen chapters of comfort and consolation flow from the fountain of the fifth evangelist so that parched people might be well-watered from the rock of salvation. Furthermore, Isaiah informs us that a Savior is to be born of a virgin (Isaiah 7:14); He will free people, heal people, and provide an eternal covenant of peace. A theology of the cross and the open tomb are set forth to make room for a new heaven and a new earth (Isaiah 53; 65:17).

Through four mighty prophetic songs of the Suffering Servant to come, Isaiah signals to all Good-News preachers the direction we, too, must take. He tells us of a Servant who looks like Jesus, sounds like Jesus, and is Jesus. Here we see Isaiah is in step with the beautiful Gospel of John, who reveals to us the words of Greeks who came to the disciples, saying, "Sir, we wish to see Jesus" (John 12:21).

The proclamation seeks to set forth the person and work of Jesus. This Gospel proclaimed always aims to go out to the many nations (Isaiah 52:10). John, the evangelist, is keenly aware of the cosmic nature of the message faithful preachers proclaim. He links the story of the Greek God-fearers coming to Philip and Andrew, disciples from the region of "Galilee of the Gentiles" (Matthew 4:15). He also connects this story with Isaiah's great Suffering Servant song (Isaiah 53:1; John 12:38).

What does this mean? It means that the alert Gospel preacher is a "simultaneous" preacher. From the pulpit, he feeds the lambs of God and at the same time reaches out to the lost as one who is holding high the One who is the God-man. The very nature of our Jesus-centered preaching is to be permeated with the message of crucified glory (John 12:20–26). In the glory of the message of the cross, we see the depth of God's love; we learn the heart of God, and we see the heavenly purpose for life.

The purpose of preaching is to hold high the person and work of Jesus, so that people hearing will "see" Jesus rooted in the story of the cross. John 3:16 is simple. Its simplicity is an example for our proclamation, because it is the only message that changes our standing before God. In first-century Corinth, the congregation had fallen under the spell of preachers who marginalized the cross, minimized the resurrection, and misunderstood the nature of Baptism and the Lord's Supper (1 Corinthians 1:18–31; 10:16; 12:13; 15:1–58). Thus, the same serpent who deceived Adam and Eve deceived many of the members in Corinth. In their spiritual stupor, the Corinthians were enamored by these preachers, who preached a different Jesus, a different spirit, and a different gospel (2 Corinthians 11:3–4).

Jesus is not just one among many saviors. He is the only Savior of the world, the Creator of the cosmos, the Preserver of mankind, and the one Mediator between God and man (Colossians 1:15–20; 1 Timothy 2:5). This Savior will bring justice to the nations, mercy to mankind, and real hope. This lively hope will be the foundation for faith toward the future. This mighty Messenger of great counsel will establish an eternal Gospel government where the wounds of a crucified and risen Savior will form a new creation (Isaiah 9:6).

With this dynamic Gospel foretold and fulfilled through Jesus the Messiah, the servant of the Lord, you as the preacher (but not limited to the preacher, also the laity in their daily vocation) have the greatest news to joyfully proclaim and comfort people. What a thrill it is to do the work that angels yearn to do. To that end, as a minister of the Gospel, each week it is a great privilege to write and deliver sermons anchored in God's Word so that the Holy Spirit feeds Christ's redeemed on the Word of the living God. Therefore, the sermon is intended to dish out the meat and milk of the Gospel. This meat and milk are the gifts of Jesus to His people who gather together in the ark of salvation to be comforted and consoled, edified and encouraged, equipped and enlightened.

For this reason, I, as a dying man, preach to dying people the life-giving message that regenerates and enhances life abundantly. In God's Word, not only do heaven's doors open for us, but also we gain a true picture of God's love for us and for all. As St. Paul tells us, the same power that raised Jesus from the dead is at work in our preaching (1 Corinthians 15:1–11). Although the resurrection of Christ is a past event, it has ongoing power in the sermon and Sacraments. In this resurrection chapter, Paul declares that Jesus was raised on the third day with ongoing life-giving power according to the Scriptures. When the saints gather together for worship and hear a sermon that is the Gospel, the Burning Bush that spoke to Moses encounters His people.

The Power of Preaching

Some years ago, I witnessed a Lutheran pastor enter the pulpit with a real stick of dynamite. You would not want to do that with today's security concerns. At that time, he did this in order to make a point. His text was Romans 1:16, "For I am not ashamed of the gospel, for it is the power of God for salvation to everyone who believes, to the Jew first and also to the Greek."

Dynamite comes from the Greek word for power (δύναμις). This is the dynamite that saves, rather than scatters and spatters. It has power to free and give burdened hearts the truth of the Gospel in such a manner that they will see themselves as the redeemed of God.

At the conclusion of the letter to the Church of Rome, the apostle Paul writes,

> Now to Him who is able to strengthen you according to my gospel and the preaching of Jesus Christ, according to the revelation of the mystery that was kept secret for long ages but has now been disclosed and through the prophetic writings has been made known to all nations, according to the command of the eternal God, to bring about the obedience of faith—to the only wise God be glory forevermore through Jesus Christ! Amen. (Romans 16:25–27)

These words highlight and emphasize the power of the Gospel at work as it is preached into the hearts and ears of the people. The words of Paul in Romans 1 and 16 are used by the South Dakota District President, Rev. Scott Sailer, on his stationery to encourage pastors to be faithful in their preaching of the glorious Gospel. It is his good way to enjoin pastors to keep the main thing the main thing.

The word *Gospel* by its very definition means "Good News." The reformers explained it thus:

> The Gospel is properly a doctrine that teaches what a person should believe, so that he receives forgiveness of sins with God. In other words, it teaches that God's Son, our Lord Christ, has taken upon Himself and borne the Law's curse and has atoned and paid for all our sins. Through Him alone we again enter into favor with God, receive

> forgiveness of sins through faith and are delivered from death and all the punishments of sins, and are eternally saved.
>
> Everything that comforts, that offers God's favor and grace to transgressors of the Law, is, and is properly called, the Gospel. It is a good and joyful message that God will not punish sins, but will forgive them for Christ's sake. (FC SD V 20–21)

The Gospel has power that flows from the Word. It is the same word that brought creation into being. The Gospel has power of restoration, rescue, redemption, and salvation.

The prophet Isaiah speaks of this power, saying,

> For as the rain and the snow come down from heaven and do not return there but water the earth, making it bring forth and sprout, giving seed to the sower and bread to the eater, so shall My word be that goes out from My mouth; it shall not return to Me empty, but it shall accomplish that which I purpose, and shall succeed in the thing for which I sent it. (Isaiah 55:10–11)

This is the glorious Gospel that changes our status in the sight of God. The most dramatic event in my ministry took place when I observed firsthand the power of the Gospel at work in the life of a former Satan worshiper. When the woman and I began to visit, I learned much about how she served Satan and the things she did. I challenged her to study the Word of God with me and see the difference. After a lengthy period of instruction, she became a follower of Jesus and confessed the faith. Her life changed forever. No longer a slave of Satan, she joyfully worshiped the only true God and Lord, Jesus Christ. This is the dynamite of the Gospel at work in people's lives. Not to scatter, but to gather; not to blow up, but to bless; not to put to death, but to make alive.

Article VII of the Augsburg Confession teaches about the harmonious proclamation of the Gospel—in all its articles. There are many facets of the Gospel. At the core, Jesus Christ died and rose for us sinners.

The Scriptures are given to us for the sake of the Gospel. Luther said that the Bible, "the writings of the prophets and the Law," is the "the swaddling clothes in which [Christ] was wrapped and the manger in which He was laid. . . . In these

He is wrapped, they contain Him, they speak only of Him and bear witness of Him" (AE 76:81–82). Theology is Christology. The better we understand the person and work of Jesus, the more clearly we shall see the Father, recognize the Spirit, and celebrate the God of love—the triune God.

Here are some of the fabulous facets of the Gospel. The Gospel in this sense is like a diamond.

- Jesus died for all (2 Corinthians 5:15).
- We are saved by grace alone through the gift of faith in Jesus (Ephesians 2:8–9).
- Jesus saves via Baptism (1 Peter 3:21).
- Jesus grants us His body and blood for the forgiveness of sins (Matthew 26:26–28).
- Jesus descended into hell with a vivified risen body to proclaim decisive victory over the devil in the devil's own backyard (1 Peter 3:18–22).
- Jesus perfectly fulfilled the Law for us (Matthew 5:17).
- Jesus' blood constantly cleanses us from all sin (1 John 1:7).
- Jesus sends to us the Holy Spirit through His Word and Sacrament (Matthew 28:16–20; Acts 2:38–40).
- Jesus' pardoning love makes us new creations (2 Corinthians 5:17).
- Jesus sends His Spirit to dwell in us and pray for us (Romans 8:11).
- Jesus prays for us 24/7 as our great High Priest (Romans 8:34).
- Jesus fulfilled all the ancient prophecies perfectly in order to make salvation possible (Acts 10:43).

- Jesus dwells within us in love (Galatians 2:20).

- In love, in Christ, God planned our salvation before the world began (Ephesians 1:3–5).

- Jesus will grant to us a new, restored, forever-young body (Philippians 3:20–21).

- Jesus works everything together for our good (Romans 8:28).

- Christ appeared to Abraham, bringing about a miracle birth to prepare the way for the creation of a great spiritual nation (Genesis 18).

- Christ wrestled with and blessed Jacob (Genesis 32:22–32).

- Jesus reveals to us the love of God the Father (John 14:9–11).

- Through the gift of faith in Jesus and Baptism, we become members of Abraham's family (Galatians 3:26–29).

- Jesus is the Suffering Servant Isaiah foretold who would die and rise for us (Isaiah 53).

The Gospel-centered pastor takes Acts 10:43 seriously and sees Christ throughout the Scriptures and proclaims all the articles of the Gospel. This is our power!

These are just some of the fabulous facets of the Gospel. A preacher will try to bring out these facets in harmonious manner so there are no contradictions and there is no watering down of the Gospel. No additives. Only Jesus, Jesus only! Jesus did it all. "Paid in full—It is finished!" declares one more fabulous facet of the Gospel.

The Perils of Preaching

It has been five hundred years since the fuse for the Reformation was lit on October 31, 1517, by an Augustinian monk, Martin Luther. One of the great blessings of the Reformation was that the role of preaching was elevated by Martin

Luther in what he preached and how he proclaimed the Gospel with passion. Before the Reformation, the sermon was often a moral lesson, short on Gospel and long on Law—similar to what we see being done today by many evangelical television preachers. The clergy were not well grounded in the Scriptures, and so the sheep were poorly fed—rather than eating on the green lush Word of the Gospel, they were eating dried-up straw.

Now we have gone from Gutenberg to Google. Today, technology overwhelms people with information and underwhelms them with Gospel revelation. It is not uncommon in congregations today to see people texting other people during the sermon on subjects totally foreign to what is being proclaimed. The cyber age has shortened attention spans and deepened the challenge of the pastor to connect with the saints during the sermon. While there is still nothing new under the sun, a preacher today must marshal every good tool possible in service of the Gospel when he preaches. He must rely on the Holy Spirit's power to use him in spite of himself for the sake of the Gospel and the benefit of the saints.

Luther knew firsthand the perils of preaching in his day. Most preachers are unaware that Luther suffered such deep burnout in the ministry that he boycotted the pulpit in 1530. He abruptly quit preaching, and for nine months, he refused to mount the pulpit. He had had it. He was totally fed up with "the swine of Wittenberg" and their "ho-hum" attitude toward the grace of God.

Maybe it was because the average German male drank eight beers a day in Wittenberg. After all, there were nearly 180 personal breweries in Wittenberg in those days, in a town of 240 households. The Germans drank a good deal of beer, in part, because the water was so bad. Perhaps this reality made the work of the Holy Spirit through the Gospel more sobering than usual, taking longer to brew.

Certainly, there is the age-old problem of people taking the Gospel for granted (even we do). At first, people are so excited, so thrilled, so joyful, and then the world begins to distract them. People can lose their first love in marriage, but also in their relationship to their bridegroom, Jesus Christ. To the Church at Ephesus, Christ said, "Repent, and do the works you did at first" (Revelation 2:5).

It is salutary for pastors and parishioners to learn from Luther's 1530 crisis. Before it, Luther had been preaching sometimes four sermons a day and over two hundred forty sermons a year. This heavy workload, together with all his other responsibilities, ill health, his father's death, and threats on his own life in the year of the Augsburg Confession, caused him to wear out and burn out. Luther suffered deep disappointment because so many of the people in Wittenberg seemed bored with God's Word and were lukewarm in response to Luther's passionate preaching on the goodness of God in Christ. Luther despaired. He needed to retreat and be repaired.

Luther experienced firsthand the perils of preaching. This is comforting. It is instructive to preachers today also to beware of the pitfalls of preaching. Modern preachers, too, can suffer burnout.

Luther himself summarized the perils of preaching. When he spoke of the unholy trio of "the devil, the world, and our own sinful flesh," he captured in a nutshell the peril that the pulpit produces. These three realities continually manufacture the vermin sermon with rat-infested legalism and lawlessness obscuring Christ and bringing to the world endless toxicity.

Here are some of the perils of preaching on the part of the preacher and the listener.

Peril 1: Poor Listening Skills

Going from Gutenberg to Google, people in our society have lost the ability to listen well. "Hear me out!" is the cry of the Spirit through the prophets. "Pay close attention" is the continual plea of the holy writers. For the pastor as well as the people in the pew, careful listening is a prelude to a burning-bush experience when one comes to hear the Spirit and the Good Shepherd proclaiming through the pastor the blessed Good News of our salvation.

Pastors should listen well to the people by visiting with the saints and learning from them their fears, anxieties, challenges, and needs. A pastor who is invisible among the members of the congregation he serves will be a pastor not visible in the pulpit on the Lord's Day. A pastor with a tin ear to the voice of the people will not be able to join their real needs to the healing voice of the Good Shepherd.

Similarly, the laity do well to turn off their cell phones and turn their attention to the voice of Jesus speaking through the voice of their pastor. The saints and their pastor should be in dialogue on Sunday morning. If the listeners are paying close attention to the message, the pastor is paying close attention to their needs, and both listeners and pastor are paying close attention to the story of God's pardoning love in Christ, a Day of Pentecost will arise.

Peril 2: Lack of a Dominant Gospel Note

A good Lutheran sermon, that is, a good evangelical sermon, will have Law and Gospel preached side by side. The Law will kill. The Gospel will make alive.

The Law will slay. The Gospel will save. The Law will show us our rebellion. The Gospel will show us our Redeemer. In tandem, these two divine revelations bring necessary death and needed resurrection. But the dominant note of the sermon must be Gospel!

C. F. W. Walther, the American Luther, in Thesis XXV of *Law & Gospel*, wisely wrote, "You are not rightly distinguishing Law and Gospel in the Word of God if you do not allow the Gospel to predominate in your teaching."[4] In the same lecture, Walther enjoins pastors to make sure the Gospel is supreme. He asserted, "Jesus Christ was the marrow and substance of Paul's entire preaching, the golden thread that ran through all his sermons."[5]

Such an approach, Walther taught, would enable the pastor to "step up to your pulpit with joy."[6] It would also allow an unconverted guest in the service to have the opportunity to be converted—called by the Gospel. The temptation for pastors to allow the Law to be the dominant note is great, because on a short term, one can seemingly gain good external results. I have personally known a pastor who said to his blood-bought people during a sermon that they don't deserve the grace of God. In essence, this is true. We don't deserve the grace of God. That is a gift, as Paul reminds us in Ephesians 2:8–9. But the Law should not be the dominant note in the sermon. Such preaching will do great harm to the preacher as well as the parishioner in the pew.[7] Pastors do well to read *Law & Gospel* once a year. Parishioners also will find this book immensely insightful, comforting, and a conduit of joy so that they, like a good evangelical pastor, can be helpers of joy.

Peril 3: Failing to Work with the Original Languages

There are so many thrilling insights in the Greek New Testament and in the Hebrew and Aramaic Old Testament. Luther was a superb exegete. He translated the Bible from the original languages into the language of the people. The difference in working well with the original languages versus only the English is like the difference between watching a program on a black and white screen versus Blu-ray. The insight the verb tenses give, the vividness that arises from the original languages, and the beauty of the Bible in its spectacular repetition,

4 C. F. W. Walther, *Law & Gospel: How to Read and Apply the Bible*, ed. Charles P. Schaum (St. Louis: Concordia, 2010), 455.

5 Walther, *Law & Gospel*, 458.

6 Walther, *Law & Gospel*, 458.

7 Walther, *Law & Gospel*, 461.

rhythm, and rhyme is sublime. A humble, Christ-centered pastor working with the original languages will be surprised by joy and in turn bring to God's people added grace upon grace with a sharper sword. Consider these two quotes:

> The more a theologian detaches himself from the basic Hebrew and Greek text of Holy Scripture, the more he detaches himself from the source of real theology! And real theology is the foundation of a fruitful and blessed ministry.[8]

> In order that those who are not more familiar with it may have instruction and guidance for reading the Old Testament with profit, I have prepared this preface to the best of the ability God has given me. I beg and really caution every pious Christian not to be offended by the simplicity of the language and stories frequently encountered there, but fully realize that, however simple they may seem, these are the very words, works, judgments, and deeds of the majesty, power, and wisdom of the most high God. For these are the Scriptures which make fools of all the wise and understanding, and are open only to the small and simple, as Christ says in Matthew 11[:25]. Therefore dismiss your own opinions and feelings, and think of the Scriptures as the loftiest and noblest of holy things, as the richest of mines which can never be sufficiently explored, in order that you may find that divine wisdom which God here lays before you in such simple guise as to quench all pride. Here you will find the swaddling cloths and the manger in which Christ lies, and to which the angel points the shepherds [Luke 2:12]. Simple and lowly are these swaddling cloths, but dear is the treasure, Christ, who lies in them. (AE 35:236)

Here are a couple examples of the use of the languages and the nuances they reveal:

My parents came to the United States from Israel for the first time for my wedding. I took them around to show them different sights and sounds of the town we lived in. A neighbor lady made beautiful dolls out of pheasant feathers. We stopped at our neighbor's shop, and she showed us what she had created.

8 Heinrich Bitzer, ed., *Light on the Path: Daily Scripture Readings in Hebrew and Greek* (Grand Rapids: Baker, 1982), 10.

She also informed us that she had more items at her house if my parents would like to see them. They agreed. My future in-laws were also with us. However, my father-in-law chose not to go; instead, he would wait for us. We said we would be back in twenty to thirty minutes. Unfortunately, we were gone for over two hours. When my mother saw my father-in-law sitting at the steps waiting for us, she saw his irritation and said, "Nabil, if someone touched your father-in-law's nose, he would bleed." She could read the signs.

In the Book of Numbers, we have these words: "The Lord is slow to anger and abounding in steadfast love" (Numbers 14:18). But the Hebrew literally means God has not gotten angry. Because, in the words of my mother's colloquialism, if He had, He would have bled. The wrath over the sin of humanity would have reached His nostrils, and He would have unleashed His venom on us. That is what my mother meant.

By the use of the original language, we see God's clear revelation of who He is and what He does for us sinners. The words tell us what a loving and gracious God we have. He is not easily angered. He is patient with us and desires to teach us His unfathomable grace, which He gives freely. To put it another way, when Moses was led by the Holy Spirit to write these words: "The Lord is slow to anger and abounding in steadfast love," he made known to us the will of God. His desire to have all come to a knowledge of the truth and be saved is of prime importance.

In 1 Corinthians 15:3–4, the apostle Paul declares, "For I delivered to you as of first importance what I also received: that Christ died for our sins in accordance with the Scriptures, that He was buried, that He was raised on the third day in accordance with the Scriptures." In his careful use of the Greek grammar, the apostle is showing through the use of the perfect tenses that there is ongoing and continuous power at work in the bodily resurrection of Jesus from the dead. Jesus' resurrection is not merely a mighty past event. The same power that raised Jesus from the dead is at work in every Baptism (1 Peter 3:21), and in the Lord's Supper (1 Corinthians 10:16), and in the preaching of the Gospel (Romans 1:16). The preacher gets to dish this out to the saints in the pews.

Peril 4: Using Complex Language

Preaching with charity means preaching with clarity. Preaching with clarity means using simple language in service of the Gospel. When I left the seminary for my first call, I visited with the pastor who had encouraged me to study for the

Office of the Ministry. His words of advice were precious and made a profound impact on my ministry. He said, "Brother Nabil, now that you have graduated from the seminary, remember to speak to your people at their level. This way, all people in the congregation will understand your message. Amen!"[9] I have taken his advice to heart and applied it in my ministry to the saints I have been privileged to serve so that the gates of hell will not prevail against them.

Luther himself sought to preach to children, to the unlearned, to the common person. He had a knack of preaching simple sermons that taught deep truths. He loved, in particular, preaching on the Gospel of John, for this Gospel taught profound truths in simple language. This Gospel greatly influenced Luther's preaching style.

Peril 5: The Elijah Syndrome

In 1 Kings 19, we have the story of a tired and tattered prophet and preacher, Elijah. Distant from the consolations of brother prophets, physically tapped out, and depressed from a flight from the theology of the cross, Elijah wanted out of the ministry as well as this life. The poor man was like many preachers in the pulpit and people in the pew today. Overwhelmed and under-rested!

All too often today, we have beleaguered, exhausted pastors preaching to "weary and heavy-laden" members. The life-giving message of the Gospel when delivered in a death-giving fashion to parishioners is not a good meeting of the minds, nor spirit. By the mercies of the One whose love refreshes us, rejuvenates us, and restores us in Jesus Christ, people and pastors must encourage one another to avoid Elijah syndrome.

The Letter to the Hebrews, likely a sermon, was preached to a congregation suffering sagging attendance (10:25), and its people were moving about with drooping hands and weak knees (12:12). As Thomas Long put it, "They are tired—tired of serving the world, tired of worship, tired of Christian education, tired of being peculiar and whispered about in society, tired of the spiritual struggle, tired of trying to keep their prayer life going, tired even of Jesus."[10]

It is ironic how we who believe so strongly in salvation by grace and not by works can easily work ourselves to death attempting to please man instead of

9 The Rev. Howard Shane, a dear friend of mine and my former pastor while attending Our Redeemer Lutheran Church, Sioux Falls, South Dakota, encouraged me to enter the ministry and had a great influence on me regarding what it really means to be a pastor. He has shaped me to be the man of God I am today.

10 Thomas G. Long, *Hebrews*, Interpretation: A Bible Commentary for Teaching and Preaching (Louisville: Westminster John Knox Press, 1997), 3.

God. By grace, we must take care to avoid Elijah syndrome and find ways not to let the wearying agenda of the world grind us into a self-justification lifestyle. For pastors, staying in touch with pastoral conferences where pastors meet and stay anchored in the Word daily will be most salutary. Continuing education is also a refresher on so many levels. Only a pastor with a well-rested body, soul, and spirit can deliver the life-giving message of a living Savior in a life-giving manner to a tired and weary people in the pew.

Peril 6: Procrastination

How vital it is to get to the sermon early. Pastors who wait too long to prepare their sermon will encounter far more anxiety. Also, a sermon begun early has the benefit of a pastor correlating through the whole week all kinds of useful information that can be used in the sermon. Along the way in the homiletical gestation process, the pastor can share with the saints the meaning of his text, the central truth he has mined from it. When he does, he will find that the laity often give wonderful specific examples suitable and helpful for the sermon to provide rubber-hits-the-road wheels to make the sermon even more concrete and less abstract. Preparing a sermon in advance enables the pastor to take words and turn them into pictures rather than delivering a half-baked sermon.

Peril 7: Forgetting the Message of the Cross!

It is so easy to slip into a theology of glory. We yearn for heaven on earth. Members want to see big numbers. People want to drag into the present some of the good-old heyday memories of the 1950s when churches were growing. However, living in a postmodern age when Christianity is increasingly met with more and more hostility, we need to recall our strength; a theology of the cross will bring comfort and consolation to all weary travelers in the wilderness of life.

God's deepest demonstration of His love and power and glory was the death of His beloved Son upon the cross. To an ancient church living in postmodern conditions in a place called Corinth, St. Paul wrote, "We preach Christ crucified" (1 Corinthians 1:23). This message, joined with the good news of the bodily resurrection of the Lord Jesus (1 Corinthians 15:3–4), is ever to be the core and center of our preaching.

Jesus' passion is to be our passion; His mercy is to be our mercy and His love our love. When it isn't, we have forfeited a marvelous opportunity to preach Christ crucified and the fruit that His supreme sacrifice provided for condemned sinners in need of rescuing from eternal death and damnation. The whole reason we have forty days of Lent is to study the details of the message of the cross and the infinite love of God in flesh made manifest. If this is not the core of our preaching, we are most to be pitied.

Peril 8: Failure to Be in the Word

So often we pastors are like starved cooks. We dispense God's Word to others in a sermon or Bible study. We continually offer up portions of the Bread of Life—the milk and meat—in our preaching and teaching. However, we fail to partake of it ourselves in daily Scripture reading and devotions, and we are the poorer for it—in life and in the pulpit. The public person must be a private person or we will not be good in public. And above all, we must hide away with God's Word so that we, too, can encounter the Burning Bush through His living Word to be equipped for every good work.

It is a sad truth, but many a hardworking pastor will tell you it was not until retirement that he got a chance to study the Bible more diligently. "I never read the whole Bible through until I retired," lamented one pastor. The demands of their office and the press of requests often distract pastors from a well-rounded reading of God's Word. On the other hand, pastors who saturate their minds and marinate their souls in the daily devotional study of God's Word will find their preaching able to appropriate from the fullness of Scripture in a more meaningful and powerful manner.

There are many other perils of preaching not listed above. Luther himself often felt he was a failure for some of the sermons he delivered. He once said, "I have often been disgusted with myself when I came from the pulpit."[11] But this was Luther's honest way of asserting he was mindful of the great responsibility given with the privilege of preaching—the life-giving and life-changing Word of God.

The Privilege of Preaching

St. Paul also felt the high heavenly privilege in preaching the Gospel. In Ephesians 3:8, he writes of being "the very least of all the saints," yet God gave him grace to proclaim to the Gentiles the unfathomable riches of Christ. Paul, who encountered the risen Lord on the road to Damascus, who saw the outskirts of paradise, who was called to be an apostle, could never get over the privilege that

11 *Four Hundred Years: Commemorative Essays on the Reformation of Dr. Martin Luther and Its Blessed Results, in the Year of the Four-hundredth Anniversary of the Reformation*, ed. W. H. T. Dau (St. Louis: Concordia, 1917), 205.

he, the chief of sinners, was called to preach about the length, height, breadth, and depth of God's love (Ephesians 3:17–19). He saw the importance of this message in making dead people alive by the power of the Gospel. For only the Gospel works salvation (Ephesians 2:1–10) and equips the saints with the full armor of God (Ephesians 6:10–18).

For pastors, it is also a privilege. By the calling of Christ through His congregations, we are blessed to proclaim the most important message to the world. Through the preached Gospel, we are graced with the privilege to impact lives for all eternity. Through the preached Gospel, we make special friends for all eternity (Luke 16:9).

For people in the pew, hearing the Gospel is also a privilege. All of us yearn for true love, significance, and security. Only through the Gospel story of Christ's love are we able to know we are loved, we have significance in life, and we have security through the powerful unbreakable promises of the risen Savior. The details of His redemptive story enrich lives, enhance lives, and save lives so that we might become complete and righteous humans in the way that only God's love in Christ can bring about. The privilege of encountering the Burning Bush through a Law-Gospel sermon rooted in Christ beckons us to see the glory God gives whenever we allow the Spirit through Word and Sacrament to bring to us rich resurrection realities. By preaching that is rooted in Christ and anchored in His perfect saving work on our behalf, we carry out a sacred duty with an awesome responsibility.

I, as a servant of the Most High God, am privileged to share the Good News in a word—a sermon. A sermon is an audible meal written by the Holy Spirit to be delivered by His servant, the called pastor. This feast is prepared not for the palate but for the eardrum! It is received from the pulpit just as the communicant receives the very body and blood of the crucified and risen Christ at the altar.

The privilege of preaching is sharing the message of grace that travels to the ear. This feast flows to the heart, bringing with it the soul-feeding comfort and strength that is found only in the forgiveness of sins, which is the gift of faith. The divine speech is intended to be heavenly food for hungry souls who are walking and wandering in this wilderness to sustain them throughout their daily walk. As the saints are gathered by the Holy Spirit in the presence of Jesus around His altar, they receive by faith what they need—to hear again and again that they are loved, cared for, forgiven, and greatly blessed by the God who gives His unmerited grace in Christ, our Savior. With this blessed meal, there is the guarantee from Christ Himself that the gates of hell will not prevail against the Church.

When my father-in-law was dying, the last time I saw him, he said, "Nabil, my body is getting weaker and weaker. But my spirit is getting stronger. I thank my Savior for His Word that brings me comfort in the face of death. I will not see you again this side of heaven, but look forward to seeing you in heaven." Within three weeks, he was with the Lord. What a testimony to the mighty power of God's Word in the lives of His people. This is what the publisher of the Good News is sent by God to accomplish—to reveal God's purpose for the lives of His people.

For this reason, a caring, loving undershepherd works joyfully and faithfully to put before the saints the finest food the Savior offers. Weekly he seeks the counsel of the Holy Spirit to help him prepare a meal that will feed those who are hungry and remove the burdens of those who are troubled.

Richard Caemmerer stated, "The preacher works for God. God is making bare His holy arm. He is speaking His Word to people. He is summoning them to repentance. He is life and peace to them. He proposes to do this through His servant who speaks for Him. The preacher says words; but they are to be the Word of God."[12]

It is truly a great blessing for a pastor to offer the goods that Jesus gives to His beloved—forgiveness of sins, peace, comfort, love, and light—goods the Savior dishes out to help them be men and women of God during their earthly pilgrimage. As Caemmerer emphasized, "'It pleased God through the folly of what we preach to save those who believe' (1 Corinthians 1:21). These words of St. Paul suggest that preaching is God's own act of rescuing men from death. It is God's saving Word to men."[13]

As pastors, it is the highest honor to share the Word of the living God with His blood-bought children, whom we are to nurture and care for. These are not simply words that we are given to preach, but words that change our status before God for eternity. They are His words, given to your lips, dear pastor and people.

Our precious, baptized, redeemed, forgiven, blood-bought, and heaven-bound people are being attacked from every front. They are burdened; and at times, Satan plants the seed of doubt in their hearts, which challenges them not to believe the message that God loves them unconditionally. Therefore, the message of the sermon ought not confuse but clarify. Indeed, it ought to clearly

---

12 Richard R. Caemmerer, *Preaching for the Church* (St. Louis: Concordia, 1959), 18–19.

13 Caemmerer, *Preaching for the Church*, 3.

speak only Christ, Christ only and always. It ought not burden but bless. It ought not damn but deliver. It ought not be for entertainment but for vivification of dead people so that they might live under the Rock Eternal and drink from the fountain of grace.

The preacher has the privilege to serve as a mouthpiece of the living God. To be the lips of Jesus and the voice of the Spirit is amazing. This privilege, joined with Christ's passion, moves the preacher to work hard to deliver faithfully the most important news in the universe. Thomas Long captures well my internal joy:

> To be a preacher is to be entrusted with the task of speaking the one word that humanity most urgently and desperately needs to hear, the glad tidings of God's redemption through Jesus Christ. To be a preacher is to be a midwife of the word. . . . Indeed, we do not create the word; we do not establish the time of its arriving; we cannot eliminate the labor pains that surround it; but we serve with gratitude at its coming and exclaim with joy at its birth.[14]

The privilege to preach the glad tidings of the riches of God's grace is such a joy. God brings a clean thing out of an unclean thing—by sheer grace. Being an ambassador for Christ is greater than being an ambassador for any king, president, or earthly ruler. What a privilege it is to herald the greatest news on earth!

Conclusion

Preaching is an amazing privilege given with eternal purpose and ongoing power. In a world that is quickly devolving, it signifies the glorious reappearing of the Savior. More than ever, the message of the Gospel alone provides us with faith based on Jesus' perfect work done for us.

---

14 Thomas G. Long, *The Witness of Preaching*, 3rd ed. (Louisville: Westminster John Knox Press, 2016), 13.

Study Questions

1. What three facets of the Gospel do you most enjoy your pastor accenting?

2. What are some perils in preaching that were not listed?

3. Is it possible to extend the benefits of a sermon preached by writing down its main point and keeping a record of the main points of every sermon for a whole year?

4. Would doing the above help us in our faith walk as it is easy for a sermon's message to be forgotten like a morning dream?

5. How might we pass along the message of a sermon to extend a Holy Spirit or burning-bush moment—through a letter, phone call, or a conversation over coffee, Facebook, Twitter, and others?

6. How might such a habit draw more people into the church for their joy and edification?

14 The Gates of Hell and Defending the Faith against Them

The Resurrection Changes Everything: A Twenty-First Century Apologia

Rev. Dr. Herbert C. Mueller Jr.

"Have no fear of them, nor be troubled, but in your hearts honor Christ the Lord as holy, always being prepared to make a defense [an apologia] to anyone who asks you for a reason for the hope that is in you; yet do it with gentleness and respect."

—1 PETER 3:14–16

There are two approaches to life, and only two. The universe is open, or it is closed. Life is a gift that comes from outside us, or life is a natural element that simply exists. There is an intelligence that wrote the information into our DNA, the code of life, or else it all arose of itself, organizing itself by chance. Is this universe—the only universe we know—fine-tuned for life, or is it one of a billion or more possible universes, and it just happens that this one is conducive to life?[1] Either an outside intelligence designed the makeup of all matter, placed the earth at just the right distance from the sun, with elements in just the right proportions to sustain life, or else we are all here as the result of a wildly improbable throw of the dice. There are no other viable possibilities.

1 The concept of the so-called multiverse is the pure speculation that, because the universe we live in is so complex and so finely tuned, there "must" be millions of other universes to cover all the possibilities. This idea, however, lacks any empirical evidence.

How would we know? How can we tell which option is true? Do we all just get to decide for ourselves? Does it make any difference which one we choose? Even if we do conclude there is an Intelligence, yes, a Creator, how shall we distinguish between competing versions of "His story"? Are there many avatars of the divine, as the Hindus claim? Or are we called to submit to the eternal will of Allah? What makes the Christian "story" stand out? If we do allow for the existence of the divine, how do we know our version is the right one?

Others say there are many paths, but those who travel any of them arrive at the same place at the end. Many years ago, I heard the parable of three rings. A father had three sons. Originally, he made a golden ring for his sons to share, but he soon had to make two more rings so that each son could have one. No one knew which was the original, but each one had a ring. That's how some explain the relationship between the three "Abrahamic" faiths: Judaism, Christianity, and Islam. Yet there are fundamental and profound differences between even these monotheistic faiths. For this reason, some give up altogether. "We will never know for sure," they say, "so just pick one." Or, increasingly, pick none of the above.

Yet, Christians believe there is a sign imprinted on all of history, if you are willing to consider it, something that rises above all else, as clear evidence of God's activity among humans. The mark of an open universe, this sign is quite unlike anything else. The eternal signpost, both of God's intervention in human affairs as well as His unchanging love for all people, is the cross and resurrection of Jesus Christ.

The Resurrection Changes Everything

The bodily resurrection of Jesus from the dead is ongoing assurance from God Himself that Jesus Christ is Lord and is worthy of our trust. In a world full of competing voices, the purpose of this essay is to boost your confidence in this heart of our faith, the resurrection of Jesus from the dead.[2] That's because *the resurrection changes everything*. Anyone who is unsure of the fact that Jesus

---

2 There are many good resources for apologetics and defenses (*apologia* is the Greek word in 1 Peter 3:15) of the reason for the hope that is within us. Several works consulted for this chapter include Timothy Keller, *Making Sense of God: An Invitation to the Skeptical* (New York: Viking Press, 2016)—a serious and well-reasoned book; Gregory Koukl, *The Story of Reality* (Grand Rapids: Zondervan, 2017)—written in an easy-to-read style, but quite thorough; Alex McFarland, *10 Answers for Atheists: How to Have an Intelligent Discussion about the Existence of God* (Minneapolis: Bethany House, 2012)—includes a great list of other resources regarding apologetics; and Eric Metaxas, *Everything You Always Wanted to Know about God (but Were Afraid to Ask): The Jesus Edition* (Ventura, CA: Regal, 2010)—breezy Q & A format, but well considered. These all provide (and there are many more) helpful arguments for the existence of God and for the resurrection, though they do not much reference the Means of Grace or the Sacraments. The Lutheranism 101 series from Concordia Publishing House is therefore also a "must." The books in this series explore various topics on what we as Lutherans believe and teach.

rose from the dead will also be less confident in other areas of apologetics and witness: creation versus evolution, the exclusive claims of Christianity, and so on. However, when a person is fully convinced that Jesus Christ did rise bodily from the dead and that He is alive today, ruling over all creation for the sake of His Church, such conviction shows a confidence in the Christian message that is not easily shaken. Certainty about the death and resurrection of Jesus and the reason for it—the boundless love of God—profoundly changes how that person thinks of others and approaches them. St. Paul testifies:

> For the love of Christ controls us, because we have concluded this: that one has died for all, therefore all have died; and He died for all, that those who live might no longer live for themselves but for Him who for their sake died and was raised.
>
> From now on, therefore, we regard no one according to the flesh. Even though we once regarded Christ according to the flesh, we regard Him thus no longer. (2 Corinthians 5:14–16)

Our adversary, the devil, would love to turn the cross and resurrection into just another fairy tale people give up when they become adults. Indeed, if there is no resurrection, the whole New Testament loses its meaning and becomes one of many religious myths. The Bible recognizes this when it says, "If Christ has not been raised, your faith is futile and you are still in your sins" (1 Corinthians 15:17). But if Christ truly did rise bodily from the dead, "The firstfruits of those who have fallen asleep" (1 Corinthians 15:20), that fact permeates everything else we know and believe about ourselves, the world, and God Himself. If the resurrection happened, the universe is not a closed system where material things and physical processes are the sum total of all things. Christianity is not one more religion (set of rules and regulations) among the many, but is the confession of faith that Jesus Christ is the world's only Savior and Redeemer. There is meaning and purpose, there is good and evil, sin and death, but also beauty, consciousness, true forgiveness, life itself as gifts given by God. Indeed, real life, eternal life, is found *only* in Him.

Faith Fits the Facts

The original source of the doubts that trouble our minds is the one who, from the beginning, has been asking, "Did God really say?" Yet, knowing Jesus has defeated the devil, Christians trust that there is no way "the gates of hell" (Matthew 16:18) can prevail against His Church. We do not have to retreat in the face of the "new atheists." We can have courage in our witness. The atheist cannot answer a simple question: why is there something rather than nothing? The Christian faith is not contrary to fact, but in reality fits the actual facts better than a materialistic view. The word of the cross and the resurrection of Jesus both call us to account before God and also provide the resolution to our deepest problems. All this, because the resurrection of Jesus actually happened. The message of the cross, while foolishness to the unbelieving world, is, because Jesus lives, the power of God for salvation for everyone who believes. St. Paul explains, "We preach Christ crucified, a stumbling block to Jews and folly to Gentiles, but to those who are called, both Jews and Greeks, Christ the power of God and the wisdom of God. For the foolishness of God is wiser than men, and the weakness of God is stronger than men" (1 Corinthians 1:23–25).

The bodily resurrection of Jesus Christ from the dead must be the heart of our "defense of the reason for the hope that is within us." This was true in the first century. It will be true in the twenty-first century. Christianity is not primarily a matter of moral behavior—although we do speak of Christian morals—but Christianity is about Christ, crucified for our sins and bodily raised from the dead according to the eyewitness testimony of Scripture. Without Christ, without His life, His death in our place, His resurrection, His ascension to the right hand of God, and His return to rescue us, there is no Church, no Christian faith. This might seem obvious in the extreme, but we must be clear about it. We are convinced that Christ Jesus, the eternal Son of the Father, true God and true man, is God's final and complete revelation of Himself in this world. We have come to know that His life and His death on the cross are the complete payment for the sins of the world—mine, yours, and everyone's. Christ made perfect satisfaction before God for all sinners. How do we know? Of this, God "has given assurance to all people by raising Him [Jesus] from the dead" (Acts 17:31).

Of course, if you have begun with the assumption that the universe is a closed system, you will find this "faith talk" to be mumbo-jumbo, an ancient superstition. "Science has proven there is no god," or "Scientific investigation will eventually explain how it all works, if it has not already."[3] Simply because the scientific method can do much to tell us how the universe works does not answer the question why there is something rather than nothing. That is a theological question that goes beyond the ability of science. Why, for example, does the universe give evidence of a beginning, as almost all scientists now acknowledge?[4] Why should the universe be comprehensible at all to us? The fact that it is understandable implies there is a Mind behind it. Why does the universe behave according to mathematical and physical laws that are knowable to us? Why are the properties of matter and the physics that govern those properties conducive to life? Why are the earth and solar system so finely tuned as to support and protect life?[5] Why does the universe contain information and conform to mathematics? The very DNA in every living cell consists of information coded in a language that is transferred whenever the cell multiplies. In every other case, for information to be added to a system, there must be an intelligence behind it. How did the information in our cells' DNA originate? Critics of Charles Darwin's theory of origins (i.e., "macro-evolution") point to examples of "irreducible complexity" at even the cellular level as evidence of intelligent design. We have not the space here to go into all of these debates, as fascinating as they are.[6] They do show, however, that it may be just as much a "leap of faith" (probably more!) to believe the universe arose by chance as it is to believe there is a divine intelligence behind it all. The idea that we must leave God out of our explanations of the universe is actually not true "science" but is a philosophical position one has taken before examining the evidence itself. The *assumption* "there is no God" rules out, even before one begins, any evidence that might point to an Intelligent Designer.

If, on the other hand, we allow that the universe is open, not closed, we are free to consider the evidence of design found throughout the creation. If our minds are not closed to the possibility, we are open to recognize that information

3 Such a statement assumes too much. Alex McFarland observes, "Absolute scientism, which puts ultimate value on empirical science, basically refutes itself, because it fails to acknowledge the limits and presuppositions of science. Absolute forms of scientism make claims about science that are not scientific, but philosophical in nature. . . . God's existence cannot be proven, so He doesn't exist" (*10 Answers for Atheists*, 44). See also Commission on Theology and Church Relations, *In Christ All Things Hold Together: The Intersection of Science and Christian Theology* (St. Louis: The Lutheran Church—Missouri Synod, 2015), 6ff, for further explanation of "scientism."

4 The most common theory is that the universe began with an instantaneous expansion of a singular point from which all matter and light have arisen, the so-called big bang. Many scientists at first resisted the idea because it posited a beginning, but the cosmological evidence is overwhelming. We say, of course! "God said, 'Let there be light,' and there was light" (Genesis 1:3). Scientific observation tells us there was a beginning, but we need Scripture to show us *God* is the reason for the beginning.

5 Keller, *Making Sense of God*, 219.

6 Michael J. Behe, *Darwin's Black Box: The Biochemical Challenge to Evolution* (New York: The Free Press, 1996), 39. "By *irreducibly complex* I mean a single system composed of several well-matched interacting parts that contribute to the basic function, wherein the removal of any one of the parts causes the system to effectively cease functioning."

added from outside the system may be evidence for an intelligent source. This accords with common sense. Nothing cannot produce something. There must be an actor, a cause. We know of no other chain of events without a beginning. As long as you do not beg the question by assuming God is not possible, then the fact that there is something, that there is a fine-tuning that supports life "makes much more sense in a universe in which there is a creator and designer."[7] This is what theologians call "the natural knowledge of God" written into nature, both in us and outside of us (see Romans 1:18–20).

Why do human beings have a sense of right and wrong, of good and evil? Scripture explains that something of God's moral standard remains written on the human heart (Romans 2:14–16). If God does not exist, where does that universal knowledge come from? How would it have "evolved"? This sense of moral obligation inherent in human beings is much more plausible in a universe created by a personal God to whom we are morally responsible and accountable. However, in a closed universe, where God is excluded, there is no real explanation beyond evolutionary speculation that it somehow enabled our ancestors to survive. But why should that be? The same can be asked of human consciousness and self-awareness, as well as our ability to comprehend the world and form ideas. To insist there must be an evolutionary or purely materialistic explanation is to assume there cannot be anything beyond what we can see. Again, that is a philosophical assumption, not a scientific fact. Concepts of art and of beauty, our ability to reason, to think, to speak, to be self-aware, to appreciate elegant music, to work with mathematics, to form ideas of justice and fairness, all make much more sense in a universe created and sustained by an intelligent, conscious, idea-making creator God.

These traditional arguments for the existence of God do not yet reveal the gracious nature of God or His desire to have a loving relationship with His human creatures. Nor do they explain the problems of evil, or why people suffer, or how our relationship to God may be restored. Suppose we do grant that God exists. Suppose we even grant that all people are responsible for their actions and are accountable to Him for how they live, good or evil. There is nothing uniquely Christian about such a conclusion. What makes the Christian worldview better? How do we defend against those who would say that another view is just as true? Present culture not only allows a place for every religious idea, but it also somehow has further decided that every variety of religion has equal (or no)

7 Keller, *Making Sense of God*, 219.

value. As a member on the fringes of my last parish told me, "Well, pastor, we're all trying to get to the same place, and who's to say which way is best?" "Coexist," the bumper sticker says. In this climate, the worst *faux pas* is to claim you have the right way, the real truth, and that others are wrong. Religious "pluralism" has become the new orthodoxy.

Enter the apostle Peter. He was hauled before the temple authorities to answer how he had healed a man lame from birth. They were "greatly annoyed because [Peter and John] were teaching the people and proclaiming in Jesus the resurrection from the dead" (Acts 4:2). When the authorities asked, "By what name did you do this?" (Acts 4:7), Peter did not equivocate, "Well, you can believe whatever you want, that's okay by me." He was clear: "Let it be known to all of you and to all the people of Israel that by the name of Jesus Christ of Nazareth, whom you crucified, whom God raised from the dead—by Him this man is standing before you well" (Acts 4:10). He went on to say, "And there is salvation in no one else, for there is no other name under heaven given among men by which we must be saved" (Acts 4:12). What gave Peter the right or authority to say that? Only this: the resurrection of Jesus, which was the reason the authorities were so annoyed with him in the first place! The resurrection was the inconvenient (to the authorities) evidence that God Himself was behind all this new activity.

Just days before, Peter had proclaimed before literally thousands of people on Pentecost:

> Men of Israel, hear these words: Jesus of Nazareth, a man attested to you by God with mighty works and wonders and signs that God did through Him in your midst, as you yourselves know—this Jesus, delivered up according to the definite plan and foreknowledge of God, you crucified and killed by the hands of lawless men. God raised Him up, loosing the pangs of death, because it was not possible for Him to be held by it. For David says concerning Him,
>
> "I saw the Lord always before me,
> for He is at my right hand that I may not be shaken; . . .
> For You will not abandon my soul to Hades,
> or let Your Holy One see corruption. . . ."

> This Jesus God raised up, and of that we all are witnesses. Being therefore exalted at the right hand of God, and having received from the Father the promise of the Holy Spirit, He has poured out this that you yourselves are seeing and hearing. . . . Let all the house of Israel therefore know for certain that God has made Him both Lord and Christ, this Jesus whom you crucified. (Acts 2:22–27, 32–33, 36; read also the whole chapter)

There is a pattern of proclamation here that shows up over and over in the Book of Acts.

I. **Prophecy is fulfilled in Jesus.**
II. **Jesus is attested to you by signs and wonders.**
III. **He was delivered up according to God's plan.**
IV. **You crucified Him.**
V. **But God raised Him up.**
VI. **Just as David prophesied that death could not hold Him.**
VII. **So God raised Him up from the dead.**
VIII. **Of that we are witnesses.**
IX. **God has made Him both Lord and Christ, this Jesus whom you crucified.**

What was the response? "When they heard this they were cut to the heart, and said to Peter and the rest of the apostles, 'Brothers, what shall we do?' And Peter said to them, 'Repent and be baptized every one of you in the name of Jesus Christ, for the forgiveness of your sins, and you will receive the gift of the Holy Spirit" (Acts 2:37–38).

In their proclamation, the apostles reflected Jesus' own claims. To know Him is to know God (John 8:19). To see Him is to see God (John 12:45). To receive Him is to receive God (Mark 9:37). Only through Him can anyone come to know God (Matthew 11:27; John 14:6). Only God forgives sins, and, yes, Jesus forgives sins (Mark 2:1–12). Jesus even takes on the divine name, "I am" (John 8:58), claiming thereby to be "Yahweh" Himself, who appeared to Moses in the burning bush (Exodus 3:14). People at the time knew exactly what He was saying, because they took up stones to kill Him for blasphemy.[8] Where did Jesus get this

8 See Keller, *Making Sense of God*, 238–39, for a more complete list.

authority? What is His proof? If the resurrection is a fable, a myth, something borrowed from pagan sources, these are empty claims. But if it's true? That changes everything!

Paul's Testimony in Athens

We find another prime example of the apostolic pattern of witness in Paul's speech before a crowd of skeptics in Athens. He began with something they knew:

> Paul, standing in the midst of the Areopagus, said: "Men of Athens, I perceive that in every way you are very religious. For as I passed along and observed the objects of your worship, I found also an altar with this inscription: 'To the unknown god.' What therefore you worship as unknown, this I proclaim to you." (Acts 17:22–23)

Having established a connection with his hearers, Paul moved toward the heart of his message:

> The God who made the world and everything in it, being Lord of heaven and earth, does not live in temples made by man, nor is He served by human hands, as though He needed anything, since He Himself gives to all mankind life and breath and everything. And He made from one man every nation of mankind to live on all the face of the earth, having determined allotted periods and the boundaries of their dwelling place, that they should seek God, and perhaps feel their way toward Him and find Him. (Acts 17:24–27)

God is the source of everything. The reason there is *not* nothing is God. All human beings, made by God from one man, are equal before God. God determines where they live. God desires that they seek Him.

> Yet He is actually not far from each one of us, for "In Him we live and move and have our being"; as even some of your own poets have said, "For we are indeed His offspring." Being then God's offspring, we ought not to think that the divine being is like gold or silver or stone, an image formed by the art and imagination of man. (Acts 17:27–29)

With the premise established, Paul testifies to the resurrection.

> The times of ignorance God overlooked, but now He commands all people everywhere to repent, because He has fixed a day on which He will judge the world in righteousness by a man whom He has appointed; and of this He has given assurance to all by raising Him from the dead. (Acts 17:30–31)

Here it is. This makes Christianity different from all other religious systems. Jesus Christ is the one by whom God commands repentance—a complete change of mind and heart. Jesus Christ is also the one by whom God will hold us all accountable, for He will come to be the judge of the living and the dead. Why? Because Jesus is the One who rose from the dead. This message is both inclusive and exclusive. It is for "all people everywhere." No one is left out. Yet it is also completely exclusive. There is only one way to come in—repentance. You have to admit you need Him, and admit you are dying and need resurrection.

God's Path to Us

God created human beings in His image, good and perfect, to know Him. But beginning with the first man, Adam, all humanity is in rebellion against God. We do not do as we ought and we also actively sin against God's moral commands. Consequently, human life is broken. We experience suffering, and everyone will die. Death is not original to God's creation but is the reproach that covers all people (see Isaiah 25:6–9). We could never free ourselves from this predicament, but God Himself has acted. We could never follow any path to God, but God has made His path to us. He took on our human flesh in Jesus Christ. He kept His own commands in our place. He received in Himself the punishment we deserve for our sins.

> Since therefore the children share in flesh and blood, He Himself likewise partook of the same things, that through death He might destroy the one who has the power of death, that is, the devil, and deliver all those who through fear of death were subject to lifelong slavery. . . . Therefore He had to be made like His brothers in every respect, so that He might become a merciful and faithful high priest

> in the service of God, to make propitiation for the sins of the people. (Hebrews 2:14–15, 17)

To "make propitiation" is to "take the rap," to endure in our place all the wrath we deserve because of our sin. Therefore, when God raised Jesus from the dead, He promised to raise to eternal life all who by faith find their refuge in Him. Jesus Himself testified: "For this is the will of My Father, that everyone who looks on the Son and believes in Him should have eternal life, and I will raise him up on the last day" (John 6:40). And again, Jesus said, "I am the resurrection and the life. Whoever believes in Me, though he die, yet shall he live, and everyone who lives and believes in Me shall never die" (John 11:25–26). By His Spirit in His Word, we call Him Lord (1 Corinthians 12:3). Now He promises, through the pen of His apostle,

> If we confess our sins, He is faithful and just to forgive us our sins and to cleanse us from all unrighteousness. If we say we have not sinned, we make Him a liar, and His word is not in us.
>
> My little children, I am writing these things to you so that you may not sin. But if anyone does sin, we have an advocate with the Father, Jesus Christ the righteous. He is the propitiation for our sins, and not for ours only but also for the sins of the whole world. (1 John 1:9–2:2)

None of this is our doing. Jesus took the whole load on Himself. It is a gift received by faith. It can never be earned but is given freely to all who believe.

> What does it say? "The word is near you, in your mouth and in your heart" (that is, the word of faith that we proclaim); because, if you confess with your mouth that Jesus is Lord and believe in your heart that God raised Him from the dead, you will be saved. For with the heart one believes and is justified, and with the mouth one confesses and is saved. For the Scripture says, . . . "everyone who calls on the name of the Lord will be saved." (Romans 10:8–11, 13)

And how does the Spirit work faith in us that we actually do call on the name of the Lord?

> So faith comes from hearing, and hearing through the word of Christ. (Romans 10:17)

> For since, in the wisdom of God, the world did not know God through wisdom, it pleased God through the folly of what we preach to save those who believe. For Jews demand signs and Greeks seek wisdom, but we preach Christ crucified. (1 Corinthians 1:21–23)

Even now, God is so abundant with His grace and His desire to have us for Himself that in Holy Baptism, He unites us with Christ in His death and resurrection (Romans 6:1–6), and in Holy Communion, He feeds us with His own body and blood (1 Corinthians 11:23–26). His Word does what it says, actually delivering what it promises.

Philosophical reasoning can prepare our minds for the divine, but how does God show that He is *for us*? Only in the sign of the cross, where Christ gave Himself for us. "I have been crucified with Christ," St. Paul writes. "It is no longer I who live, but Christ who lives in me. And the life I now live in the flesh I live by faith in the Son of God, who loved me and gave Himself for me" (Galatians 2:20). God for you is revealed only in Jesus, dead on the cross. But what distinguishes Jesus on the cross from the other thousands crucified by the Romans? He is God in the flesh, and He has risen from the dead. Faith in Christ will be counted as righteousness (as was Abraham's faith [Genesis 15:1–6]) for all "who believe in Him who raised from the dead Jesus our Lord, who was delivered up for our trespasses and raised for our justification" (Romans 4:24–25). This is why there is salvation in no other, for no other has risen from the dead. The resurrection changes everything!

But what if it didn't really happen? What if the resurrection is a story they made up? a myth borrowed from pagan mystery cults? some kind of group hallucination? a sinister plot? a fraud? The resurrection has been called all of that and more, and if any one of these lies of the devil were to prove true, the whole Christian enterprise falls to pieces. One of the greatest proponents of the resurrection, St. Paul recognizes exactly this in writing:

> If there is no resurrection of the dead, then not even Christ has been raised. And if Christ has not been raised, then our preaching is in vain and your faith is in vain. We are even found to be misrepresenting

> God, because we testified about God that He raised Christ, whom He did not raise if it is true that the dead are not raised. For if the dead are not raised, not even Christ has been raised. And if Christ has not been raised, your faith is futile and you are still in your sins. (1 Corinthians 15:13–17)

Our defense of the reason for our hope always comes down to this: Jesus lives! If the resurrection truly happened, then what the Scriptures say is true. If not, Christian faith would be what its critics say it is—a childish remnant of our superstitious past. But if Jesus really did bodily rise from the dead, that changes everything. Jesus does have a legitimate claim on me, and on you.

Our Hidden Motives

There may be a hidden motive in those who reject the reality of Jesus' resurrection in favor of some other explanation. As we have seen, if Jesus did rise, all people are called to repent. Everyone needs Him, because we are all dying as a result of sin. But what if I don't want to repent? What if I'm enjoying my life right now, even enjoying my sin? What if I don't feel the need to change or if I think the Christian message is simply beyond belief? Or what if I'm offended by the horrible nature of the cross, or if I am comfortable in my present situation? What then? The natural reaction is to make excuses as to why I should not have to change. Spiritually, it means I hold Jesus at arm's length. If Jesus truly rose from the dead, He would show Himself, some have said. But because He hasn't appeared to me, He must be a fraud. You see, if Jesus is a legend and the resurrection a myth, such a person can go on much as he has before. If Jesus is considered a good man or even a great moral teacher, someone may even seek to emulate Him, but that doesn't necessarily require fundamental changes to one's life. Perhaps a few adjustments might be needed, but nothing too radical. So they hold Jesus at arm's length by refusing to consider a real resurrection. A good man, yes, but God in the flesh? Crucified for our sins and raised for our justification? That's too far-fetched.

At the same time, most people do have this nagging feeling, once they get to know a little of Him, that they have to do something with Jesus. Some, therefore, will remake Him in their own image, mold Him to what they want Him to be. Everyone who attempts, for instance, to go beyond the biblical witness to find "the real Jesus" ends up describing a reflection of themselves or what they think Jesus should be.

The question remains, like a thought that won't let go—what if it's true? What if He did rise from the dead? Then all the rest follows. Then Jesus is the Son of God and the only name under heaven by which we can be saved. Then Jesus does reveal God to us, Father, Son, and Holy Spirit. Then God does desire us for Himself, loving us with an everlasting love. Then we are called to die to our sin so that He might raise us to new life. For if Jesus lives, it is proof God does want to restore us, revive and forgive us, that He has an eternal claim on us. We are back on the shores of the Sea of Galilee, where the living Lord Jesus met Peter and Andrew, James and John, in their fishing boats to say, "Follow Me!" And He is just as alive today, seeking to meet us where we are, to say also to us, "Follow Me. Follow Me all the way through death to eternal life." "Truly, truly, I say to you," Jesus said, "whoever hears My word and believes Him who sent Me has eternal life. He does not come into judgment, but has passed from death to life" (John 5:24).

Reasons for a Bodily Resurrection

Let's take a closer look. We have to summarize in some detail the physical and historical evidence for the resurrection. There's actually quite a lot, and, if you are ready to consider it, the evidence is quite clear and convincing. Once you eliminate all other possibilities, you are left with the conclusion that there is no explanation other than that it truly did happen. Indeed, it's quite impossible for it not to have happened.

First, *there were eyewitnesses.* Jesus was publicly crucified. Crowds of people, friend and foe alike, saw Him die. Besides that, the Romans were experts at putting people to death. The Roman historian Tacitus, writing in the late first century, informs his readers, "Christus, from whom the name [Christian] had its origin, suffered the extreme penalty during the reign of Tiberius at the hands of one of our procurators, Pontius Pilate."[9] This did not happen in a corner. The thing was known. Speculation of any plot to take Jesus down from the cross while still alive to revive Him later simply does not fit the evidence. He was dead. The Romans were efficient. The spear thrust reported in the Gospel of

9 Tacitus, *Annals* 15:44, quoted by Metaxas, *Everything You Always Wanted to Know about God*, 18. Metaxas quotes other Roman and Jewish sources outside the Bible: Josephus, Suetonius, Pliny the Younger, and others. These are well-known to historians and do establish early secular references to Christ.

John demonstrated He was already dead (John 19:34). That's also why this note in Mark's account is important:

> Joseph of Arimathea, a respected member of the council, who was also himself looking for the kingdom of God, took courage and went to Pilate and asked for the body of Jesus. *Pilate was surprised to hear that he should have already died.* And summoning the centurion, he asked him whether he was already dead. And when he learned from the centurion *that he was dead*, he granted the corpse to Joseph. (Mark 15:43–45, emphasis added)

Note that Joseph was a prominent individual, well-known. Note that Pilate was surprised Jesus was already dead, but specifically checked with the executioner to be sure. He was dead when they put Him in the tomb. Besides, because it belonged to someone important, many people would have known where the grave was. Matthew 27:66 tells us that they sealed the stone and set a guard just in case the disciples might try to steal His body and claim He rose from the dead. Given all this, it just doesn't fit the evidence for there to have been a plot to fake a resurrection. Plenty of people saw Him die and saw Him buried, stone-cold dead.

Three days later (in the Jewish manner of reckoning), some women began to claim the tomb was empty. Soon, other eyewitnesses saw Him alive. It is quite significant that the whole Christian faith hinges on an empty tomb and a missing body. Those facts are publicly verifiable. In the same basic location and the same time frame, Jesus was killed and buried. People began to claim that He rose from the dead. Such claims could easily have been proven false (and there were plenty with the motive to try), if someone would have come up with His dead body. The people in charge who wanted Jesus dead could have easily put a stop to what they saw as nonsense simply by producing a body. But they didn't. Because they couldn't. The tomb was empty. Everyone knew the tomb was empty. It was in a public place. Anyone could go and see for themselves.

When all this was written down in the Gospels, the Book of Acts, and the letters of Paul, it was not many decades or hundreds of years later; rather, many of those who saw Him, touched Him, heard Him, who were there when He showed Himself alive, were themselves still alive when the eyewitness testimony was written down. St. Luke describes how he carefully researched all the details to set down an orderly account (Luke 1:1–4). Matthew, Mark, and John were there.

They saw it all. But so did many others. If the Gospel writers got something wrong, other eyewitnesses could correct them. This is the point Paul makes in writing,

> I delivered to you as of first importance what I also received: that Christ died for our sins in accordance with the Scriptures, that He was buried, that He was raised on the third day in accordance with the Scriptures, and that He appeared to Cephas [Peter], then to the twelve. Then He appeared to more than five hundred brothers at one time, most of whom are still alive, though some have fallen asleep. Then He appeared to James, then to all the apostles. Last of all, as to one untimely born, He appeared also to me. (1 Corinthians 15:3–8)

This letter, a primary source, written about twenty to twenty-five years after the resurrection, is striking for several reasons. You will note that Jesus appeared to many different specific people, including five hundred or more who saw Him at the same time. Paul expressly states that many were still alive when he wrote. What does this mean? If you don't believe me, go talk to them, Paul is implying. They can tell you. They saw Him. Each of the four Gospel writers remembers different details—these are not contradictions, but indications there was no collusion between them. The records we have bear the characteristics of eyewitness testimony.

What is even more amazing is that the very first eyewitnesses were women. In that culture, no one considered the testimony of a woman to be reliable. So, not only is Jesus elevating women by appearing to them first, but also if the resurrection were a story concocted by men later, the last thing they would have done would have been to make the women of their group the first to see Him. This small detail is actually quite telling. In fact, when the women first came to the men to tell them they had seen the risen Lord, the whole thing seemed to them (the men!) to be "an idle tale, and they did not believe them" (Luke 24:11). But the reason all the Gospel writers have the women seeing Jesus first is because that's what happened. The women were the first eyewitnesses. Carefully considered, this fact increases the reliability of the Gospel record.

One more factor regarding the empty tomb is pertinent. Not only was it publicly known where the tomb was, but there had also even been a guard posted. But look what happened to the guard! When they saw the angel of the Lord roll away the stone to expose the empty tomb, Matthew reports they became as dead men (28:4). They themselves saw *why* the tomb was empty!

> Some of the guard went into the city and told the chief priests all that had taken place. And when they had assembled with the elders and taken counsel, they gave a sufficient sum of money to the soldiers and said, "Tell people, 'His disciples came by night and stole Him away while we were asleep.' And if this comes to the governor's ears, we will satisfy him and keep you out of trouble." So they took the money and did as they were directed. And this story has been spread among the Jews to this day. (Matthew 28:11–15)

So they had to be bribed to spread the story that while "we were not doing our jobs, the disciples came and stole the body." One does not normally have to be bribed to tell the truth, but generally one needs to be paid off to spread a lie.

In general, the accounts of the resurrection appearances of Jesus bear the mark of authenticity. Would the disciples to whom Jesus appeared on the way to Emmaus have admitted, "We just didn't recognize Him for the whole way," if it were not true? (See Luke 24:13–35.) Later that evening, when Jesus came through the locked doors to show Himself to the disciples, they behaved just as we might expect. They were afraid because they thought He was a ghost. But Jesus said,

> "Why are you troubled, and why do doubts arise in your hearts? See My hands and My feet, that it is I Myself. Touch Me, and see. For a spirit [a ghost] does not have flesh and bones as you see that I have." And when He had said this, He showed them His hands and His feet. And while they still disbelieved for joy and were marveling, He said to them, "Have you anything here to eat?" They gave Him a piece of broiled fish, and He took it and ate before them. (Luke 24:38–43)

Not only did Jesus identify Himself by His wounds, but He also ate—and ghosts don't eat. And there were at least ten there to see it. When Thomas (who was not there that night) refused to believe the others, Jesus came the next week to show Himself specifically to Thomas. Jesus said to him, "'Put your finger here, and see My hands; and put out your hand, and place it in My side. Do not disbelieve, but believe.' Thomas answered Him, 'My Lord and my God!'" (John

20:27–28). Not only do the disciples react just as we might expect, but also Jesus directly addresses any doubts they might have when they couldn't believe their eyes. In writing his Gospel, John is also aware of our needs: "Jesus did many other signs in the presence of the disciples, which are not written in this book; but these are written so that you may believe that Jesus is the Christ, the Son of God, and that by believing you may have life in His name" (John 20:30–31).

Now let's consider what happened to the disciples as a result of the resurrection. How about some "before" and "after" pictures?

Peter before: Yes, he loudly boasted of his loyalty even to the point of cutting off the ear of one of those who had come to arrest Jesus, but a short while later, accused by a slave girl of belonging to Jesus, he denies Him three times: "I don't know the man!" (see Mark 14:66–72).

Peter after: Standing before thousands, he proclaims, "This Jesus [whom you crucified] God raised up, and of that we all are witnesses" (see Acts 2:32, 36).

Peter, James, and John before: They fell asleep in the garden when Jesus had asked them to watch and pray (Mark 14:41).

Peter and John after: [Peter said,] "And now, brothers, I know that you acted in ignorance, as did also your rulers. But what God foretold by the mouth of all the prophets, that His Christ would suffer, He thus fulfilled. Repent therefore, and turn back, that your sins may be blotted out, that times of refreshing may come from the presence of the Lord, and that He may send the Christ appointed for you, Jesus" (Acts 3:17–20).

"Now when they saw the boldness of Peter and John, and perceived that they were uneducated, common men, they were astonished. And they recognized that they had been with Jesus. But seeing the man who was healed standing beside them, they had nothing to say in opposition. But when they had commanded them to leave the council, they

> conferred with one another, saying, 'What shall we do with these men? For that a notable sign has been performed through them is evident to all the inhabitants of Jerusalem, and we cannot deny it. But in order that it may spread no further among the people, let us warn them to speak no more to anyone in this name.' So they called them and charged them not to speak or teach at all in the name of Jesus. But Peter and John answered them, 'Whether it is right in the sight of God to listen to you rather than to God, you must judge, for we cannot but speak of what we have seen and heard'" (Acts 4:13–20).

All the disciples before: They argued who is the greatest but then ran away at the first sign of trouble (Luke 22:24–27; Mark 14:50).

All of the disciples after, when the authorities were jealous: "They arrested the apostles and put them in the public prison. But during the night an angel of the Lord opened the prison doors and brought them out, and said, 'Go and stand in the temple and speak to the people all the words of this Life.' And when they heard this, they entered the temple at daybreak and began to teach" (Acts 5:18–21).

What changed them? What gave them this courage? How did these frightened rabbits become bold witnesses? What moved them to suffer all rather than deny Jesus? Yes, there were times when even Peter needed correction by Paul, but not ever because any of them changed their mind about the resurrection. They all were killed rather than change their testimony (except for John, who lived to old age). Could a fraud, a hallucination, a plot surrounding a lie have that power? No, they were eyewitnesses. They were there, as John later wrote:

> That which was from the beginning, which we have heard, which we have seen with our eyes, which we looked upon and have touched with our hands, concerning the word of life—the life was made manifest, and we have seen it, and testify to it and proclaim to you the eternal

> life, which was with the Father and was made manifest to us—that which we have seen and heard we proclaim also to you. (1 John 1:1–3)

Suppose for a moment, however, that they did make it up. Imagine one of the disciples in that circumstance in a dialogue with his executioner.

Executioner: Burn this pinch of incense to Caesar to worship him as Lord, and I will let you go. Otherwise, you are going to die just like your so-called Savior, Jesus.

Disciple (thinking): Hmm . . . What should I do? We stole the body, hid it, and made it all up. Now I'm in a spot. It's been a good run, I guess . . .

Executioner: Hurry up!

Disciple: Okay, okay. No, I won't burn the incense. I will not give up my Savior.

Executioner: You've made your choice.

Disciple: So be it.

Such a conversation is absurd on the face of it. All the disciples went to their deaths absolutely convinced Jesus was alive and that Jesus would raise them from death as well. None of them ever changed their story. They were not deluded. They did not make it up. Their testimony of the resurrection is true.

Then there is the case of Saul turned Paul. Saul was a well-known young man from a good family who studied under one of the most highly regarded rabbis in history. Saul was far more advanced than his contemporaries. The high priest had given him authority to arrest these blasphemers, these upstart followers of Jesus. Suddenly, while on his way to arrest more, he threw it all away. He gave up his former life and joined his enemies, even changing his name from Saul to Paul. He left behind his reputation, his social standing, and everything he had worked his whole life to have. He set it aside in favor of traveling thousands of miles, subjecting himself to lashings, stoning and beating to the brink of death, shipwrecks, starvation, imprisonment, all so that he could tell people that Jesus is the Son of God, crucified and raised from the dead to take away their sins. So he did this because he was bored with his nice life? Not a chance! No, as he told everyone who would listen until they chopped off his head for doing so, he did it because he had met Jesus, risen from the dead. It defies belief to think he would have made such a change for the sake of a lie. Only a real resurrection—and Paul's having witnessed the resurrected Christ—could have effected such an about-face (see Acts 9:1–22; 22:1–21; 26:12–23).

Next we have the explosive growth of Christianity in the years immediately following Jesus' death. During His three-year career, Jesus had many followers, numbering in the thousands. He fed them, healed them, drove out demons, even raised the dead. One would think that His death would have killed His movement. In fact, there were others in that time—messianic pretenders who rose up, gained a following for a time—but the crowds melted away when they were killed. But Jesus was different. Within weeks of His death, there were three thousand followers, then five thousand, then countless more. All of this in the same locale where Jesus had been killed *and all within weeks of His death.* Why? What happened? The only possible explanation is that Jesus truly rose from the dead. One of the authorities, when they were deciding what to do with the apostles and their testimony of the resurrection, made this point quite forcefully:

> A Pharisee in the council named Gamaliel, a teacher of the law held in honor by all the people, stood up and gave orders to put the men outside for a little while. And he said to them, "Men of Israel, take care what you are about to do with these men. For before these days Theudas rose up, claiming to be somebody, and a number of men, about four hundred, joined him. He was killed, and all who followed him were dispersed and came to nothing. After him Judas the Galilean rose up in the days of the census and drew away some of the people after him. He too perished, and all who followed him were scattered. So in the present case I tell you, keep away from these men and let them alone, for if this plan or this undertaking is of man, it will fail; but if it is of God, you will not be able to overthrow them. You might even be found opposing God!" (Acts 5:34–39)

What do we have at this point? The body is nowhere to be found. The tomb is empty. There are dozens of initial eyewitnesses. We have emboldened followers. Enemies converted. Hundreds who saw Him at the same time, telling everyone they know they saw Him alive with their own two eyes. They're all willing to die rather than change their minds. Word of that would get around!

And yet, there's even more! We have seen that Jesus claimed to be God— "Whoever sees Me sees Him who sent Me" (John 12:45). He forgave sins as only God can do. At His trial, when they asked Him, "Are You the Christ, the Son of the Blessed?" Jesus said, "I am, and you will see the Son of Man seated at the right hand of Power, and coming with the clouds of heaven" (Mark 14:61–62). This is exactly what His followers proclaimed of Him from the very beginning, that He is the Christ, the Son of God. In that culture, to claim to be God was blasphemy. That's why the temple authorities condemned Jesus to die. So why would people steeped in that culture immediately speak of Him in divine terms? Before His death, Peter calls Him "the Holy One of God" (John 6:69). After His resurrection, Peter, quoting Psalm 16, again calls Him God's "Holy One" (Acts 2:27). That's blasphemy, unless, of course, it's true. What could move them to make such a claim? There's only one viable answer—only a bodily resurrection. Sometimes it is said that the early Christians copied pagan mystery cults, or followers of Mithras, and their stories of dying and rising gods. But the reality is probably the other way around, since mystery cults did not make much of dying and rising until *after* Jesus had lived and died and rose. So who was copying whom?[10]

Finally, we have Sunday itself. For centuries, the command of God was drummed into the people of God to worship on the seventh day. Remember the Sabbath Day to keep it holy! Suddenly, and almost immediately, these Jewish believers in Jesus began to worship on the first day of the week, calling it "the Lord's day" (Revelation 1:10). Something enormously important had to have happened on that day to effect that change. Yes, only a bodily resurrection will do! Scripture says of the first believers, "They devoted themselves to the apostles' teaching and the fellowship, to the breaking of bread and the prayers" (Acts 2:42). Paul writes of the Lord's Supper, "As often as you eat this bread and drink the cup, you proclaim the Lord's death until He comes" (1 Corinthians 11:26). So it has happened that every Sunday for nearly two thousand years, at places all over the world, Christians have gathered to proclaim His death and resurrection and to receive Him in His Supper. That in itself is an ongoing sign of the resurrection.

10 Every year around Easter or Christmas, certain cable television channels breathlessly promote shows that purport to explain (away) the facts of the Gospel. A number of articles found online at www.tektonics.org/copycat/mithra.php explain that any similarities between Christianity and Mithraism are most likely due to followers of the Persian/Roman God Mithra expropriating Christian ideas rather than the other way around.

Only a living Jesus can give us His true body and blood under the bread and wine for the forgiveness of sins.

Remember the words of that former enemy converted by the risen Christ: "If in Christ we have hope in this life only, we are of all men most to be pitied. But in fact Christ has been raised from the dead, the firstfruits of those who have fallen asleep" (1 Corinthians 15:19–20). In other words, if Jesus did not bodily rise from the dead, there is no Christianity. But if He did rise, then He is who He claims to be, and the implications are world-changing! It would, as they said, "Turn the world upside down" (Acts 17:6).

Here is the evidence:

- Eyewitness testimony.
- Authentic accounts of Jesus' appearances.
- It all took place in one locale.
- All agree the tomb was empty.
- There was no body to be found.
- All this was written down while the witnesses were still alive.
- The guards at the tomb had to be bribed to spread a lie.
- The change in the disciples.
- The case of Saul turned Paul.
- Explosive growth of Christianity, beginning from where it all happened.
- Calling Jesus the Son of God from the beginning.
- Sunday and the Lord's Supper as signs of the resurrection.

Certainly, we could expand this list, but none of this works if Jesus is still in the grave. None of this is possible if the resurrection is a fraud, a delusion, or a plot of some kind. There is only one possible conclusion left—Jesus did rise from the dead.

His Resurrection Changes Everything!

Now let's consider the difference the resurrection makes for other areas of our apologetic task. What about our view of creation and the value of human life? We do not here intend to rehash the whole evolution vs. creation debate, but wish to note only this: the "engine" of evolution is death, while the resurrection shows God to be the God of life. So-called macro-evolution (the idea that all life can be explained without God by means of "natural selection") is said to work because all things die and are replaced eventually by forms of life presumably better adapted for survival. Even to say that God worked through evolution to give us the variety of life we have today (so-called theistic evolution) means that the God of life created by means of death.[11] Yet Scripture calls death "the last enemy" (1 Corinthians 15:26). In contrast, the resurrection of Jesus is the beginning of the end for death. Our God is not in the death business; He is in the business of raising the dead. In Scripture, death is not the engine of any progress, but rather the result of sin. Death is not what God intended for His human creatures but is an unrelenting evil, tearing apart lives and relationships. The Gospel proclaims that Jesus Christ, through death (and resurrection), destroyed the one who has the power of death, namely, the devil (Hebrews 2:14). Without Christ, death is final, the end, a black hole from which there is no return. The best the evolutionist can say is that our decomposing flesh becomes food for other living things, and maybe we live on in the memory of others. But God desires to raise the dead. Jesus even disrupted one funeral procession that He met with a resurrection (see Luke 7:11–17). At the end of time, there will be one grand celebration, not of death, but of resurrected life in Christ.

The resurrection of Jesus also changes how we look at the creation itself. Because God is the God of life, we see His creation as His gift to sustain this life. Because "the earth is the LORD's and the fullness thereof" (Psalm 24:1), He calls us to care for the creation as His stewards. At the same time we recognize the

11 The CTCR document *In Christ All Things Hold Together* recognizes this contradiction. Trying to harmonize evolution and Genesis "subverts the Christological core of Scripture" because it makes death an integral part of creation rather than the result of sin (p. 12).

brokenness inherent in all things because of sin, we also know the creation will be restored perfectly when Christ returns, because Scripture says, "The creation waits with eager longing for the revealing of the sons of God. For the creation was subjected to futility, not willingly, but because of Him who subjected it, in hope that the creation itself will be set free from its bondage to corruption" (Romans 8:19–21).

The resurrection of Jesus needs to permeate how we look at all of human life. Evolution leads people to believe that some lives are more valuable than others. Some lives are expendable if they are perceived to be inconvenient or in the way of one's desires. It is no coincidence that the forces defending abortion are often opposed to biblical values and Christian morals. But God Himself has placed infinite value on every human life. Christ became human for us to suffer our death, to receive what we deserved for our sins, and then to rise again that we might have life.

> You were ransomed from the futile ways inherited from your forefathers, not with perishable things such as silver or gold, but with the precious blood of Christ, like that of a lamb without blemish or spot. He was foreknown before the foundation of the world but was made manifest in the last times for the sake of you who through Him are believers in God, who raised Him from the dead and gave Him glory, so that your faith and hope are in God. (1 Peter 1:18–21)

In contrast, our present secular culture has been called a "culture of death."[12] Too often, death is seen as the solution to a problem. If a child is not wanted, many believe abortion is acceptable. We soften it with words like "pro-choice," but the death of this child in the womb becomes the solution. Someone is old and decrepit? Why not provide them with *euthanasia*—a Greek term meaning "good death"—that is a much softer way to say it. When a person denies the Creator and accepts the idea that human beings are not unique but the product of random evolutionary processes, this removes any real foundation for morality. Without a Creator, without a source of life outside us, there can be no objective right or wrong. Truth becomes something every person may construct for himself. Even

12 "In our present social context, marked by a dramatic struggle between the 'culture of life' and the 'culture of death,' there is need to develop a deep critical sense, capable of discerning true values and authentic needs" (John Paul II, *Evangelium Vitae* ["The Gospel of Life"], March 1995, https://w2.vatican.va/content/john-paul-ii/en/encyclicals/documents/hf_jp-ii_enc_25031995_evangelium-vitae.html).

the most basic of human relationships, marriage between one man and one woman, becomes whatever humans want to make of it, if there is no living God.

God's Decisive Intervention

The Gospel of Christ's resurrection breaks into all of this with something completely different. God is the God of life, and the life is in His Son. God has intervened decisively in our house of death, has broken in to bring life. We in the Church have been given a message of life, not death. The resurrection of Jesus gives us courage to testify that God's living Word remains sure. That's because it is the living voice of Jesus Himself, the God-man, the Word of God made flesh, crucified and raised from the dead. Christian morality is not a human construct evolving through the ages but is revealed in Christ's Word. God's instructions are not for us to mold to our liking, but we are to be molded by that Word and called to account where we have fallen short. A bodily resurrection also shows that what we do with our bodies does matter to God. Notice the sweep of immoral human behavior in the following reference and then note the antidote: "Do not be deceived: neither the sexually immoral, nor idolaters, nor adulterers, nor men who practice homosexuality, nor thieves, nor the greedy, nor drunkards, nor revilers, nor swindlers will inherit the kingdom of God. And such were some of you. But you were washed, you were sanctified, you were justified in the name of the Lord Jesus Christ and by the Spirit of our God" (1 Corinthians 6:9–11). This does not mean Christians are without sin. Far from it. However, it does mean that the Church at her best knows how to deal with sin. She has been sent by her living Lord Jesus to forgive sins, to proclaim repentance and forgiveness of sins in His name to all nations (Luke 24:47). Those who hear and believe are transformed by the Word of forgiveness. Of course, if there is no resurrection of Jesus, none of this means anything. But because Jesus lives, He stands behind His Word to assure us it is true.

Functional Universalism?

A focus on the resurrection will negate the attraction of "functional universalism." This is the idea that all people whom we consider to be reasonably good will go to heaven no matter what they believe. It is "functional" universalism because the ideas may not be fully formed. One finds it even in some people who profess faith in Christ; such people, when pressed, allow that God will probably accept the good Muslim or the good Hindu into heaven. People commonly say, "He never went to church, and I don't know if he believed or not, but he was basically a good person." In contrast, Jesus not only claimed to be the way, the truth, and the life and the only way to the Father (John 14:6), but He also insisted,

> "I am the living bread that came down from heaven. If anyone eats of this bread, he will live forever. And the bread that I will give for the life of the world is My flesh." The Jews then disputed among themselves, saying, "How can this man give us His flesh to eat?" So Jesus said to them, "Truly, truly, I say to you, unless you eat the flesh of the Son of Man and drink His blood, you have no life in you. Whoever feeds on My flesh and drinks My blood has eternal life, and I will raise him up on the last day." (John 6:51–54)

When a person says something to the effect, "Well, I don't think Jesus meant to be that exclusive," or "Could the church have added that later?" such thinking may betray lack of confidence in the resurrection and the centrality of the cross. While visiting congregations as part of my pastoral work, I noted that, when a parish's efforts in the task of reaching people outside the congregation with the Gospel appeared anemic or ineffective, there was often an underlying attitude: "We don't have many mission opportunities. Most people in our town go to church already." Or, as someone once told me, "I believe in Jesus as my Savior, so don't get me wrong, pastor. But if a person believes something else and is really sincere about it, who am I to tell them they're wrong?" Although such a person may not describe it this way, "functionally" it is universalism.

In contrast to this, the fact that Jesus did rise bodily from the dead makes His words come alive as He sent the Church to proclaim repentance and forgiveness of sins in His name (Luke 24:47). Because St. Peter had seen, talked with, and even ate with the resurrected Lord, he was also able to say,

> And we are witnesses of all that He did both in the country of the Jews and in Jerusalem. They put Him to death by hanging Him on a tree, but God raised Him on the third day and made Him to appear, not to all the people but to us who had been chosen by God as witnesses, who ate and drank with Him after He rose from the dead. And He commanded us to preach to the people and to testify that He

> is the one appointed by God to be judge of the living and the dead. To Him all the prophets bear witness that everyone who believes in Him receives forgiveness of sins through His name. (Acts 10:39–43)

Years later, near the end of his earthly life, Peter would write, "I will make every effort so that after my departure you may be able at any time to recall these things. For we did not follow cleverly devised myths when we made known to you the power and coming of our Lord Jesus Christ, but we were eyewitnesses of His majesty" (2 Peter 1:15–16). Because he was convinced of the resurrection of Jesus, St. Paul was able to speak this way of his impending death:

> It is my eager expectation and hope that I will not be at all ashamed, but that with full courage now as always Christ will be honored in my body, whether by life or by death. For to me to live is Christ, and to die is gain. If I am to live in the flesh, that means fruitful labor for me. Yet which I shall choose I cannot tell. I am hard pressed between the two. My desire is to depart and be with Christ, for that is far better. (Philippians 1:20–23; see also vv. 24–26)

Many more examples of Scripture can be given that make sense only if the eyewitness testimony of the apostles is true—that Jesus bodily rose from the dead. So it does matter in whom we trust. Mohammed is dead and buried. The Buddha died as well. Hindus believe in an endless cycle of reincarnation. But Jesus promises, "I will not leave you as orphans; I will come to you. Yet a little while and the world will see Me no more, but you will see Me. Because I live, you also will live" (John 14:18–19). Without a real resurrection, those are empty words. But because Jesus is alive today, Jesus, and Jesus alone, can make good on that promise. That is why in the Creed, we not only confess that "on the third day He rose from the dead," but we also express our confidence in "the resurrection of the body," namely that we, too, shall rise. Paul makes the same connection in words often read at the graveside: "Our citizenship is in heaven, and from it we await a Savior, the Lord Jesus Christ, who will transform our lowly body to be like His glorious body, by the power that enables Him even to subject all things to Himself" (Philippians 3:20–21).

A healthy focus on the resurrection of Jesus combats the doubts that give rise to "functional universalism." Again, it was the resurrected and living Lord Jesus who sent His Church to all people everywhere: "Make disciples of *all nations*, baptizing them in the name of the Father and of the Son and of the Holy Spirit, teaching them to observe all that I have commanded you. And behold, I am with you always, to the end of the age" (Matthew 28:19–20, emphasis added). Every other world religion says, "Do this, do that, and you will live." The Christian message calls everyone to confess, "I have not done it, not done enough. But Jesus has. Jesus did it all for me. And Jesus lives to forgive me and to take me home to Himself." Only Jesus says, "In My Father's house are many rooms. If it were not so, would I have told you that I go to prepare a place for you? And if I go and prepare a place for you, I will come again and will take you to Myself, that where I am you may be also" (John 14:2–3). Only Jesus bodily rose from the dead.

Our defense of the reason for the hope that is within us, our efforts to spread the Good News of Jesus, to invite others to "come and see," rest completely in the resurrection. If Jesus did not bodily rise, we are wasting our time talking about Him, but if He truly did rise, that changes everything. Here's a humble illustration: God has blessed me with a nice car. It's comfortable, gets good fuel mileage, and has just enough power. My car will take me many places, but if I begin to think it will take me all the way to Germany, I'm going to be mistaken. No matter how sincerely I believe it, when I come to the edge of the big water called the Atlantic Ocean, my car will not take me across. Other religions may help you live an outwardly good life, but when you come to the edge of a big water called "death," you will have no way to cross. Only Jesus, who has been there and come back, can bring you across. This is why St. Paul writes,

> Whatever gain I had, I counted as loss for the sake of Christ. Indeed, I count everything as loss because of the surpassing worth of knowing Christ Jesus my Lord. For His sake I have suffered the loss of all things and count them as rubbish, in order that I may gain Christ and be found in Him, not having a righteousness of my own that comes from the law, but that which comes through faith in Christ, the righteousness from God that depends on faith— that I may know Him and the power of His resurrection, and may share His sufferings, becoming like Him in His death, that by any means possible I may attain the resurrection from the dead. (Philippians 3:7–11)

Christianity is not at heart a list of rules, but trust in the living Lord. All other religious leaders from the past are dead and gone. You can go and visit their graves. But in Jerusalem, there is the Church of the Holy Sepulchre built over where Jesus was buried. That grave is empty. There is NO BODY there, for Christ is risen!

What about Suffering?

Now we come to one of the biggest questions, one of the biggest objections atheists may raise. What about suffering? How do you account for suffering? Why do good people have pain? Why am I hurting? It seems a senseless evil to me.[13] How does Jesus address this? Most people live with the vague impression that the universe itself is broken. Or else they have concluded the universe is oblivious to human suffering. Some philosophies say we suffer because we are working out some bad "karma," or are being punished by God or the universe. The friends of Job in the Bible came to him with this idea, essentially: "Job, admit it. You have sinned against God; that's why this evil has happened to you." Others say we suffer because the powerful oppress the weak, and only the fittest survive. But then we all die anyway. This leads some to rage against a cold and unfair universe. Others will calmly, even proudly, accept their fate with a brave exterior covering their inner hopelessness. In the end, Christians are asked to explain the mystery of suffering while the atheist has to explain everything else.

In the death and resurrection of Jesus, God does not explain our suffering—He triumphs over it. He does not give a logical, reasoned-out philosophy of pain, but He Himself comes to suffer with us, to cry out on the cross, "My God, My God, why?" (Mark 15:34). The risen Jesus is now able to come to us in our suffering to sustain us. He can even use our suffering in His gracious hand to mold us according to His will (FC SD XI 48–49). Then, because the end of His suffering and death is His resurrection from the dead, He promises to raise us, so we can say with Paul, "I consider that the sufferings of this present time are not worth comparing with the glory that is to be revealed to us" (Romans 8:18).

This is God's basic *way of operating*. He raises the dead. First Jesus, then you and me. He calls the lowly. He lifts up the humble. He finds the lost. Throughout the biblical story, God does not often choose the strong and the powerful, but

13 McFarland observes: "In order to say that suffering is evil, a person must have some standard of good. But where does the atheist get this standard? On the basis of atheism, we're all the products of chance, time and an undirected process known as evolution. If survival of the fittest is the rule of nature, then who's to say what's really good or evil" (*10 Answers for Atheists*, 165).

frequently the dominated, the powerless, and the marginal. In Genesis, God often picks not the firstborn, but the second son: Abel rather than Cain, Isaac rather than Ishmael, Jacob over Esau, Joseph instead of Reuben. Working with women, it's often not the young and beautiful: it's old infertile Sarah, not young Hagar; unloved Leah, not lovely Rachel.[14] As the story progresses, God stands with the slaves in Egypt to deliver Israel. Moses is the outcast who doesn't speak well. The judges often come from the smaller tribe, those of low status. David the king is the youngest of eight sons. Do you see the pattern? "He raises the poor from the dust and lifts the needy from the ash heap, to make them sit with princes, with the princes of His people. He gives the barren woman a home, making her the joyous mother of children" (Psalm 113:7–9). It's God's basic way of operating—resurrection.

In the New Testament, Jesus consorts with the rich and poor alike, not as "good" and "moral" people might expect. He attracts tax collectors and sinners, calling them to repent and follow Him (Luke 15:1–2). He is concerned with the little, the last, the least, and the lost. He even raises the dead—it's always His go-to plan. This is not simply because people love an underdog but has to do with ultimate reality. We are all dying sinners. The rich and the powerful. The poor and the outcast. We all end up in the grave. So Jesus Christ Himself was abandoned by most of those closest to Him, including, for a time, even His Father. He was the victim of a miscarriage of justice who died in disgrace, helpless; and He suffered it all willingly, for us. Christians are not saved by finding in themselves the strength to escape death by their great deeds, but we receive by faith the salvation Christ worked for us. Now in His Word, in Baptism and His Supper, He gives His gifts of the forgiveness of sins and resurrection to life. The Word delivers what it promises.

"Pull yourself together! Master yourself! Get control of your situation. Be strong; you can do it!" is one approach the world takes. Another is to control others by playing the victim. But Jesus says, in essence, "You cannot do it. You have to rely on Me." A salvation earned by moral effort would favor the strong, the competent, the privileged. But salvation as a gift of God in the death and resurrection of Jesus favors the failed, the outsiders, the weak, because it goes only to those who know salvation *must* be sheer gift. When you know you are as good as dead, then you come to appreciate above all else the One who raises the dead. That's because the Bible is not principally the story of great heroes of

14 I am indebted to Keller, *Making Sense of God*, 206, for this way of framing these concepts.

faith; rather, it is the record of God intervening in the lives of people who don't deserve it, often resist it, and don't always appreciate it: people like you and me. People like those we know and meet every day. That is what changes us. That is what gives new life, for "God chose what is low and despised in the world, even things that are not, to bring to nothing things that are, so that no human being might boast in the presence of God" (1 Corinthians 1:28–29). By His resurrection, Jesus does not *explain* suffering and death, but triumphs over them. We matter to God, soul and body, because we will be raised, soul and body, to eternal life.

Our Twenty-First Century Apologia

We face many challenges to the Christian faith. Claims made for "scientific facts" lead some to conclude that Christianity is outmoded, no longer a reasonable alternative. On the opposite side, we have the rise of militant Islam, advocating faith in and obedience to a god, but not the God who reveals Himself as Father, Son, and Holy Spirit. New objections to traditional Christian morality have arisen and quickly come to dominate the culture. What was unthinkable to most a mere twenty-five years ago has become the new orthodoxy. Oppose at your peril these challenges to Christian faith and morals. Our purpose here, however, is not to dissect these cultural battles, but to imbue you, dear reader, with biblical confidence to face this twenty-first-century future with the same courage and grace of the Christians of the first century. What was it that gave them a holy boldness to proclaim Christ? What filled their hearts with courage to face down their opposition? What gave them a graciousness toward their accusers that, even if they were martyred, many more found attractive? Why is it said that "the blood of the martyrs is the seed of the Church"?[15] There is one deciding factor. The resurrection of Jesus made all the difference. No bodily resurrection? No Church. But common people, ordinary fishermen, tax collectors, and sinners convinced of the resurrection of Jesus, along with many more attracted to their message, all filled with the Holy Spirit by that message, were formed by the Spirit into the Church.

Even in the face of possible persecution, you have the same source of courage and grace under pressure—the Holy Spirit working through the Word of Christ and the Sacraments of Baptism and Holy Communion. Your faith will be shown

15 A more accurate rendition of this popular quote from Tertullian, a Church Father writing about AD 197 to the persecuting authorities, reads, "The more you mow us down, the thicker we rise; the Christian blood you spill is like the seed you sow, it springs from the earth again, and fructifies the more" (*The Apology of Tertullian*, trans. William Reeve, Ancient and Modern Library of Theological Literature, vol. 31 [London: Griffith, Farran, Okedon & Welsh; Newberry House, 1889], 143).

in what you say and how you live. Worldly wisdom will not do; only the cross of Christ. Vague assurances will not cut it. Only the promise of resurrection in Jesus. Will you speak and act in such a way that people ask you, "Please tell me what is the reason for the hope that spills out of you"? Listen to their concerns, then point them to Jesus, raised from the dead, and invite them to come with you to hear more of Him.[16]

On a trip to the Holy Land, I had the privilege of visiting the site of the first-century city of Caesarea Philippi. Philip, one of the sons of King Herod the Great, wishing to impress the Roman Emperor Tiberius Caesar, built a city with temples dedicated to a myriad of pagan gods. Into the side of a cliff are carved dozens of little shrines, each one containing a niche for an idol of wood or stone.

It is significant that Jesus had led His disciples into this same region of Caesarea Philippi and there began to ask them, "'Who do people say that the Son of Man is?' And they said, 'Some say John the Baptist, others say Elijah, and others Jeremiah or one of the prophets.' He said to them, 'But who do you say that I am?'" (Matthew 16:13–15). No question is more important than this.

"Simon Peter replied, 'You are the Christ, the Son of the living God'" (Matthew 16:16). Note that well. The living God, not the four hundred or so stone idols around them, but the living God. He is the God of the resurrection, who finds the lost, lifts up the downtrodden, forgives the sinner, and raises the dead. "And Jesus answered him, 'Blessed are you, Simon Bar-Jonah! For flesh and blood has not revealed this to you, but My Father who is in heaven'" (Matthew 16:17).

No one will be convinced by force of human argument, but the Father draws them by the Spirit to the living Jesus. "No one can come to Me unless the Father who sent Me draws him" (John 6:44). Christ continued: "I tell you, you are Peter ["Peter" means "little rock"], and on this rock [meaning bedrock or foundation stone] I will build My church" (Matthew 16:18). Simon Peter is the "little rock." The "big rock," however, is Peter's confession of faith that Jesus is "the Christ, the Son of the living God" (Matthew 16:16). "On this rock," Jesus promises, "I will build My church and the gates of hell shall not prevail against it" (Matthew 16:18).

The rock is our confession of Christ, the Son of the living God, the One crucified for our sins and raised again for our justification. But the promise belongs to Jesus. "I will build My church!" If Jesus is dead and buried like any other crucified man, there is no confession, no Church. Because Jesus lives,

16 The Lutheran Church—Missouri Synod Office of National Mission is implementing a series of evangelism workshops entitled *Every One His Witness*. See www.lcms.org/witness-outreach.

not just "in spirit" but bodily raised from the dead, He will keep His promise. "I will build My church and the gates of hell shall not prevail against it." Why? The evil one cannot stand against the Resurrected One. Because Jesus lives, the devil is defeated.

From this victory also flows the great gift of forgiveness. Jesus continues, "I will give you the keys of the kingdom of heaven, and whatever you bind on earth shall be bound in heaven, and whatever you loose on earth shall be loosed in heaven" (Matthew 16:19). Here Peter stands for the apostles. Later Jesus gives the same keys to the Church (Matthew 18:18). This is how Jesus builds His Church. Yes, when we confess Him, and when we bind and loose sins in His name, we do the speaking. But it's His Word, and His Word actually "delivers the goods," for standing behind the promises is the living and glorified Son of God, whom John heard say, "Fear not, I am the first and the last, and the living one. I died and behold I am alive forevermore, and I have the keys of Death and Hades" (Revelation 1:17–18). This is the One we serve. He is our sure defense.

Is the universe open or closed? The resurrection of Jesus shows that God Himself has entered our reality to intervene for us. Are there many paths to God? Or just one path from God to us in Jesus? Is God really there? Does He care? The bodily resurrection of Jesus is the irreversible sign that God shows up and with everlasting love has compassion on all He has made (Isaiah 58:8). The apologia needed for the twenty-first century will be the same as the first. The resurrection of Jesus is clear confirmation that He is the way, the truth, and the life (John 14:6). Whatever we face in the future, we are called simply to confess Him before the world. The resurrection of Jesus changes everything!

> If Christ had not been truly raised
>   His Church would live a lie;
> His name should nevermore be praised,
>   His words deserve to die.
> But now our great Redeemer lives;
>   Through Him we are restored;
> His Word endures, His Church revives
>   In Christ, our risen Lord. (*LSB* 486:3)

Study Questions

1. How does the bodily resurrection of Jesus affect your outlook on life? your view of reality? your experiences in our present culture?

2. How do the cross and resurrection of Jesus work as sure signs, both for the existence of God and His intervention in human affairs?

3. What are the implications for you of the fact that only Jesus has crossed "the big water" called death and come back?

4. Have you met anyone who tries to hold the risen Jesus at arm's length? Or have you done so yourself? What was your motive?

5. Explain in your own words how the cross and resurrection show both the inclusive and exclusive nature of the Christian message. How does the resurrection provide "the reason for the hope that is within you"?

6. How convincing for you are the reasons presented for trusting that Jesus truly did rise from the dead? Why? Does the resurrection give you confidence that the gates of hell shall not prevail? How?

7. How does the resurrection change how we view our present culture? the question of suffering? the mission of the Church? the reliability of God's Word? what we do in our bodies?